Development Theory in Transition

Magnus Blomström
and Björn Hettne

Development Theory in Transition

The Dependency Debate and Beyond: Third World Responses

Magnus Blomström
and Björn Hettne

Zed Books Ltd., 57 Caledonian Road, London N1 9BU

Development Theory in Transition was first published by
Zed Books Ltd., 57 Caledonian Road, London N1 9BU, UK,
and 171 First Avenue, Atlantic Highlands, New Jersey 07716,
USA, in 1984.

Cover designed by Walter Castro.
Printed and bound in the United Kingdom at the
Bath Press, Avon.

Second impression, 1985
Third impression, 1987
Fourth impression, 1988

British Library Cataloguing in Publication Data

Blomström, Magnus
Development theory in transition : the
dependency debate and beyond : Third World
responses.
1. Developing countries—Economic conditions
2. Economic development
I. Title II. Hettne, Björn
330.9172'4 HC59.7

ISBN 0-86232-270-7
ISBN 0-86232-271-5 Pbk

Contents

Figures

Preface

Two years ago we published a book in Swedish entitled *Underdevelopment and Dependency. The Latin American Contribution to Development Theory*. Parts of that book are incorporated in the present work and we are grateful to Henrik Lutzen for the translation. This book differs from the earlier one, however, in the sense that we have presented a more elaborated account of the dependency debate in other Third World contexts (the Caribbean, Asia and Africa). The earlier analysis has thus been extended to include Third World contributions to the theory of development. Furthermore, we have tried to present a more detailed discussion of the alternatives to the dependency approach and to assess their relevance.

We are indebted to several colleagues and friends for interviews and fruitful discussions during the work on this book. Particularly we would like to mention Samir Amin, George Beckford, M.R. Bhagavan, David Court, Theotonio Dos Santos, Johan Galtung, Goran Hyden, André Gunder Frank, K.S. Jomo, Kabiru Kinyanjui, Khor Kok Peng, Rajni Kothari, Claude Meillassoux, Rex Nettleford, Gabriel Palma, Pedro Paz, Octavio Rodriguez, Carl Stone, Osvaldo Sunkel and Pedro Vuskovic. We are also grateful to Mats Lundahl, Robert Molteno and Ronaldo Munck for helpful comments on earlier drafts. Eugenio Rovzar organized a seminar on a draft at CIDE in Mexico City at the end of 1981 and a similar seminar was organized by Harry Goulbourne at the University of the West Indies in Kingston. These seminars were most important during the course of the work. Annika Forssell, Lilian Landqvist and Anita Oxenham typed successive drafts with care and great skill. Finally, we appreciate the financial support given by the Swedish Agency for Research Co-operation with Developing Countries (SAREC).

Magnus Blomström
Björn Hettne
Gothenburg, 1984

Introduction

Purpose of the Study

This book gives an outline of the growth of development theory from a Third World perspective. Our hypothesis is that the traditional and still far from abandoned thinking on development is based on experiences which are specific to the Western world and that the claim to universal validity must therefore be repudiated. A truly universal theory of development must reflect the development experiences of different societies. Since the global dominance of Western development theory is based on intellectual penetration (from the centre to the periphery), it is important to consider 'the voices from the periphery' in this context.

The Latin American debate on the problems of underdevelopment is probably the most extensive discussion on development in the Third World and therefore a valuable contribution to modern social science. It has not only criticized the 'conventional' development theory, i.e. the theories that were shaped during the 1950s, but also acted as a catalyst in the forming of a more relevant and less ethnocentric development theory. Thus, the Latin American debate on underdevelopment and dependency constitutes not only the starting point for this book, but also its core.

The debate began during the last years of the 1940s when a group of Latin American economists working for the UN Economic Commission for Latin America (ECLA) criticized the traditional theory of international trade and its development effects. The ECLA group argued that the economic relations between 'Centre' and 'Periphery' tended to increase the gap between rich and poor countries. This argument later became the starting point for a long polemic. The critique of the ECLA thinking came not only from orthodox, liberal economists, but also from Marxists. Nevertheless, during the 1950s the ECLA theories became accepted as development strategy for many Latin American regimes. This strategy required an active government involvement in the economy, protectionism and industrialization through import substitution.

After the expansion during the 1950s had turned into the stagnation of the 1960s, criticism of the ECLA ideas became more outspoken, but also more theoretically consistent. The criticism from the left is most relevant for the later development: it came from three directions: (1) from a younger, and more radical generation of ECLA economists, (2) from the so-called neo-Marxists associated with the American journal *Monthly Review*, and (3) from Marxists of the European tradition. These criticisms have been the starting point for various schools within the Latin American debate on dependency and underdevelopment, which has already gone well beyond its geographical boundary and now forms part of the international theory of development.

A secondary purpose is therefore to account for the dependency and dependency-related debate in other parts of the world. Thirdly, it is our ambition to pinpoint the significance of the dependency school for the current trends in development theory.

The Sociology of Paradigm Change

One of the purposes of this book is thus to illuminate the mechanisms behind and preconditions for the spread of the dependency theory outside Latin America, and the emergence of what we call 'secondary centres' of the dependency debate. This raises a number of intricate questions. We must be able to distinguish between those ideas that are diffused and those that originate spontaneously. Latin America is not the only underdeveloped continent that has been described as 'dependent'. *Au contraire*, a number of dependency theorists have claimed that dependency is a fundamental trait of the process of underdevelopment in Latin America, as well as in Asia and Africa.

It is an established fact that dependence (varying in degree from country to country) is an *historical situation* in most nations in the Third World; it is, furthermore, quite likely that dependence has manifested itself in the form of a more or less articulate *notion of dependence*. In Latin America this notion was expressed in the concept of *dependencia*. We shall, therefore, define dependency theory as an 'export commodity', consisting of the ideas of the Latin American dependency school. In other words, we distinguish between dependence as an historical situation and the various expressions of the idea of dependence; among the latter we distinguish, in turn, between those expressing a general notion of dependence and its special, Latin American manifestation: dependency theory. The *diffusion* refers to the spread of this theory only; we shall thus attempt to distinguish between the theory and the notion. As will be seen, India had a term for the notion of dependence (the Drain) long before dependency theory, as defined above, got there. In the Caribbean, the notion was formulated simultaneously with the arrival of the theory from Latin America, which resulted in a partly independent dependency theory. Both of these cases serve as illustrations of the discussion above.

It is necessary to deal briefly with how a scientific approach comes into existence and how it changes. According to the so-called 'positivist' view, scientific knowledge develops continuously through the empirical testing of hypotheses. Thomas Kuhn has introduced a radically different view, namely that scientific development is a discontinuous process (Kuhn, 1962). He claims that scientific development is the result of a series of revolutions, called paradigm changes. A paradigm sums up the scientist's views about what should be the object of scientific research and how to go about solving scientific problems. The formulation of a certain paradigm is followed by a period of 'normal science', i.e. a science which is governed by that paradigm. Kuhn compares this to doing a jigsaw puzzle: the pieces can be fitted together because of some overall expectation about the layout of the puzzle. When the pieces no longer fit together, the paradigm no longer serves its purpose – the paradigm is contradicted by the reality. The 'paradigm crisis' is characterized by a frantic search for a new paradigm, until a new paradigm has been established, and the pieces fit together again. This constitutes the scientific revolution.

It is important to keep in mind that the original intent of Kuhn's theory was to explain the development of theories pertaining to the natural sciences, physics in particular. Many regret the fact that this concept has been transferred to, and used in, the social sciences and the humanities. But, in spite of the somewhat different conditions, the paradigm concept is obviously needed, although scientific revolutions in Kuhn's sense are rare. In this book we therefore see the tension between the modernization paradigm and the dependency approach as a conflict of paradigms.

There was a growing discrepancy between the modernization paradigm and the real world during the 1960s. The underdeveloped countries did not follow the path staked out by the developed countries – a path that was supposed to lead to material growth and democracy. Instead, underdevelopment grew, as did the cleft between the rich and the poor countries. The pieces no longer fitted together. At this point the dependency school appeared to offer a better basis for a theory of development. In our opinion, the paradigm concept is an aid to the understanding of how the theory of development has developed. Whether or not it is relevant to other branches of the social sciences shall be left undiscussed.

The transfer of the paradigm concept from the natural sciences to the social sciences creates one problem which has been succinctly formulated by Albert O. Hirschman:

> The career of development economics in the last 25 years illustrates one of the crucial differences between the natural and the social sciences. In the natural sciences, as Thomas Kuhn has shown, the formulation of a new paradigm is followed by an extended period in which the paradigm is fully accepted and the labours of 'normal science' are devoted to its verification, application, and further extension. In the social sciences, on the other hand, the enunciation of a new paradigm not only gives rise to similar sympathetic labours, but is often followed almost immediately by a persistent onslaught of qualification, criticism, and outright demolition that is very much part of normal

> social science. This situation explains the distinctive intellectual climate of the social sciences: here the confident belief in a genuine cumulative growth of knowledge, so characteristic of the natural sciences, hardly ever has a chance to arise.
> (Hirschman, 1977, p. 67)

The overthrow of one scientific approach by another, a so-called change of paradigm, is a process which occurs not only at the conceptual level. Certain scientific ideas dominate, not only because of their ability to convince, but also because of the position of power of those who, for various reasons, happen to consider the ideas correct and suitable. The criteria of suitability are rarely stated, and vary from the simple fact that the scientist is familiar with these ideas rather than with the alternatives, to a general correspondence between the ideas and government policies. In order to understand a change of paradigm, it is necessary to study the institutional conditions behind the scientific production of a society. Although we do not intend to develop a theory about the changes of paradigms, we would like to mention some of these institutional conditions which we find relevant, e.g. the general stage of development of what we call the academic infrastructure.

As far as the spread of the dependency theory is concerned, it is necessary to study the extent to which a development theoretical tradition can be said to have existed in that area at all, either as an independent tradition, or as a research area within a particular scientific discipline. It is also necessary to examine whether or not this tradition is compatible with the dependence perspective, and the extent to which it corresponds with the country's general development efforts. It is also important to examine the process of decision-making at the universities (e.g. student influence), their relative autonomy *vis-à-vis* the government, and how isolated they are from society in general. Do alternative institutions intercept new signals with greater ease than the more bureaucratic and unwieldy universities? How did this conflict of paradigms express itself as a power struggle at the universities? These are the kind of issues we shall take up in connection with the spread of the dependency theory in the Caribbean, Africa and Asia.

Outline of the Study

The book is organized in the following way: the first chapter deals with the birth and growth of modern development theory until the 1960s. This growth occurred mainly within the discipline of economics but new 'dimensions' were later added via contributions from sociologists and political scientists. The theory of development thus burst its economic fetter and became more and more interdisciplinary in nature. Certain perspectives appeared both in economic and sociological, as well as political, analyses of the problems of underdevelopment. Most scholars in those days saw development in an evolutionary perspective, in which the concept of underdevelopment was defined in terms of observable differences between rich and poor countries. The true meaning of development was to bridge these gaps by means of an imitative process in which the less developed countries gradually assumed the qualities of the industrialized nations. The analysis of the qualities which were to be imitated was shared by economists, sociologists and political scientists, so that some specialized in economic structure, some in human attitudes and social institutions. Naturally, geographers, social anthropologists and psychologists also contributed, but we have not attempted to provide a complete description of this *eurocentric phase* of the growth of the theory of development. The primary purpose of this chapter is to provide a background for the critical tradition which started in the Third World, primarily in Latin America. First, however, we shall deal with some other prerequisites for the growth and development of this tradition.

Chapter 2 provides the background to the Latin American debate on underdevelopment. First the conflict between classical Marxism and so-called neo-Marxism is dealt with. The growth of the latter was intimately connected with the interpretation of the Latin American reality. The Marxian tradition had the same simplistic, evolutionary view of the development of the Third World which we have found in the traditional theory of development. In addition the Latin American communist parties acted as the diplomatic tools of the Soviet Union, a fact which did not enhance the analytical powers of the Marxian tradition. During the 1950s and the 1960s a less traditionally bound Marxist school was created, while at the same time a different revolutionary practice developed in Latin America: 'guevarism'. As a second source the chapter introduces the ECLA and the early Latin American debate on development. We argue that the comparatively strong Latin American tradition of the social sciences is one important reason why an independent and critical social science first developed in this region. In this context, the ECLA played a key role. All this affected the growth of the dependency school, but before presenting the ideas of this school we also deal with its critique of traditional development theory. In our opinion this contribution has been overlooked, particularly since it was to a very large extent responsible for undermining conventional development theory, thus creating the basis for the emergence of a more relevant theory of development.

Chapter 3 outlines the rise of the Latin American dependency school. We describe its chronological development by discussing its central figures and their major contributions, and conclude with a more analytical summary of the theoretical positions of the dependency school. In our opinion, earlier characterizations and summaries have been oversimplified, partly because they have been polemically oriented, and partly because attempts have been made to identify the theoretical positions of the dependency school by means of a one-dimensional analysis. We believe that by using several theoretical dimensions, we have been able more correctly to describe various different theoretical positions within the school. Certain ideas are, however, common to the majority of the proponents of the dependency school:

– Underdevelopment is intimately connected with the expansion of the industrialized capitalist countries.
– Development and underdevelopment are different aspects of the same universal process.
– Underdevelopment cannot be considered as the original condition in an evolutionary process.
– Dependency is, however, not only an external phenomenon but is also manifested in different ways in the internal (social, ideological and political) structure.

Recently, the theory of dependency has been subjected to an increasing and partly successful criticism, which we describe and attempt to explain in Chapter 4. First, we deal with the not so easily bridged gap between conventional development theory and the dependency school. In this area there was no debate, only a poignant silence. However, a belated debate started between orthodox Marxists and proponents of the dependency school. This debate later had significant effects on both the dependency school and Marxism.

The following three chapters (5 to 7) deal with the spread of the dependency theory to other parts of the Third World. Outside Latin America we have found three important centres of dependency discussion: the Caribbean (Guyana, Trinidad and Jamaica), West Africa (Senegal) and East Africa (Tanzania). Through interviews with social scientists in these areas we have attempted to trace the spread of the theory of dependence as well as factors which have facilitated this process. In the case of Asia we have found a negative reaction to this theory, whereas it was accepted in Africa. The Caribbean area has not only accepted the dependency perspective, but has developed a parallel view of its own. We also review the criticisms in the 'secondary centres' of the dependency school. In this context the Indian discussion is of particular relevance as well as the actual development of a number of economic strategies contradicting basic tenets of the dependency theory.

We shall also discuss the cases of Jamaica and Tanzania, whose governments have tried to apply the theories of dependency practically. Even at this level we find that the efforts of the dependency school have been less successful.

In Chapter 8 we attempt to summarize current trends in the theory of development. Here we wish to emphasize the dependency school's role of catalyst in the development of a relevant theory of development. It is not yet a complete and consistent theory of development. In our opinion there are three distinct traditions which all display traces of the catalysing effect of the dependency school. First, we have the world System Approach, which may be seen as the successor of the dependency school. Secondly, we have a revitalized Marxism, freed of eurocentrism, whose mode of expression primarily is the current debate on modes of production. The 'new' Marxism may be viewed as a direct consequence of the challenge from the dependency school. Thirdly, we have the more established tradition which has also been freed of its ethnocentrism and false development optimism; it now includes a consciousness of the ambiguous and diversified nature of international economic relations. This development should also be seen in the light of the dependency school's criticism of the conventional theory of development.

1. The Emergence of Modern Development Theory

The modern theory of development dates back to the end of the Second World War. The interest in the problems of development increased, particularly since a number of European colonies in Asia and Africa began their struggle towards political independence at that time, and were thought of as potential allies in a bipolar world.

The early attempts at constructing development theories were marked by the fact that the concepts of development and economic growth were considered to be synonymous. It was therefore quite natural that economics played a dominant role in this context. Thus the beginnings of the modern development theory should be seen in the light of the development of the economic discipline.

It is customary to identify three distinct phases in the history of economic thought: the classical, the neo-classical and the Keynesian. The most significant representatives of the classical period are usually considered to be Adam Smith, David Ricardo and Thomas Malthus, who, suffice it to say, had a marked interest in the problems of economic development – an interest which, in modern terms, had a wide, interdisciplinary perspective. A number of the problems with which the classical school concerned itself are consequently found in modern discussions of development theory. Adam Smith, for example, provides a thorough discussion about the causes of increasing productivity, which he relates to the division of labour and the size of the market. Malthus is best known for his treatment of the problems of population growth, while Ricardo provided an analysis of the distribution of production among the various classes in society, and of how this distribution in turn affects economic development.[1]

The Marxist Tradition

The mainstream of the continued development of economic theory replaced the classical approach by the neo-classical one, with one important exception – Karl Marx. Although Marx is often considered to belong to the classical school because of his use of the classical conceptual apparatus, Marxist theory developed its own tradition. Before taking a look at the neo-classical school, we shall therefore deal with the Marxist view of development.

Marx

Marx based his studies of various societies on a materialist interpretation of history.[2] According to this approach, the analysis of the development of a society must begin from the process of production, which, in turn, contains two crucial aspects – the *forces of production* and the *relations of production*. In terms of Marxian political economy the forces of production are generally assumed to be the sum of the material conditions of production – raw materials, tools, machines, etc. – as well as the human beings themselves, with their knowledge and experience. The relations of production are the relations between human beings during the process of production, exchange and distribution of the material utilities in a society. The forces of production and the production relations together form the *mode of production*. This mode of production constitutes the society's *economic structure*, and since, according to Marx, this is the determining factor, he uses it as his point of departure in the analysis of the historical development.

The forces of production develop and are renewed continuously, along with human knowledge of nature and technological development. However, a given state of productive forces requires appropriate relations of production, i.e. appropriate social relations which govern the use of the productive forces. This implies that the social relations must be changed and adjusted to the state of the forces of production. Even the opposite causal relationship may be valid, so that the social relations affect the state of the productive forces.

According to Marx, the origins of all historical changes may be found in the conflict between the forces and the relations of production. When the latter do not correspond to the former, development in a society is slowed down, and the obsolete social relations must be disposed of and replaced by new and more advanced ones.

This structural change does not come about automatically. In a class society there will always be those who benefit from the old (obsolete) production relations, and who will not voluntarily relinquish their positions. The result is therefore a struggle between different classes in society.

The reason for the conflict between the forces of production and the social relations is that the latter are more sluggish than the former. After a while the conflicts within a given mode of production become too great; a *social revolution* is the inevitable result. The old mode of production is then replaced by a new and 'higher' one, which incorporates new social relations that are better adjusted to the state of the productive forces. The process starts over again, but this time at a higher level of economic development.

In order to provide a reasonable explanation of historical development by means of historical materialism, it is not sufficient to analyse the economic base. It is also important to study such factors as ideology, religion, laws, etc., or what is usually called the *social superstructure*, and how it affects development. This superstructure can periodically precipitate the development of the base, and periodically slow it down or stop it completely. The superstructure, however, does not exist on its own; its character is, in the final analysis, determined by the requirements of the economic base. Marx mentioned several different modes of production, which, successively, should replace each other as the development of the forces of production progressed. Thus, feudalism was the predecessor of capitalism, and capitalism that of socialism and communism. In order to reach a state of socialism all societies, including the less developed ones, were required to pass the various stages of capitalist development. However, Marx doubted that the less developed countries were capable of accomplishing this on their own. Later, we shall see that he often considered these countries to be 'primitive' and incapable of starting a process of development by themselves. Colonialism was therefore, according to Marx, a necessary evil. Despite the fact that colonialism was both cruel and ruthless, it was necessary for the elimination of the pre-capitalist modes of production and the introduction of capitalism.[3]

According to Marx there was no difference between the kind of capitalism developed in the colonies and that developed in Europe. In a famous passage from *Capital* he states: 'The industrially more developed country shows the less developed one merely an image of its own future.' Thus, Marx did not believe in a continued expansion of European imperialism. Instead the less developed countries would develop a more autonomous kind of capitalism, similar to that which later developed in the USA (Kiernan, 1974.) From this we might conclude that Marx, like Engels, shared the common 19th Century view that development (capitalism) was universal and inevitable. A more detailed study of Marx's views on the non-European countries may be found in Chapter 2.

Lenin

Subsequent generations of Marxists did not question the inevitability and progressive nature of capitalism.[4] Lenin's concrete description of the development in Russia during the late 19th Century however indicates a consciousness of the fact that capitalist development in less developed regions is more complex than suggested by Marx's analysis. In his book *Capitalist Development in Russia* (written during the period 1896-9), Lenin provides a more refined and elaborate analysis of the complex interplay between a developed and a less developed region. This book was written as part of a polemic with the so-called Narodniks, who claimed that capitalist development was not possible in Russia, mainly because Russia, as compared to other countries, was far behind in terms of industrialization. Nor did they believe that capitalist development was necessary in order to reach socialism. They believed that the old, Russian agrarian society contained a system built on common ownership, and that that system might form the basis for future socialism in Russia.

Lenin, on the other hand, claimed that not only was capitalism possible in Russia, but that it had developed already. What the Narodniks saw as an *obstacle* to the development of capitalism (e.g. the high level of unemployment), Lenin saw as a direct result of capitalism. He claimed that the Russian rate of development, partly as a result of imperialism, was actually slower than that of the more developed capitalist countries, but that capitalism nevertheless was a progressive force in Russia (Sutcliffe, 1972, p 183). Lenin's views on capitalist development in Russia may be summarized as follows: he found capitalism to be both politically necessary and economically possible, and showed by means of concrete studies that it was, in fact, developing. However, certain traditional (pre-capitalist) structures remained as an obstacle to its further development, and they were not going to disappear as quickly as Marxists previously had thought. Actually, capitalist development in less developed countries (Russia) was now, for the first time, seen not only as a process in which pre-capitalist structures were destroyed and replaced by something new, but also as a more complex process in which external and internal structures interacted. The capitalist development in Russia would therefore become some kind of 'slow motion replay' of the development in Western Europe (Palma, 1978, p 893).

The early Marxist theoreticians who dealt with imperialism did not question Marx's idea of the progressive role played by capitalism in the less developed countries (in the developed countries, however, capitalism was considered to have reached a greater degree of maturity, and was therefore no longer as progressive). What they did question was his analysis of the interaction between the developed and the less developed countries. Here Marx had taken the easy way out by disregarding the importance of political independence. He had not realized the way in which colonial ties affected industrial development in the less developed countries, and thus overestimated the possibility of introducing capitalism through colonialism.

Lenin, who may be considered the most important of the early theorists of imperialism, did not find that exporting capital to the less developed countries would automatically lead to capitalist development:

> The progressive effects of capitalism, on the contrary, are not to be seen there (in the colonies), despite the infiltration of foreign capital. When the dominant imperialist power needs social support in the colonies, it joins forces, first and foremost, with the ruling classes of the old pre-capitalist system – the feudal-type landlords, the commercial and money-lending bourgeoisie – against the masses.[5]

According to Lenin, the obstacle to capitalist development in the less developed countries should be looked for in the colonial ties to the mother country. If these ties could be broken, capitalist development was indeed possible. The problems which would then face the countries, e.g. that of the late start of industrialization, would, in many ways, be similar to those facing Russia at the end of the 19th Century.[6] He thus believed in the progressivity of capitalism in the less developed countries, once they had become politically independent.

The Neo-classical and the Keynesian Contribution

As mentioned above, the classical economic theory was replaced by the neo-classical one. Here we search in vain for the classical economists' long-term perspective.[7] The attention is now focused on static, microeconomic relations. The main issue was how the market mechanism could optimally distribute the resources in society. In terms of development theory, the neo-classical school is merely a parenthesis.

John Maynard Keynes's theoretical contribution on the other hand meant that macroeconomic problems returned as the key issue in economics. In times of depression and high unemployment in the industrialized countries, the problem was to employ existing, but poorly utilized, factors of production. Keynes argued that the aggregate demand, and its various components (consumption and investment) were of strategic importance. An increase in expenditure which, in turn, increased aggregate demand would eventually lead to an increase in the level of economic activity and a decrease in unemployment. Thus, Keynes was primarily interested in short-term problems of stabilization. Since the problems of underdevelopment are radically different from those of the Depression, he did not directly contribute to the theory of development.

These long-term problems, which Keynes intentionally disregarded, were instead developed by two other economists – Evsey Domar and Roy Harrod.[8] Independently of each other, and with somewhat different premises, they managed to show the intimate relationship between an economy's rate of growth on the one hand, and its level of saving and investment on the other. Their growth model, named after them, later formed the basis for modern growth theory, in which saving and investment are considered to be the central force behind economic growth.

The Harrod-Domar model greatly influenced development theories during the 1950s. Development and growth were considered to be synonymous in theoretical discussions during this period, i.e. development was more or less considered to be synonymous with capital formation. W.A. Lewis has provided a classical passage in this context:

> The central problem in the theory of economic development is to understand the process by which a community which was previously saving and investing 4 or 5 per cent of its national income or less, converts itself into an economy where voluntary saving is running at about 12 or 15 per cent of national income or more. This is the central problem because the central fact of economic development is rapid accumulation (including knowledge and skills with capital).
> (Lewis, 1955, p 155).

The great majority of economists thus saw no difference between 'underdeveloped' and 'undeveloped' countries during the 1950s. By looking at the observable differences between industrialized countries and underdeveloped countries attempts were made at describing the level and various aspects of underdevelopment. The problem of underdevelopment was therefore characterized as being one of shortage, i.e. shortage of capital.

Rostow

Walt Rostow's doctrine, which played an important role during the late 1950s and the 1960s, was a typical expression of this perspective. According to him there were five stages through which all societies had to pass in order to reach a self-sustaining economic growth:

1. The traditional society;
2. the pre take-off stage;
3. take-off;
4. the road to maturity;
5. the society of mass consumption.

In the traditional society the level of technological knowledge was so low that it imposed an upper limit on per capita production. The economic prerequisites for a 'take-off' were created during the second stage, and many of the characteristics of the traditional society were then removed. Agricultural productivity increased rapidly, and a more effective infrastructure was created. The society also developed a new mentality, as well as a new class – the entrepreneurs.

The third stage, the take-off, was the most crucial for further development. It was during this period, covering only a few decades, that the last obstacles to economic development were removed. The most characteristic sign of having reached the take-off stage was that the share of net investment and saving in national income rose from 5 per cent to 10 per cent or more, resulting in a process of industrialization, where certain sectors assumed a leading role. Modern technology was disseminated from the leading sectors while the economy moved towards the stage of maturity. The economic structure changed continuously; certain industries stagnated while new ones were created. The state of maturity was gradually reached – as was the ultimate goal, the mass consumption society. The citizens could now satisfy more than their basic needs, and consumption was shifted towards durable goods and services.

According to Rostow, international relations did, in fact, speed up the process of development, but had little to do with underdevelopment. Rostow differed from the early development theorists by his much broader approach (he saw his 'theory' as an alternative to the Marxist theory), but the key element in his thinking was, nevertheless, the process of capital formation.

Balanced v. Unbalanced Growth

The early development theories' interest in capital formation may also be seen from the debate on development strategies. The most prominent question in this context was that of a balanced or an unbalanced growth. The proponents of the former often based their arguments on the logic of the vicious circle: since standard of living, saving, investments and purchasing power kept each other locked at a low level it was quite possible that limited efforts, such as the establishment of industries, would not succeed in disturbing the low-level equilibrium and breaking the vicious circle. What was needed was a whole series of industrial establishments supporting each other both on the demand and the supply side. The support on the supply side lay in the fact that the production was complementary; the support on the demand side in the fact that a 'package' of industries together generated a purchasing power which guaranteed that the entire output could be sold.

Complementarity might therefore be said to be the key concept in the strategy of balanced growth. As far as the investment programme was concerned, the level of ambition varied with the level of complementarity. It might be a matter of complementarity between different light industries, between light and heavy industry, between industry and agriculture, and, in its most ambitious form, between industry, agriculture and infrastructure.[9]

The debate initiated by the proponents of balanced growth was quite extensive. From where were the underdeveloped countries to obtain required administrative capacity for the carrying out of a balanced growth programme, and from where were resources for investments to come? The questions were legion and the concept of balanced growth was criticized from various quarters,[10] notably by Albert Hirschman (Hirschman, 1958). He claimed that the greatest flaw in the theory of balanced growth was the assumption of ample supply of the one factor which in reality was truly scarce in the underdeveloped countries – namely decision-making and entrepreneurial skills. In his opinion it was better to concentrate the few decision-makers available in these countries in a few sectors, rather than spreading them over the entire economy. The expansion of one sector was certain to create bottlenecks in others; an incentive to expand would thus be created in the sectors in which the bottlenecks had arisen. A classic example of this kind of situation is the relationship between various technical innovations in the spinning and weaving mills in England during the industrial revolution. A realistic strategy which took the lack of both economic resources and administrative capacity into account was therefore thought to consist of an investment programme which intentionally created bottlenecks as a further incentive to economic development. Thus, Hirschman proposed an unbalanced growth as an alternative to the balanced growth strategy.

The debate gradually subsided, basically because those for and against balanced growth had more in common than sometimes seemed to be the case. A number of arguments were carried over into the general discussion of economic planning in underdeveloped countries, and in a planning context one cannot, *a priori*, assume that a suitable planning strategy should be based on balanced or unbalanced growth.

Trade and Development

According to the early development economists, international relations had nothing to do with underdevelopment. On the contrary, they thought these contacts had a positive effect on the process of development. We shall therefore consider how the neo-classical economists viewed the then most important relation between nations, i.e. foreign trade.

The neo-classicists considered foreign trade to be an effective 'engine of growth' and were therefore in favour of free trade. They pointed out that historical experience, both in developed and less developed countries, had shown that a large part of the economic growth had been generated by exports. The gains from trade were both of a static and a dynamic nature. Static, or as they were also called, direct gains were generated by using existing resources more effectively. The dynamic gains were indirect and generated by trade.

The so-called neo-classical theory of trade deals mainly with questions of a static nature. Its central argument is the theory of comparative costs, which says that a country may raise its level of consumption above what would have been possible in a state of autarky, by specializing in the production and foreign sale of commodities which, relatively or comparatively, have the lowest costs of production. The world as a whole, as well as each single country (including the less developed ones) obtain more goods, at a constant level of factor input, through an international division of labour in which all nations specialize and export only those commodities which they can produce cheaply.

The theory of comparative cost dates back to David Ricardo. Its modern version was mainly developed by Eli Heckscher (Heckscher, 1919) and Bertil Ohlin (Ohlin, 1933). They succeeded in going a step further than Ricardo by showing that not only did comparative advantages of cost determine the pattern of international trade, they also explained why one country was capable of producing certain commodities cheaper than others. Different countries had different relative supplies of production factors, and that was what determined what commodity would give the country a comparative cost advantage. A country should specialize in and export those commodities the production of which used resources in good supply. A country which had a relatively good supply of labour, compared to capital, should have a comparative advantage of cost in the production of commodities which used more labour than capital, and should therefore export labour-intensive commodities and import capital-intensive ones from countries with relatively ample supplies of capital.

The theory furthermore stated that free trade would raise the participating countries' level of welfare, as well as, and this was important, lead to a factor price equalization between the countries. The wage differences between the developed and the less developed countries would, for example, be reduced, which, in turn, would lead to a more equal, international distribution of income.

In addition to these direct and positive effects from free trade the neo-classical economists also saw a number of indirect effects, which, in fact, had already been studied by such classical economists as Smith and Mill.

The neo-classicists, however, used them as further arguments for free trade (see e.g. Viner, 1953 and Haberler, 1959). One indirect effect was the fact that trade would make material factors available, such as new machinery and raw materials which, in turn, would speed up economic development. It was thought that the trade would transfer both technical and administrative know-how to countries that needed it. To the countries which had fallen behind other countries in the process of development and industrialization this latter effect was particularly important, because 'they might learn from the pioneers' experiences, both their successes and failures, as well as their mistakes'. A third, indirect advantage from trade was that it promoted free competition. Increased competition was thought to raise efficiency and lead to faster growth.

The modern development theoretical discussion has re-examined the effects of foreign trade. Economists from the Third World have been most active in this process of re-examination; the most influential of them, Raúl Prebisch, will be dealt with in detail in a later chapter. The best-known Western economists who have criticized the neo-classical theory of trade are Hans Singer, Gunnar Myrdal and Dudley Seers.

In 1950 H.W. Singer published an article in which he questioned the development effects of international free trade (Singer, 1950). In the existing international division of labour the periphery produced and exported raw materials while the centre specialized in producing manufactured goods. According to Singer this division of labour was an obstacle to the economic development of the periphery, since the underdeveloped countries producing raw materials were subjected to deteriorating terms of trade *vis-à-vis* the industrialized countries. Thus, the gains from foreign trade were concentrated to the 'centres' and did not raise the welfare in all the countries trading with each other, as claimed by the neo-classical theory of trade. Contrary to what those in favour of free trade had suggested, the periphery should not specialize in and export commodities in which it had comparative advantages, but should instead attempt to change the whole structure of comparative advantages. In other words, the periphery should invest in industrialization.

Gunnar Myrdal went one step further by pointing out that the so-called 'backwash' effects from trade might lead to 'underdevelopment' (Myrdal, 1957). The neo-classical theory of trade stated that development in one part of the world would lead to development in other parts through various 'spread' effects. An increase in income in one country would lead to an increased import requirement and hence to an increase in production in another. However, Myrdal thought that free trade, rather than equalizing incomes in different countries, would tend to aggravate the differences. In his opinion, an expansion of the market would often favour those countries which already possessed developed industries since countries with a relatively small industrial basis (e.g. small-scale industries and handicrafts) fall behind when competing with the larger and more developed industries. Although free trade in the short run might have certain positive spread effects, they would, in the long run, be offset by the negative backwash effects.

Early Structuralism

In 1963 Dudley Seers published a classic essay in which he rejected the current economic theory's claim of universality. He stated that the theory was only valid in a special case, namely that of modern industrial capitalism (Seers, 1963). Like Singer and Myrdal, Seers had worked for the UN during the 1950s. Their experiences in this international service formed the basis for their critique of current economic theory. Although the concept of 'paradigm' was not widely used at the time, it is striking to see how Seers's reasoning implies some kind of paradigm crisis and anticipates a new paradigm.

> This paper is the reaction of an economist who, after several years of work overseas on problems of economic development, had had an opportunity to reflect on the usefulness of his subject. If the tone is rather sharp in places, I must ask the reader to understand that close personal contact with the problems of backward countries instils, for many reasons, a sense of urgency and some impatience. Economists seem very slow in adapting themselves to the requirements of the main task of the day – the elimination of acute poverty in Africa, Asia and Latin America – just as the previous generation of economists failed to cope realistically with economic fluctuations until after the depression had brought politically catastrophic results.
> (Ibid., p 77)

Thus Seers compared the Keynesian revolution to the current development theoretical problems of the time, to which he saw no quick solutions ('Nobody burns his lecture notes until the next generation is already thundering at the door'). However, he did have certain ideas about potential sources of new ideas, i.e. from Raúl Prebisch and the Economic Commission for Latin America (ECLA), where he himself had been working during the 1950s. He also mentioned Myrdal, Singer and Nurkse, but 'Prebisch lives closer to the seismic fault from which the tremors are emanating' (ibid., p 79). In other words, he saw the light coming from Latin America; if a name must be tacked on to this approach, it should be 'early structuralism'.

Some of the early development theorists tried to form a structural view of underdevelopment. Let us for a moment turn to sports for an example (Van Benthem van den Bergh *et al.*, 1972). Instead of seeing the process of development as a race, we might look at it as a league of commercially run football teams. Some of the teams are more successful. They can now purchase the poorer teams' best players; thus the poorer teams tend to deteriorate even further, and the possibilities of improving their league standings all but vanish.

Thus, underdevelopment is primarily a problem of relations rather than a problem of scarcity, according to the structuralist view. In a given structure, be it domestic or international, value will regularly be added to certain positions, whereas others, relatively speaking, will be deprived of value. Development for one of the parties will therefore tend to imply underdevelopment for the other, depending on their relative positions within the structure binding them together. Consequently, development to the misfavoured and underdeveloped party must imply that its position in the structure will change, or that the structural relation is broken.

We might illustrate the meaning of a structural analysis, and how it differs from the views exemplified by Rostow's theories, by taking a closer look at the much used concept of dualism.[11] Basically, dualism refers to observable contrasts between different economic sectors, or between (rich and poor) regions in the world. The controversy over the concept is due less to dualism as an empirical phenomenon than to its causes. A descriptive study of dualism might simply confirm that what is abundant in the developed countries (capital, technology, know-how, health, initiative, etc.) is truly scarce in the underdeveloped ones. It is not possible to come to any important conclusions about causal relationships at this level of analysis. However, at the structural level of analysis it is a matter of analysing systematic (structural) relations between both parties and how these, in turn, are related to the observed differences in levels of development. Depending on the kind of problem being studied, this analysis can be done at the sector, regional or international level.

Starting at the sector level, the most influential work was done by W.A. Lewis (Lewis, 1954 and 1955). He claimed that an underdeveloped country's economy was dual, i.e. that it consisted of two sectors – one industrial and the other agricultural. In Lewis's development model the agricultural sector serves as a labour reserve for the industrial sector. The latter is thus capable of expanding, due to this 'hidden capital-reserve', until the labour surplus in the agricultural sector is used up. As will be shown in a later chapter dealing with the Caribbean development debate, this model was based on experience from Puerto Rico, and was primarily intended as a strategy for the industrialization of Jamaica.

Another well-known example of dualism is Java, with its 'traditional' rice farms and modern plantations. Java was actually the basis from which the original concept of dualism was developed. During the early 20th Century the Dutch economist J.H. Boeke described Java as a dual society, and described dualism by referring to the differences between Western and Eastern mentality. Fifty years later the American social anthropologist Clifford Geertz produced a structural explanation of dualism in Java. Geertz demonstrated the structural relations between the sectors, and clearly pointed to the mechanisms which gradually aggravated underdevelopment in Java (Geertz, 1963).

Gunnar Myrdal is usually counted among the early students of structural relations at the regional level.[12] He rejected the theory of equilibrium and claimed that the original change in a system does not necessarily bring about a reaction which forces the system back into a condition of equilibrium. On the contrary, subsequent changes may drive the system further away from the original condition of equilibrium in what Myrdal himself called a *cumulative causal process*. Consequently the problems of regional disequilibrium will grow successively worse. Because of 'external economies' industrial investments will be shunted into areas where investments have previously been made, thus leading to financial impoverishment in other regions. The most active age groups are drawn to the expanding region, while the stagnant regions are depleted, both in terms of labour and potential entrepreneurs. Services, administration and political organizations are concentrated in the expanding region, which, in addition to economic superiority, now also gains political superiority. After a while the stagnant region reaches a lower limit in terms of schools, hospitals, communications, etc., at which moment its autonomous life ends. Its continued existence now becomes dependent upon what, in the expanding, dominating region is called regional policy. In this way underdevelopment can be a created process.[13] Myrdal's theory of cumulative causation as well as other early structuralist theories of 'vicious circles' can be seen as predecessors to the dependency approach.

The Modernization Paradigm

The earliest modern theory of development was purely economic and based upon simple models of growth, in which capital formation was the key factor. These models had been developed with a view to purely Western conditions. Their application to the problems of the underdeveloped countries revealed an immense gap between fact and theory. The subsequent theoretical development may be seen as an attempt to fill this gap. The problems of population growth were noticed first; the concept of capital was expanded to include health care and education; attitudes and institutions were brought into the theoretical discussion; the political factors were eventually given the important position they deserved. This entire process of theoretical development implied a dramatic end to the narrow, economic, model-oriented view that had influenced the earlier discussions of development theory. An increasing number of disciplines were included, and development theory has gradually grown towards a more independent and interdisciplinary field of research. At the same time it has become necessary to abandon all attempts at creating *the* theory of development.[14]

To a relatively limited extent this movement towards multi- and interdisciplinary approaches meant that scientific ethnocentricity was abandoned. The new and relevant factors which were gradually brought into the discussion were usually identified by a comparison between the developed and underdeveloped countries. The disciplines that now began to participate in the theoretical discussion, however, repeated the early mistakes of development economics by mechanically applying their methods and approaches to the situation of underdevelopment. It was difficult to break the ethnocentric perspective and to change culturally determined premisses. The bias was furthermore increased by the fact that most of the social sciences in the Third World displayed little or no independence, but rather mechanically imitated Western methods.

In spite of the increasing complexity of development theory as it grew more interdisciplinary, it is nevertheless possible to distinguish in the new approaches the same basic evolutionary framework that was so characteristic of Western cosmology. Most contributions – whether economic, political, sociological or psychological – were rooted in a basic paradigm, now most commonly referred to as 'the modernization paradigm'. Development was seen in an evolutionary perspective, and the state of underdevelopment defined in terms of observable differences between rich and poor countries. Development implied the bridging of these gaps by means of an imitative process, in which the less developed countries gradually assumed the qualities of the industrialized nation. The task of analysing the qualities to be imitated was shared between economists, sociologists and political scientists, so that some specialized in economic structures, others in human attitudes, social institutions and political development.

Modernization means different things to different people on different occasions. The concept has been used in at least three senses: as an attribute of history, as a specific historical transitional process and as a certain development policy in Third World countries (Smith, 1973, p 61). It is the third meaning which is most relevant in the context of development theory, but the problem is (and that probably accounts for the appeal of the modernization perspective) that the three meanings are blurred. Modernization policies (implying a rationalization and effectivization of economic and social structures) are not only seen as elements of a development strategy but as the working out of universal historical forces (the first sense) which bear a strong resemblance to the transition from feudalism to capitalism in Western economic history (the second sense). Thus, there are among the modernizers both fundamentalists, who believe in development as a basically repetitive process, and less rigid proponents, who see modernization merely as one aspect of social change. It is the existence of the former approach, where development is an endogenous process, realizing the potential inherent in more or less embryonic form in all societies, depending on their level of social development, which makes it possible to talk about a paradigm.

We shall here discuss some well-known theories within the modernization paradigm from different social sciences. They have been chosen to illuminate both the central core and the borderlines of the paradigm.

Sociology

Since the main contributions to modernization theory came from sociology, it is appropriate to start with this discipline. There are many 'grand theorists' in this tradition but the central figure was Durkheim. In the division of labour and in the postulate of structural differentiation he saw the motive force of modern societies. It should, however, be noted that the classical theorists were mainly concerned with the transition from 'tradition' to 'modernity' in Western Europe, although the general relevance of this scheme is sometimes implied. It is also of importance that classical views were usually rather ambivalent *vis-à-vis* the process of modernization, as shown by Durkheim's concept of *anomie* and Marx's preoccupation with alienation. A third relevant observation is that modernization theory as part of the larger evolutionary tradition, of which it forms the most recent tradition, conceives of social change as a *basically* endogenous process. We emphasize 'basically', since external variables were often called upon to explain how the process of modernization was triggered off, as in Marx's and Engels's famous statements on the function of colonialism to drag stagnant societies into history. However, the potential for modernization lay dormant in the societies concerned. For those most faithful to the paradigm, modernization was a universal process characteristic of human societies rather than a concrete historical process taking place in specific societies during specific periods.

The classical framework appears in its modern form in Talcott Parsons's pattern variables: particularism-universalism, ascription-achievement and diffuseness-specificity. To complete this chain of influences, Bert Hoselitz was the first to apply Parsons's pattern variables to the problem of development and underdevelopment (Hoselitz, 1960). According to him, society went through development or modernization as particularism, ascription and diffuseness were replaced by universalism, achievement and specificity. In practice, modernization was very much the same as Westernization, i.e. the underdeveloped country should imitate those institutions that were characteristic of the Western countries. Thereby Marx's prophecy that the backward country saw the image of its own future in the more developed one would come true.

To give a deviating example from sociology, we may briefly refer to Barrington Moore's *The Social Origins of Democracy and Dictatorship* (1966) in which the unilinear scheme which was so characteristic of the modernization paradigm is abandoned altogether and instead three historically relevant paths to modernization are identified: the classic bourgeois revolution (Britain), revolution from above (Germany) and revolution from below (Russia). Here we find no determinism in the analysis of the transition and no assumption of convergence after the transition. In accordance with the modernization paradigm, Moore's theory of development considers endogenous factors only. This is, of course, more realistic for large countries, such as India and China, than for small countries, like Tanzania and Jamaica but even in those cases chosen by Moore, the international system should in fact have been given a more prominent role in the analysis (Skocpol, 1979).

Economics

Probably the most well-known economic contribution within the tradition of modernization theory is that of Walt Rostow, who, as was pointed out above, conceived development as a number of stages linking a state of tradition with what Rostow called 'maturity'. This development was analysed primarily as an endogenous process. Rowtow's doctrine, which played an important role during the late 1950s and early 1960s, was a typical expression of the Western development paradigm. It is interesting to compare his analysis with that of Alexander Gerschenkron, which differs in three important respects from Rostow's. In our view, these differences demonstrate to what degree one can depart from the basic premisses of a paradigm without breaking it. First of all, Gerschenkron's analysis of the industrialization process in Europe concerns a specific historical process, whereas Rostow's stages are supposed to be universally valid. Secondly, what appear as preconditions for take-off in Rostow's analysis, here come out as results of the process of development. This process can be initiated in spite of lacking preconditions, through what Gerschenkron calls 'processes of substitution'. The most important factor is the state, whose activities can compensate for lack of entrepreneurship, capital markets, etc. Thirdly, the international context enters Gerschenkron's analysis as an important causal factor, which, through the possibility of substitution, enables a country to take advantage of other countries' technology and thereby skip stages. In spite of these differences, which clearly point to the weakness in the modernization paradigm, we could possibly consider Gerschenkron's contribution as 'normal science' (showing dangerous anomalies) within the modernization paradigm.

The problem of underdevelopment, as we know it today, had no place in this paradigm. There was only an original stage of backwardness, on which should follow a process which released the forces of modernization. These forces were seen as inherent in all societies and in so far as there was need for a theory of underdevelopment, its function would be to analyse 'barriers to modernization' and 'resistance to change'. Gerschenkron realistically pointed out the multilinearity of this process, but even in his analysis one finds the normative position that countries, after having achieved their take-off (which Gerschenkron termed the 'Big Spurt'), should return to the 'normal' track of development.

Political Science

Rostow's stages were basically derived from the distinction between 'tradition' and 'modernity' which is well known from classical sociology and the Weberian analysis of ideal models. Maine described the transition between the two states of *status* versus *contract*, Durkheim spoke of *mechanical* versus *organic* solidarity and Tönnies about *Gemeinschaft* versus *Gesellschaft*. There is no denying that more or less sophisticated versions of this paradigm existed, but in its more simplistic form the modernization paradigm served as a development ideology, simply rationalizing cultural colonialism. Nowhere was this as clear as in the field of *political science*, where the tradition of studying change was much weaker than in sociology.

The political modernity, which was to be achieved by 'political development', was modelled on the parliamentary democracy of the British type or (when North American theorists were involved) a presidential democracy of the US type. In fact this genre was dominated by North American scholars and their framework was partially derived from the pattern variables mentioned above. Gabriel A. Almond was the intellectual leader of the new movement and the major work showing the way was *The Politics of the Developing Areas* (1960), edited by Gabriel Almond and James S. Coleman. As Samuel Huntington points out, this work deals with comparative politics rather than political development (Huntington, 1971, p 299). The 'developmental approach' came six years later (Almond and Powell, 1965). Here, political development was seen as an aspect of the wider process of modernization, marked by three criteria: structural differentation, subsystem autonomy and cultural secularization. Other authors stressed different criteria but most of them saw political development as a complex concept (i.e. it included several dimensions) and as an element of modernization. For this reason they were trapped in the same teleological illusion as the sociological modernization theory. The content of political development or political modernization was implicitly identified with the institutional differences between the Western democracies and various traditional political systems. Political scientists who went out to study the 'developing area' in the 1960s thus borrowed freely from their more experienced relatives: economics (political development) and sociology (political modernization). Naturally these field experiences had a sobering effect on theory.

A study which may be said to fall within the modernization paradigm, while at the same time partly contradicting it, is David Apter's *The Politics of Modernization* (1965). A distinction is here made between a 'reconciliation system' and a 'mobilization system'. The former corresponds to a modern, pluralistic political system, whereas the latter constitutes a transitional phase between traditional and modern. Having worked in Africa, Apter realized that this transition implied immense social tensions and that therefore a more or less dictatorial political organization was needed. This may be compared to Gerschenkron's processes of substitution during the 'Big Spurt'. The mobilization system and the big spurt should consequently be seen as temporary deviations from the normal, evolutionary path, and the idea of 'back to normalcy' is implicit in both theories. This idea reveals the impact of the modernization paradigm but at the same time the recognition of abnormalcy indicates a divergence from the paradigm.

Of the liberal optimism implied in the political modernization approach not very much remains today. Almond himself refers to 'the missionary and Peace Corps mood' prevailing during the 1950s and early 1960s (Almond, 1970, p 21). In a critical review of political modernization theory Donald Cruise O'Brien points out that the increasingly tense international situation has aroused the academic interest in *political order* rather than *political change* (Cruise O'Brien, 1979). Occasionally the abstract concept of 'order' is substituted for a more brutal, but more precise language. However, this falls outside our present concern with modernization theory, although it exemplifies how changing academic concerns reflect the spirit of the time.

Growth and modernization theories were, of course, not completely dominant during the 1950s and 1960s, nor did they escape criticism. The modernization paradigm has been subject to strong criticism from social scientists in the Third World, particularly in Latin America. Since this belongs to the prehistory of 'dependency' we shall deal with this criticism in the next chapter.

After the critical foundation had been laid by the Latin Americans the modernization paradigm came into disrepute even in the West and there have been a number of analyses of its rise and fall (Smith, 1973; Roxborough, 1979). This critique not only concerns modernization theory as such, but the whole tradition of evolutionism and functionalism of which it forms part. Smith divides his criticism into four different lines of attack. *Methodologically* neo-evolutionism is based on comparative statics which neglect both the sources and the route of change. From a *logical* point of view there is, for example, the mistake of equating serialism with causal explanations of transitions. *Empirically*, it is easy to point out that any effort to classify societies using indicators of tradition and modernity soon breaks down. From a *moral* point of view, finally, the most clear-cut objection is the unabashed ethnocentrism implied in the modernization approach, which as we shall see, was one reason for the Latin American critique.

On the winding road towards a theory of social change there are many mistakes, both major and more trivial. Modernization theory certainly belongs to the first category. If one can speak of a paradigm in development theory, the modernization perspective provides us with one. It has a long tradition in Western social thought. It was, mainly thanks to the doctrine of endogenism, logically coherent. It dominated several social sciences in the 1950s and 1960s. It had a great appeal to a wider public due to the paternalistic attitude towards non-European cultures. This is turn created the rationale of development aid, as well as the forms it took. It is probably correct to say that the general outlook of modernization theory still constitutes the popular image of developing countries. In the academic world, however, modernization theory became outdated in the early 1970s, whereas the more pragmatic tradition of development economics continued in spite of the emergence of a rival approach, to be discussed later.

Notes

1. See e.g. Hoselitz (1960) and Robbins (1968) for the role of development theory in the history of economic thought. Adelman (1961) is a study of classics from a modern growth theoretical perspective.
2. Here it should be pointed out that a detailed description of the method of historical materialism is not within the scope of this book.
3. It is interesting to note that, during the later part of his life, Marx himself questioned this on several occasions during the debate on Russia; instead,

he attempted further to develop the theory, although he had obvious theoretical problems which he was never able to solve. A detailed discussion of this may be found in Eric Hobsbawm's *Introduction to Marx* (1964). Hobsbawm also shows that Marx's view approached that of the Narodniks (see below): 'It is interesting, that – somewhat unexpectedly – his [Marx] views inclined towards those of the Narodniks, who believed that the Russian village community could provide the basis of the transition to socialism without prior disintegration through capitalist development. This view does not follow from the natural trend of Marx's earlier historical thought, was not accepted by the Russian Marxists (who were among the Narodniks' opponents on this point) or by subsequent Marxists, and in any case proved to be unfounded. Perhaps the difficulty Marx had in drafting a theoretical justification of it reflects a certain feeling of awkwardness. It contrasts strikingly with Engels' lucid and brilliant return to the main Marxist tradition – and to support for the Russian Marxists – when discussing the same topic some years later (Hobsbawm, in Marx, 1964, pp 49-50).

4. Lenin, for example, writes as follows: 'The progressive historical role of capitalism may be summed up in two brief propositions: increase in the productive forces of social labour, and the socialization of that labour. But both these facts manifest themselves in extremely diverse processes in different branches of the national economy' (Lenin, 1956, p 595).
5. These observations, formulated by Lenin during the Comintern Congress in 1920, are taken from Cardoso (1977) p 7. A detailed analysis of Lenin's views on this question may be found in Singer (1976).
6. A more detailed discussion of this may be found in Palma (1978).
7. Joseph Schumpeter is an important exception. He carefully studied growth and development problems. See, e.g. Schumpeter (1934).
8. Harrod (1948) and Domar (1957). A summary may be found in Kregel (1972).
9. This is an attempt to create a synthesis of balanced growth theoreticians, who all have their own version of what balanced growth should be. The most influential of these works were done by Rosenstein-Rodan (1943), Nurkse (1953) and Lewis (1955).
10. The theory of balanced growth is criticized from various points of view in e.g. Fleming (1955); Bauer and Yamey (1957); Hirschman (1958); Kindleberger (1958); Streeten (1959); and Singer (1964).
11. The concept of dualism is briefly discussed in Barber's contribution in Streeten (1970) and in Brookfield (1975).
12. Myrdal (1957). When Myrdal talks about regions, he does not mean regions within a country only. A region may also consist of several countries, which is why the same kinds of mechanisms work at the international level. See also our earlier discussion of Myrdal.
13. We shall return to the subject of structural analyses at the international level on several occasions. It should, however, be mentioned that what the authors who dealt with this level did study was how various historically given relations between different parts of the world affected the development in those parts. It was primarily authors in the Marxist tradition who dealt with this subject. Raúl Prebisch was the best known among the non-Marxist authors.

14. Towards the end of the 1960s, one economist, Benjamin Higgins, summarized the theoretical development as follows: 'The appeal to the other social sciences for help has also been heeded. Sociologists, psychologists, political scientists, anthropologists are flocking to the development field . . . Yet we seem as far from a general theory as ever. Indeed the flood of new knowledge seems to make generalizations of a kind useful for policy purposes in all developing countries more and more hopeless . . . It is my view that no Newton will appear, no breakthrough will occur. Development is not that kind of problem' (Higgins, 1968, p 843). Salvatore Schiavo-Campo and Hans W. Singer come to the same conclusion in the introduction to *Perspectives of Economic Development* (1970): 'a theory of economic development has not emerged, at least not in the same sense that we can identify a price theory, or a pure trade theory, or even a theory of growth. For development is not merely economic growth it is growth accompanied by structural social and economic change. It is perhaps inevitable that the impossibility of using a ceteris paribus approach to problems of development should engender difficulties in constructing a unified theoretical framework.' It is obvious that it is not only the complexity of problems that stand in the way of constructing a unified theory, but also ideological and political differences. 'A single body or theory about development is as unlikely to emerge as it is about any other major social theme engendering political conflict and sharp intellectual divergences' (Bernstein, 1973, p 21). These quotations express the general feeling of resignation among those who worked with development theory during the 1960s. In Kuhn's terminology (Kuhn, 1962) one might describe this stage as a 'paradigm crisis'.

2. Background to the Dependency Approach

The *dependency approach* originated in the extensive Latin American debate on the problems of underdevelopment, which was a most valuable contribution to modern social science. Not only did it contain an effective criticism of the modernization paradigm, it also provided an alternative perspective and still functions as a catalyst in the development theory which is taking shape at present.

The dependency school emerged from the convergence of two intellectual trends: one often called 'neo-Marxism', and the other rooted in the earlier Latin American discussion on development that ultimately formed the ECLA (the United Nations' *Economic Commission for Latin America*) tradition.

The concept of neo-Marxism reflects a certain dualism in Marxist thinking, i.e. on the one hand the traditional approach, focusing on the concept of development and taking a basically eurocentric view, and, on the other, a more recent approach, focusing on the concept of underdevelopment and expressing a Third World view. Of course, much controversy has arisen as to the continuity or discontinuity of these two approaches. To the orthodox Marxists, the main body of neo-Marxist thinking is more or less incompatible with the classic Marxist framework. This complex issue will be dealt with in the first part of this chapter.

A second important background to the dependency school was the more indigenous Latin American discussion on underdevelopment, reflecting specific economic and intellectual experiences in various Latin American countries, particularly during the depression of the 1930s. This economic crisis dramatized the dimensions of Latin American dependence. It initiated more systematic economic research, and it necessitated a policy of import substitution, later systematized into a development strategy. If we add to this the early works of the Argentinian economist Raúl Prebisch we have the background story of ECLA, a story that forms the second part of the chapter. The third part deals with the Latin American critique of the modernization paradigm. This critique is an integral part of those theoretical trends that lead to the dependency approach.

Marxism versus Neo-Marxism

Marx and the Third World

It would be absurd to apply Marx's description and conclusions about 19th Century European capitalism to the so-called problems of the underdeveloped countries of today. It would be equally absurd to blame Marx for the futility of such an undertaking. In this context we shall, however, treat Marxism as a system of thought which has been mechanically applied to the problems of underdevelopment. Our purpose is not to criticize Marx, but to point out that the intellectual development in the Third World has been greatly influenced by the fact that Marxism, as well as a number of other systems of thought, was introduced as an ideology rather than as a theory.

Before the Russian Revolution, Marxism was mainly represented by a few, often poorly translated, publications. The subsequent large-scale distribution of Marxist literature was more a matter of political zealousness than a response to intellectual demands. This is not one of the brightest chapters in the history of Marxism, but it is important to the development of the dependency school, particularly since the latter was a reaction against schematic Marxism and the analytical weakness and political inefficiency of orthodox communism.

In one of their more pamphleteering moods, Marx and Engels stated that the future of the backward country is reflected in that of the more developed country: through the rapid improvement of the instruments of production and vastly improved communications the bourgeoisie forces all nations, including the most barbarian ones, into civilization. The low prices of goods is the heavy artillery with which it shoots down all Chinese walls, and the means by which it forces the capitulation of the barbarians' stubborn hate of foreigners. All nations are forced to adopt the bourgeois mode of production – unless they want to be ruined; it forces upon itself the introduction of so-called civilization, i.e. becoming bourgeois. In other words: the bourgeoisie creates a world in its own image.

Marx's thoughts about 'the problems of underdevelopment' did not differ significantly from the prevailing 19th Century evolutionism.[1] The Third World rested, peacefully and unsuspectingly like a sleeping beauty, waiting for the Western world's Prince Charming to awaken the process of development, if not by a kiss, then by the sword. In one of the most frequently quoted passages on the non-European world, Marx foresees an industrial revolution in India as the inevitable result of the English-built railways.

> You cannot maintain a net of railways over an immense country without introducing all those industrial processes necessary to meet the immediate and current wants of railway locomotion, and out of which there must grow the application of machinery to those branches of industry not immediately connected with railways. The railways system will therefore become, in India, truly the forerunner of modern industry. (Marx and Engels, 1960, pp 84–5)

What Marx wrote about Asia (apart from the draft of a theory about the Asian mode of production) was mostly pure journalism, influenced by the news of the day; Marx himself considered it to be 'extra income' of little value.[2] His writings on Asia therefore offer little information to the reader interested either in Asia or the history of Marxist thinking; however, the fact that there are so few of them makes them difficult to ignore.[3]

One of the key concepts in this context is 'the Asian mode of production'. In Marx's extremely tentative formulation this concept is of little value as a description of India, or indeed of the rest of Asia. Nevertheless, it offers an important insight into the nature of Marxism, since the later published work on pre-capitalist social formations (which included a discussion of the Indian mode of production) clearly documents a 'multilinear' view of development.[4] The most remarkable aspect of Marx's analysis of the Asian mode of production, however, is the fact that he considers it to be devoid of dynamics, which therefore, in a way, legitimizes colonialism. Marx, as well as most other contemporary European intellectuals, no doubt viewed this slumbering society somewhat disdainfully; in formulating the concept he intended to add to Hegel's analysis of the superstructure (oriental despotism) by providing his own analysis of the base (the Asian mode of production).

Marx's writings about the Asian mode of production were thus based on an old European tradition of thought around the subject of 'oriental despotism'. At first it was feared and respected, but as the Turkish empire declined, these sentiments changed into disdain. Turkey was the first model, but as knowledge about Asia grew, the concept moved eastward.

Marx's contemporaries knew quite a lot about India, a little about China, and very little about Japan. When speaking of Asia, Marx mostly meant India (Kiernan, 1974, p 168). The same basic attitude is found when he does explicitly mention China. The general decline which was the result of the opium trade in China, for example, is dealt with in the following drastic terms: 'It would seem as though history had first to make this whole people drunk before it could rouse them out of their hereditary stupidity' (Marx and Engels, 1960, p 20).

Marx and Engels refer sparingly to Latin America in their extensive production. The references they do make are strongly eurocentric in nature (Aguilar, 1968, p 3), and deal exclusively with politics, such as, for example, the Mexican-American War of 1847, which Engels thought of as a fortunate and historically progressive incident: 'for such a country to be dragged into historical activity by force is indeed a step forward. It is in the interest of its own development that henceforth Mexico should be placed under the tutelage of the United States.' Marx agreed: 'All the vices of the Spaniards – boastfulness, grandiloquence, and quixoticism – are found in the Mexicans' (Aguilar, 1968, pp 66-7).

Marxism in Latin America

Apart from the basic method, Marx's own writings thus provided a poor basis for a genuinely Marxist analysis of the economic conditions and the class struggle in Latin America. European immigrants had introduced socialist ideas during the latter part of the 19th Century, but they bore the mark of anarchism rather than that of Marxism (Alba, 1968, p 37). In Latin America, as well as in most other parts of the Third World, Marxism was spread through the Communist International (the Comintern).[5]

The first Comintern congress which specifically dealt with Latin American questions was the Sixth, held in 1928. The following passage is quoted from the Comintern's declaration on Latin America, which also initiated the 'hard line'.

> In Latin America the Communists must everywhere actively participate in the revolutionary mass movements directed against the landlord regime and against imperialism, even where these movements are still under the leadership of the petty bourgeoisie. In so doing, however, the Communists may not under any circumstances politically subordinate themselves to their temporary ally. Whilst struggling for the hegemony, during the revolutionary movements, the Communist Parties must strive in the first place for the political and organisational independence of their Parties, securing its [*sic*] transformation into the leading party of the proletariat.
> (Clissold, 1970, p 78)

During the period between 1928 and the 1935 People's Front policy the Comintern enforced its 'ultra-left' line, characterized by a revolutionary puritanism which refused to collaborate with any bourgeois elements. The Nicaraguan Sandinista guerrilla for instance, was severely criticized. This line was totally unsuccessful, with the exception, of course, of deteriorating relations between the Soviet Union and the Latin American governments. The softer line, introduced after 1935, lasted until the dissolution of the Comintern in 1943; as a result of it the communist parties in several countries eventually turned into significant political forces.

Most often, however, they remained as minority groups of little or no political importance. They rarely produced thinkers of any significance, although the Peruvian José Carlos Mariátegui was an exception. His *Siete Ensayos de Interpretacion de la Realidad Peruana* (Seven Essays on the Peruvian Reality) written in 1927 remains, according to Aguilar, 'the single most important attempt to understand a national, Latin American problem in a Marxist perspective' (Aguilar, 1968, p 12). In order not to give the impression that early Latin American communism was unjustly scanty, we shall discuss Mariátegui in some detail. In *Siete Ensayos* he described the history of Peru in a dialectic perspective, from the primitive communism of the Incas to the socialism of some future age (Baines, 1972, Chap. 7). Mariátegui claimed that the Spanish conquest had meant a retardation (to feudal institutions), and that the subsequent capitalism had been perverted, partly by the foreign economic influence and partly by the domestic alliance between the bourgeoisie and the aristocracy. According to Mariátegui, the 'proletariat' was in fact the primitive, Indian population. The new Peru was to be built on the latter's collectivist traditions. His homespun, nationalistic Marxism (somewhat reminiscent of Mao Zedong) was consistent with the Comintern line up until the tightening of the reins in 1928; after that he turned into an eccentric in an increasingly streamlined communist movement.

Towards the end of his life Mariátegui became more and more isolated. His revolutionary nationalism led him to support Haya de la Torre, the populist leader of the *Alianza Popular Revolucionaria Americana* (APRA). Later Mariátegui became convinced that the APRA would follow the example of Kuomintang in China – which was quite an astute prediction. Haya de la Torre replied by accusing Mariátegui of taking orders from Moscow – which was absurd. The Comintern agents had tried to persuade Mariátegui to change his Peruvian Socialist Party (PSP) into a communist party in 1928, but to no avail. The Comintern did not, at that time, permit any independent interpretations of the Marxist-Leninist doctrine. In the spring of 1929 the first Latin American communist congress met in Buenos Aires to come to grips with the 'Mariátegui problem'. After a stormy discussion, the congress criticized Mariátegui for his 'Trotskyist' views. After his death, the PSP was changed into an orthodox communist party and a tool of the Comintern. The revolutionary throughts of Mariátegui as well as their correct interpretation are still discussed today (Choy *et al.*, 1970; Paris *et al.*, 1973).

The case of Cuba is also a good example of the contrast between the orthodox, communist party line and a more voluntaristic, revolutionary strategy. Urged by the Comintern and aided by the Mexican Communist Party, the Cuban Communist Party was founded in 1925. Cuba already had a militant, non-Marxist, radical nationalism with José Martí as its central figure. Martí had led the insurrection against Spain in 1895 and fell in combat. Those who claim that Fidel Castro was influenced more by José Martí than by Marx are probably right.

The depression created great social problems in Cuba during the 1930s, when the economy was strongly dependent on the United States. In 1933 Fulgencio Batistá led an insurrection against the dictator Gerardo Machado. Batistá enjoyed extensive popular support, although not by the Communist Party, which was illegal until 1938. Led by Blas Roca, the Communist Party played an important role in the labour movement. After 1935, when the Comintern proposed a popular front policy, the party sought allies in other groups of the left, and eventually ended up supporting Batistá. In return, he not only legalized the party, but promoted two leading communists to ministerial posts. The party changed name in 1944 and became the *Partido Socialista Popular* (the PSP). Between 1938 and 1944 the membership had grown from 23,000 to 122,000. In 1952 Batistá's dictatorship moved towards the right and the Communist Party was again made illegal. In 1959, Castro began the revolt which was carried out entirely without the support of the Communist Party. The course of events of the revolt is well known: in December 1956, 82 revolutionaries landed in Cuba from the boat *Granma*, 19 of them reached the Sierra Maestra Mountains and began the guerrilla war which led to Batistá's fall a few years later.

From a conventional communist view the Latin American society was still 'feudal' in nature, and a mobilization of the proletariat would therefore be premature before Latin America had experienced its own 'bourgeois' revolution. In other words, it was the historical task of the growing bourgeoisie to smash the 'feudal-imperialist alliance' – a task in which the proletariat was to participate. Only then would a socialist revolution be possible (the 'two-stage strategy'). The Cuban Revolution challenged this political view. Aguilar sums up the pre-Cuban phase as follows:

> Indicative of the situation of the Communist parties in this period, and a key to the internal and external conflicts that were overwhelming them was their scant participation in the most important events of the moment. Not in Guatemala in 1944, in Bolivia in 1952, or in Cuba in 1959, nor in any of the other political convulsions in Venezuela, Argentina, Colombia or Peru did the Communists play an outstanding role.
> (Aguilar, 1968, p 38)

In conclusion it might be said that the role of Marxism in Latin America was marginal until 1960 – with the exception of certain political movements (Chile) and certain individuals (Mariátegui). Around 1960 the movement suffered from yet another schism as a result of the Sino-Soviet conflict (Ratliff, 1976, p 22). In spite of the Chinese challenge, to which should be added the criticism from various 'Trotskyists', 'Castroists' and nationalist communists, and the Soviet invasion of Czechoslovakia in 1968, the Latin American communist parties have remained amazingly faithful to the Soviet Union. In terms of development strategic thinking they have been very close to the ECLA analysis (see below), and when the ECLA strategy ran into difficulties during the 1960s, they were also subjected to criticism from the dependency school. One of the best-known dependency theorists, A.G. Frank, had this to say about the Latin American communist parties:

> . . . the Latin American communist parties and their ideologues . . . have made no contribution to Marxism or any other theory that anyone has been able to discover . . . Programmatically they have been scarcely as advanced as the bourgeois developmentists from whom they differed at most in their largely Soviet-inspired and propagandist opposition to American imperialism; politically they have been little more than a tail wagged by the national bourgeois dog who used the Communist parties – temporarily excepting in Guatemala, Venezuela and Colombia – to keep a leach on the dependence theorists, the Communist parties at home and abroad loyally joined the opposition.
> (Frank, 1977, p 356)

The New Left in Latin America

During the 1960s Latin American political practice developed into something entirely different from what the official communist analysis had predicted. The peasants were more inclined to revolt than the workers, and the rural guerrilla appeared to be an alternative to organizational work within the labour movement. The 'traditional' Marxist views were consequently subjected to severe criticism from 'the left'. Furthermore, there was now a Marxist-inspired debate that did not necessarily have any connections with the Communist Party.[6] The underlying political reason for this may be sought in the Cuban Revolution.

This revolution should not have been possible, according to the conventional Marxist view, and at the beginning, the Cuban Communist Party saw Fidel Castro as a bourgeois adventurer. His success, as well as the breakthrough of Che Guevara's revolutionary appeals in other parts of the Latin American continent, undermined the communist parties' positions and forced them into a more or less radical re-evaluation of their earlier policies. Aguilar says:

> The repercussions of these events naturally went beyond the Cuban sphere. It is evident that many of the arguments that were hurled directly and obliquely at the old Cuban communist cadres – 'the bachelors of Marxism' as they were disrespectfully called by Che Guevara – could very easily be applied to nearly all the Communists parties of the continent.
> (Aguilar, 1968, p 45)

Che Guevara's ideas about the role of the peasants in the revolution and the ability of the human will to surmount objective limitations is reminiscent of Mao Zedong. Latin American Marxism became even more fragmented after the Sino-Russian conflict and Maoist ideas were allowed to grow freely, as was a less party-bound Marxism. Particularly at the universities Marxism now became a part of the intellectual climate rather than just a stilted language at communist party conventions. The 'new left' had been born.

The new left was impatient. It wanted revolution *here* and *now*. The culmination of this political line was the Latin American Solidarity Conference held in Havana in August 1967. Its motto was: 'The duty of a revolutionary is to make revolution.' The influential Venezuelan Communist Party obejcted violently to the fact that Fidel Castro had assumed the task of deciding who was and who was not a revolutionary in Latin America. Other communist parties were, however, moderate in their views. The secretary general of the Chilean Communist Party noted two tendencies in the revolutionary movement in Latin America: a proletarian one and a bourgeois-nationalist one. The latter underestimated the role played by the working class, and showed a tendency towards anti-socialism – but was, nevertheless, revolutionary. Only imperialism could profit from a polarization of these two tendencies (Ratliff, 1976, p 80). Allende's front organization was made possible through this more moderate attitude.

In October of the same year, Che was killed by the Bolivian army and a month later the 'guerrilla theorist' Regis Debray was sentenced to thirty years in prison. This was the beginning of the end of the 'voluntarist' revolutionary strategy. Castro's support to various guerrilla groups became more selective. After this it becomes necessary to make a clear distinction between Cuban political views, which gradually grew more consistent with Soviet foreign policy, and Guevarism, which may be summarized as follows:

1. The people's army (i.e. guerrilla army) is capable of winning a war against a regular army.
2. It is not necessary to wait for the objective conditions for the revolution to develop; they can be created by the guerrilla army, which thus becomes an embryonic revolutionary centre (*foco insurreccional*).
3. The armed struggle in the underdeveloped countries should primarily take place in the rural areas.

All of these three points were contrary to the long-established communist line in Latin America. Although Che Guevara in his later speeches and writings often emphasized the importance of a Marxist-Leninist *avant-garde* party, particularly for the socialist construction work, there was a lingering ambivalence when it came to formulating the theoretically correct relation between the rural guerrilla organization and the urban party organization. This ambivalence has, of course, been the source of a number of disagreements, purges and schisms in the Latin American communist parties: the disagreement about *foco* and *party*, about the continental extent of the revolutionary struggle, the relative importance of the rural and the urban guerrilla, and the question of support to popular front governments – to mention a few. However, there is no reason for elaborating on the further development of Guevarism in Latin America; its more important aspects should now be obvious. During the late 1960s the somewhat fossilized communist movement in Latin America saw Guevarism as a great theoretical and ideological challenge. Many dogmas were rejected, new questions were asked, and the conditions for a more 'Latin American' Marxism were created.

Paul Baran and the Rise of Neo-Marxism

This ideological development coincided with the development of neo-Marxism at the more academic level. It is no easy task to analyse the relationship between these two tendencies. However, it is obvious that they supported each other. Let us therefore leave the brutal political reality and take a look at the intellectual preparations made in the usually more relaxed atmosphere of the university. Here Paul Baran's *The Political Economy of Growth* (1957) must be given credit for contributing significantly to the upsurge of the 'new left' and 'neo-Marxism'.

In his analysis of the political economy of development, Baran used the concept of *economic surplus* and examined how it had been created and utilized in different social systems. The surplus was simply defined as the difference between production and consumption. Furthermore he distinguished between *actual* and *potential* surplus, the latter defined as the difference between the production that would be possible in a given geographical and technological environment, and that which may be considered to be 'necessary' consumption. Baran admitted that this concept was primitive, but it had the great advantage of being relevant: it provided insight into the irrational elements of an economic system and underlined the need for an analysis of the obstacles to a mobilization of potential resources. Baran used the concept in his analysis both of developed and underdeveloped countries but we are more interested in his views on the latter.

According to Baran, capitalism had sprung from feudalism, which in its final stage of dissolution was characterized by increasing agricultural production, by a more extensive division of labour and by capital accumulation. These processes were all prerequisite to capitalism. Western Europe had led this development by its geographically advantageous position and by its lack of natural resources, which stimulated trade, shipping and pillaging. For various reasons this process was not developed in the Third World. Plundering the colonies may not have increased the European national income by much, *but it did constitute a significant contribution to its economic surplus*, hence also to investment and economic growth. The colonies' economic surplus consequently diminished, their capital accumulation came to a halt, and their budding industries were killed by competition. In other words, development in the colonies was forced off its natural course, and was now completely dominated by imperialistic interests. The countries of the Third World (Japan being a spectacular exception) stagnated somewhere between feudalism and capitalism, and were the victims of the worst of both systems. This 'Marxist' view of the spread of capitalism differed radically from Marx's own views. Baran abandoned the view of capitalism being spread from the 'centre' to the 'periphery'; instead, he introduced the idea that 'underdevelopment' was an active process following the development in the centre.

This view, which constituted a clear break with classical Marxism, was more or less hinted at, or implicit in, Baran's analysis. It was, as we shall see, brought to its logical conclusion in the works of André Gunder Frank, in which the idea of 'the development of underdevelopment' was brought forward. The Third World seemed to be doomed to perpetual underdevelopment. No capitalist development tendencies seemed to undermine the feudal social structure. In fact Latin America, along with the rest of the Third World, were *de facto* capitalist from the very moment they were incorporated in the capitalist world economy. The Latin American bourgeoisie was parasitic and would never fulfil its historical mission of freeing the productive forces. The neo-Marxist view prescribed immediate revolutionary activity, based on guerrilla tactics, instead of the communist 'two-stage strategy'. This is where the Guevarist influence comes in. Thus, the neo-Marxists, both theoretically and practically, favoured a new line which at that time seemed to be in better agreement with the political realities than the orthodox

Marxist one. Neo-Marxism was thus the academic expression of that for which the guerrilla struggle stood at the practical-political level – a point which was often emphasized. Here are some quotes from an article which is typical of the time; it was written in 1963 by the editors of the *Monthly Review*, Paul Sweezy and Leo Huberman, after a journey through Latin America.[7]

> The only possible revolution in Latin America today is a socialist revolution.
>
> The notion that there is a powerful national bourgeoisie in these countries anxious to break away from US domination . . . is unfortunately a myth.
>
> There can be no doubt that Latin America needs and is ripe for socialist revolution, not at some distant date in the future but right now.
>
> We did not meet a single serious leftist in Latin America who is not an ardent supporter of the Cuban Revolution . . . There is just one thing that worries them, the extent to which Cuba in resisting the US, may have fallen under the domination of the Soviet Union.

The above expresses an interpretation which was so different from the prevailing Latin American Marxism that it is not without justification to speak of a change of paradigm *vis-à-vis* Marxism and, above all, in relation to established theories of development.[8] The former is, of course, the more problematic of the two. A paradigmatic cleavage between two schools is primarily characterized by a lack of communication; this criterion is relatively well met in the case of the modernization perspective versus the underdevelopment perspective. The line between Marxism and neo-Marxism is much less clear and the distinction *per se* has also been subjected to some criticism (see e.g. Taylor, 1974). An authoritative view claims that Marxism is whole and indivisible, and that the neo-Marxists have either misunderstood some basic Marxist theses (i.e. they are 'poor' Marxists), or that they should not be thought of as Marxists at all.[9] The concept of 'neo-Marxism' will probably not survive for long and we merely use it as an heuristic concept to indicate a specific stage in the history of Marxism, during which there were great gaps in the Marxist analysis of the problems of 'underdevelopment'.

The Differences between Marxism and Neo-Marxism

At this point it might be interesting to take a closer look at an attempt to identify the phenomenon of neo-Marxism and the differences between neo-Marxism and Marxism. Aidan Foster-Carter has brought forward a number of points which, in his opinion, contrast the two traditions.[10] Somewhat modified, they are as follows:

(1) *Imperialism and Nationalism:* Marxism (as interpreted by Lenin) sees imperialism in a 'centre' perspective, that is, as a stage in the development

of capitalism (monopoly capitalism); neo-Marxism, on the other hand, sees imperialism from the periphery's, or the victim's, point of view, which in turn implies that the interest has shifted from development to underdevelopment. This break with what is, for the classical Marxism, such a typical evolutionary perspective is quite important to the distinction between Marxism and neo-Marxism. Marxist-inspired leaders of the Third World, such as Mao Zedong or Amilcar Cabral have often had a nationalistic appearance which has always been more acceptable to neo-Marxists than orthodox Marxists.

(2) *Classes:* Here we find several important differences. The Marxist analysis of classes is based on specifically European experiences, while that of the neo-Marxists is based on the revolutionary struggle in the Third World – with a much more generous view of different groups' revolutionary potential. Whereas Marxists have difficulties seeing anyone but the industrial proletariat as the revolutionary class *par préference*, the neo-Marxists will tend to let the peasants play this role – claiming that the industrial workers of the Third World in reality form a 'labour aristocracy'. Marxists believe in the existence, or eventual emergence, of a national bourgeoisie in the Third World; neo-Marxists, on the other hand, see the bourgeoisie as the creation and tool of imperialism, and as such incapable of fulfilling its role as the liberator of the forces of production.

(3) *Revolution and Ethics:* The neo-Marxists view the possibilities of starting a revolution with greater optimism, even if the conditions may be unfavourable, and in this context emphasize the importance of guerrilla warfare. Marxism, on the other hand, emphasizes organization and patient party work, particularly amongst the workers. In other words, the neo-Marxists emphasize the role of the subjective factors, moral stimuli, the 'new' man, etc. Marxists retain materialism and the emphasis on 'objective conditions' that gave Marx his distinctive mark as a social scientist.

(4) *Ecology:* Marxism still shows traces of the 19th Century development optimism, and many Marxists consider the concept of scarcity to be a bourgeois invention for the purpose of legitimizing economic inequality. Some neo-Marxists now integrate the growing ecological consciousness and the demands of environmental movements with their theory of development; the blind faith in industrialism as the liberator of humanity has at the same time undergone some major revisions. Similarly, there is now a tendency to think of the cities as being parasitic, and to idealize the countryside – contrasting sharply with Marx's own comments on 'the idiocy of rural life'.

The neo-Marxist concept has caused considerable irritation among Marxists, particularly as they have been accused of being 'Palaeo-Marxists'. We shall return to this subject in connection with the Marxist criticism of the dependency school.

Obviously, the differences which we have pointed out above are merely rough indications of general tendencies. On this basis it might be difficult clearly to define two theoretical camps with contrasting but internally identical views. It might be said that neo-Marxism has accepted the changes through which Marxism has passed after its transplantation from European to non-European soil, while the Marxists have been anxious to safeguard the purity of Marxism. Contrary to Foster-Carter, we believe, as suggested above, that it is inadequate to speak of two distinct 'schools'; instead, we are witnessing a dialectic, intellectual process in which Marx is the thesis and neo-Marxism the antithesis, i.e. a phase in the universalization of the Marxist tradition. This is the way in which we shall use the concept.[11] The theoretical deficiencies in orthodox Marxism with regard to its analysis of the social conditions in the Third World are now being mended and its gaps filled, as will be discussed later on.

ECLA Development Thinking

During the inter-war period a growing number of ideas and analyses based on concrete, Latin American conditions, as well as on more systematic social science research began to appear. Until then 'social science' had mainly consisted of speculations in social philosophy, strongly influenced by European culture and social debates. The Latin American authors were isolated *pensadores* ('thinkers' or amateur philosophers) who mechanically grafted European, 18th-Century evolutionism, Auguste Comte's positivism and social Darwinism on to Latin American conditions.[12]

The indigenous analyses of Latin America which appeared at the end of the 19th Century were orgies in self-criticism and catalogues of Latin American weaknesses (Hirschman, 1971), as, for example, Bunge's *Nuestra America* (1903) and the Chilean Francisco Encina's *Nuestra inferioridad economica: sus causas, sus consecuencias* (Our Economic Inferiority: Its Causes and Consequences) (1912). The obvious conclusion from this type of analysis was the idea of economic development through imitation. In 1895, the Argentinian B. Alberdi said: 'North America is South America's great, economic example' (Hirschman, op. cit., p 275).

As a result of the First World War, the Mexican and the Russian Revolutions and repeated interventions by the US in the Latin American states' internal affairs, there was a change towards finding the faults in the surrounding world, rather than in Latin America. At the same time, the social analysis began to be based on more systematically conducted research, rather than on the *pensadores* and their more or less subjective ideas influenced by European social research and debates.

As far as the social sciences were concerned, Chile appeared to be the country providing the most favourable conditions for research, particularly in the area of economics. Systematic instruction in that subject was given as early as 1813; the economic journal *Revista Económica* was founded in 1886. The department of economics at the Catholic University was formed in 1922 and that of the Chile University in 1935. Led by President Aguirre Cerda, the Popular Front government founded the *Corporacion de Fomento de Producion* (CORFO) in 1939. This agency constituted the link between academic research and practical social planning. CORFO initiated a number of empirical studies which later formed the basis for a macroeconomic analysis, which broke a number of economic taboos because of its orientation towards domestic, economic problems. Chile developed *inter alia* a positive attitude towards central economic planning; this view was further expanded when the United Nations located the Economic Commission for Latin America (ECLA) in Santiago.

It is interesting to note that the debate on economic research resulted in a certain polarization between the economists of the ECLA and the national university on the one hand and those from the Catholic University on the other. The latter had been influenced by the Chicago School, and were known as 'Los Chicago Boys'. On a more theoretical level this conflict manifested itself in the famous debate between 'structuralists' and 'monetarists' to which we shall return below.

Raúl Prebisch and ECLA

The Great Depression in the 1930s was a great divide in economic theory in the industrialized world and it is also in these experiences that we find the roots of a specifically 'peripheral' theory of economic development. The key figure here is undoubtedly Raúl Prebisch who from 1935 to 1943 was Director-General of Banco Central in Argentina, a country that was most severely hit by the depression. The idea of a centre-periphery structure in the world economy was implicit in Prebisch's early economic policy writings concerning Argentina, in which inward-directed development and industrialization were seen as the remedy (Love, 1980, p 54). It should, however, be noted that this industrialization drive is a recurrent phenomenon, which can be structurally explained as the ideology of latecomers in development. This ideology goes back to Friedrich List and the German reaction to Britain as the workshop of the world, subsequently emerging in other industrializing countries; the United States in the mid 19th Century, Russia in the late 19th Century, Eastern and South Eastern Europe in the inter-war period, and Brazil, Chile, Argentina and Mexico in the 1930s and 1940s. It was the experiences of these countries which provided the rationale for the import substitution strategy recommended by ECLA in the 1950s.

The formulation of a distinctly Latin American view of underdevelopment and of development is intimately related to ECLA, founded in 1948 in Santiago, Chile. In addition to twenty-one Latin American countries, Great Britain, France and the Netherlands also became members.

As opposed to most of the other regional UN agencies (the economic commissions for Asia and Africa), the ECLA soon developed its own views on the problems of underdevelopment and development. The one who really should be credited with this achievement is Raúl Prebisch, who became head of the ECLA in 1950. A few years before, Prebisch had written a document, eventually to become the 'ECLA Manifest': *The Economic Development of Latin America and its Principal Problems* (Prebisch, 1950). This document begins as follows:

> In Latin America, reality is undermining the out-dated schema of the international division of labour, which achieved great importance in the nineteenth century and, as a theoretical concept, continued to exert considerable influence until very recently. Under that schema, the specific task that fell to Latin America, as part of the periphery of the world economic system, was that of producing food and raw materials for the great industrial centres. There was no place within it for the industrialization of the new countries. It is nevertheless being forced upon them by events. Two world wars in a single generation and a great economic crisis between them have shown the Latin-American countries their opportunities, clearly pointing the way to industrial activity.

From this passage it is obvious that Prebisch sought the causes for Latin American underdevelopment outside the continent, and he found them in the system of international free trade. Consequently, his first attack was on the neo-classical theory of trade. According to Prebisch, this theory supported the existing international division of labour, in which the periphery had specialized in the production of primary products and the centre in the production of industrial goods, as well as the idea that this division of labour would result in the greatest possible advantage to all the parties involved. As an example he showed what, according to the theory, would happen if technical progress was more rapid in the centre's production of industrial goods than in the periphery's production of primary products. Assuming that the fall in prices would be inversely proportional to the growth of productivity, the prices of industrial goods would fall more rapidly than those of raw materials. The periphery would then be able to purchase more industrial goods for the same amount of primary products, and thus progress would accrue to all countries of the world even without an industrialization of the periphery.

Prebisch's own empirical studies, however, showed that this prediction was not generally valid. He had found that Great Britain's terms of trade had gradually improved since 1880, and since Great Britain was predominantly an importer of primary products he concluded that during this long period the terms of trade of the primary producing countries (i.e. the periphery) had seriously deteriorated in relation to Great Britain (i.e. the centre).

Prebisch's explanation of the deterioration of the periphery's terms of trade was that most of the profits from the various increases in productivity had benefited only the industrialized countries. He also tried to show that this had not been a unique phenomenon, but a sign of underlying structural relations which the neo-classical theory of trade had not taken into account.

On the production side the theory had primarily neglected the true market structures. Technical progress may favour the producer by reducing costs (which in turn may increase profits and/or wages). Prebisch claimed that development in the centre rarely led to price reductions, mainly because of the high degree of monopolization of the factor and goods market there. The fact that imperfect competition was dominating meant that price falls could be avoided, and also that the labour unions, because of their strength, could claim a share in the technical progress in the form of increased wages.

In the periphery, the opposite was supposed to be the case. Here, the consumer received the fruits of technological change via reduced prices, mainly because primary producers operate under competitive conditions. However, in reality it was the consumer in the centre who was favoured, since technical progress in the periphery primarily occurred in the export industry. Thus, the centre would benefit both from the periphery's technical progress as well as from its own.

On the demand side it was noted that the goods produced for export in the centre and in the periphery had different income elasticities. The income elasticity of imported primary products in the centre was considerably lower than the income elasticity of imported industrial goods in the periphery. This was a result, *inter alia*, of Engels's Law, which states that the percentage share spent on food is a diminishing function of income. An increase in income in the centre would therefore lead to a lower percentage change in the demand for imported primary products than a similar increase in income in the periphery would change the demand for imported industrial goods. Thus, even the demand side held elements that would lead to a deterioration of the primary producing countries' terms of trade.

Through this analysis Prebisch came to the conclusion that the underdevelopment of Latin America was due to its reliance on exports of primary products (also called the Prebisch-Singer thesis, since Hans Singer published similar ideas at the time (Singer, 1950). Prebisch also claimed that a continued emphasis on the export of primary products would inevitably lead to a further deterioration of the periphery's terms of trade. In turn, this would affect the domestic accumulation of capital. However, the international mechanisms of equalization would function as predicted by the neo-classical theory of trade if the periphery were to export industrial goods instead. Thus, Latin America would be able to keep the fruits of its own technical progress. The natural solution to the problem was therefore *industrialization*.

As we shall see later, W.A. Lewis came to similar conclusions through his analyses of the Caribbean. However, his development strategy was rather the opposite to that which emerged in Latin America. Lewis proposed an export-oriented industrialization, whereas Prebisch's and the ECLA strategy, roughly, may be summarized as follows:

– The process of industrialization was to be speeded up by the substitution of a large part of current imports by domestic production. Initially, domestic industries were to be protected from foreign competition by tariffs and other support measures, but once their competitive ability had improved, the firms should be able to manage on their own.

– The production of raw materials would continue to play an important role in the Latin American economies. The income earned from exporting raw materials should be used to pay for imported capital goods, and thus help increase the rate of economic growth.

– Initially, foreign businesses were to help speed up the process of capital accumulation. However, there was a certain feeling of reservation towards greater dependency on foreign subsidiaries (Cardoso, 1977, p 29).

– Governments should actively participate as co-ordinators of the industrialization programme. Increased government involvement was necessary to break the chains of underdevelopment.

– Later (towards the end of the 1950s), the ECLA became the driving force behind the efforts at creating a Latin American common market in order to facilitate further industrialization.

Programmed Industrialization

If the ECLA's theoretical explanation of underdevelopment and its sketches of alternative development strategies are called the first phase, the second phase may be said to have begun when the Commission tried to translate the strategy into practical policies. The initial guidelines for this work were drawn up at a conference in Rio de Janeiro in 1953. A well-prepared policy of industrialization was said to be required if the process of underdevelopment was to be reversed, and the ECLA therefore tried to convince the Latin American governments of the necessity of this, offering to assist in the preparation of detailed development programmes for each country. The phrase *programmed industrialization* became popular.

Initially, ECLA strategy was rather coldly received by the Latin American governments, which is also why most of the Commission's development programmes remained paper exercises. This resistance to its ideas explains why the ECLA could not, and should not, propose measures that were too radical, of affected internal problems. Land reforms and other basic, structural changes never received a high priority on the list of necessary changes.

A couple of years later several Latin American governments did, in fact, begin to collaborate more closely with the ECLA: Argentina, Brazil, Colombia and Peru were among the first countries to follow ECLA strategy. The Commission could now directly influence the development strategies by offering technical assistance in their planning and application, but, what was even more important, it could influence the development process indirectly by training local planners in the ECLA way of thinking. The Commission's doctrines were therefore quickly spread across the continent.

The belief that industrialization was the remedy to underdevelopment spread not only to the Latin American countries during the 1950s, but to most of the countries in the Third World. It was generally assumed that the process through which the industrialized countries had gone was essentially repeatable, and that the current conditions in these countries were the ultimate goal of development. A well-developed industrial sector was considered to be typical of a modern society; the various characteristics of an underdeveloped society would automatically disappear in the process of industrialization. The traditional oligarchy, for example, would play a diminishing role, which would lead eventually to both economic and political democracy; this, in turn, was thought to be necessary for the development of a modern mass consumption society with a high level of technology, culture and scientific activity.

Because of their belief in progress these Latin American scholars were given the nickname *desarrollistas* or *developmentista*: the Brazilian Celso Furtado was one of them. Having experienced the rapid expansion in Brazil during the 1950s, he wrote:

> By now the Brazilian economy could count on its own dynamic element: industrial investments supported by the internal market. Growth quickly became two-dimensional. Each new impulse forward would mean an increasing diversification, a larger mass of resources for investment, a quicker expansion of the internal market and the possibility of such impulses being permanently surpassed.
> (quoted from Hirschman, 1968, p 2)

The ECLA Theory of Development

We shall now return to ECLA's theoretical work. Prebisch's analysis of terms-of-trade is usually the only one referred to in this context, but it is important to realize that ECLA and Prebisch had more to say,[13] in spite of the fact that most of the interest was focused on an analysis of the external sector.[14] They actually tried to present a complete theory of development which particularly emphasized the structural imbalances between centre and periphery. Their approach not only dealt with questions related to the theory of trade and the strategy of industrialization, but also encompassed the entire complex of development. ECLA attempted to show that *underdevelopment* is not the same as *undevelopment*, i.e. lack of development. Underdevelopment was instead to be thought of as the result of a specific process that led to underdevelopment in one part of the world and development in another.

ECLA, however, never did manage to formulate a 'general theory of underdevelopment'. Instead, a new method of analysing the complex of underdevelopment was introduced, the *structuralist method*, but in spite of that, the paradigm of modernization was never really abandoned. Apart from its rather unconventional treatment of international relations, the Commission was quite traditional. We have previously discussed the great optimism of ECLA economists about the ability of industrialization to put an end to underdevelopment. Like many other economists at the time, the ECLA theorists overemphasized the role of capital in the development process. After all, the main point was that the periphery's deteriorating terms of trade affected the accumulation of capital and consequently also the rate of economic growth.

Thus the paradigm of modernization was still pretty alive, but ECLA and its new approach formed the basis for its eventual abolition. Their structural approach, which in Chapter 1 we called 'early structuralism' was extremely important, not only in the theoretical debate on development, but also in a number of other theoretical contexts such as the 'Latin American inflation controversy'.

The cause of inflation had been keenly discussed in Latin America since the early 1950s. This debate is not as well known outside Latin America as that about the development of the terms of trade. The ECLA rarely participated officially, but some of the economists working at the Commission did. At an early point they attempted to formulate a theory of inflation which was to be an alternative to the prevailing neo-classical one, and particularly to the theory formulated by the monetarists, of whom the most extreme claimed that inflation was not a result of a given economic system, but rather a problem of 'the printing press'. Inflation was primarily due to the 'irresponsibility' of individual finance ministers, who printed too much money to cover the government's budget deficit. The solution to the problem was therefore simply 'to stop the printing presses', which essentially is the same thing as reducing government expenditures.

The structuralists, on the other hand, claimed that the Latin American countries faced several 'structural' problems which automatically created inflationary pressures. Basically they were attributable to supply inelasticities: in economies with such problems, limitations of the quantity of money would not stop inflations (except in the very long run at the cost of, for example, a rise in unemployment to unacceptable levels). The monetarists' solution to the problem, which was simply a 'proper' monetary policy, was therefore rejected. With reference to the ECLA analysis of the general process of growth in Latin America, which primarily saw development as a result of the supply of capital, the structralists criticized the organizations that followed the monetarists' recommendations (e.g. the IMF) for having far too restrictive criteria for lending money.[15]

The political recommendations made by ECLA had a common denominator – the demand for increased government involvement. It was the task of the government to correct all structural elements standing in the way of development. However, ECLA always pointed out very carefully that it did not propose a planned economy. The 'Russian' model was as vigorously rejected as the *laissez-faire* model. The market economy was to remain, but under the 'surveillance' of the government. This 'Keynesian' view played an important role in Latin America, but it was also accepted in almost all of the Third World. Since the 1950s, governments have played a much more active role in these economies than in any other part of the capitalist world.

An extensive debate followed in the wake of the ECLA. Attacks were launched from both liberal and radical corners. The debate between the liberal economists and the ECLA is of little interest to the growth of the dependency school, and is therefore not included here.[16] Of more relevance, however, is the criticism of the modernization paradigm coming from Latin American social scientists.

The Latin American Critique of the Modernization Paradigm

The economic growth of the more industrialized countries of Latin America implementing ECLA policies came to a halt during the 1960s. Instead of 'taking off into self-sustained growth' there was general economic stagnation, and, as a result of that, both social and political problems came to the fore. The shortcomings of the policy of import substitution were becoming obvious. The purchasing power was limited to certain social strata, and the domestic market showed no tendency to expand after its needs had been fulfilled. The import dependency had simply shifted from consumption goods to capital goods. The conventional export goods had been neglected in the general frenzy of industrialization; the result was acute balance-of-payment problems in one country after another. The optimism of growth changed into deep depression.

Raúl Prebisch and Celso Furtado, two veterans of Latin American development economics, now both realized that although industrialization had been initiated, it did not automatically continue by itself. Here is a comment from 1966 by Furtado: 'In Latin America . . . there is a general consciousness of living through a period of decline . . . The phase of 'easy' development, through increasing exports of primary products or through import substitution has everywhere been exhausted' (quoted from Hirschman, 1968).

The growing consciousness of the fact that economic growth – for as long as it lasted – did not necessarily have any social or political counterparts also contributed to the widespread pessimism. During the 1960s the ECLA published a report on the social situation in Latin America, together with the annual economic review. Together, these publications offered a peculiar picture of the development: on the one hand industrialization and growth, and on the other unemployment and marginalization. Many students of development saw this as confirmation of the fact that established development thinking was going through a crisis.[17]

Stavenhagen

We have already dealt with the ECLA critique of simplified growth theories and the view of foreign trade as the prime mover behind development. In this context we shall deal with a much broader discussion which questioned the entire, established paradigm of modernization. In an influential essay from 1966 the Mexican sociologist Rodolfo Stavenhagen criticized what he called 'The Seven Erroneous Theses on Latin America' (Stavenhagen, 1966).

(1) *The Latin American countries are dual societies:* This proposition states that two different and, to a certain extent, independent societies exist within the Latin American countries: one traditional agrarian society and one modern, urbanized society. The former is often associated with feudalism and the latter with capitalism, which also implies that 'feudalism' is an obstacle to development that must be replaced by progressive capitalism. Both societies are, however, in reality the result of the same process.

(2) *Progress in Latin America will come about by the spread of industrial products into the backward, archaic and traditional areas:* This thesis assumes that the modern expansive sector automatically starts a process of development in the traditional sector, that the transition from traditional to modern society is a process which inevitably includes all the traditional societies in the world today, and that the centres of modernity are nothing but the result of the propagation of elements originating in already developed countries. Stavenhagen objected to this by claiming *inter alia* that the spreading out of modern consumption goods did not imply an increase in welfare *per se*, and that it instead managed to drive out local industries and trades, and eventually led to classes of middlemen and usurers. As far as capital is concerned, the spreading seemed to go in the opposite direction – from the backward areas to the developed areas. The progress of the 'modern' area was, in reality, achieved at the 'traditional' area's expense.

(3) *The existence of backward, traditional and archaic rural areas is an obstacle to the formation of an internal market and to the development of a progressive and national capitalism:* In Stavenhagen's opinion this was false because in Latin America there was no progressive, national capitalism, nor were the conditions such that one might develop.

(4) *The national bourgeoisie has an interest in breaking the power and the dominion of the landed oligarchy:* The landowners', financiers' and industrialists' interests were, in reality, joined in the same economic groups, the same companies, and occasionally even in the same families. There is no reason why the national bourgeoisies and the land oligarchy shouldn't get along.

(5) *Latin American development is the work and creation of a nationalist, progressive, enterprising and dynamic middle class, and the social and economic policy objectives of the Latin American governments should be to stimulate 'social mobility' and the development of that class:* Those classes called the middle classes are very closely connected with the existing economic and political structure and lacked the dynamic that might make them catalysts in a process of independent economic development.

(6) *National integration in Latin America is the product of miscegenation:* This thesis suggests that the development was moving towards some kind of universal society in which the differences between the dominant white minority and the mass of natives in the rural areas would disappear. This thesis was wrong because a biological and cultural mixing does not imply a change in the existing structure *per se*. In the *internal* Latin American colonies the *mestizos* represent the local and regional ruling classes, and do in fact suppress the natives.

(7) *Progress in Latin America will only take place by means of an alliance between the workers and the peasants, as a result of the identity of interests*

of these two classes: This thesis has primarily been examined by the orthodox left, but the workers' and peasants' interests were, in reality, not identical. In Latin America it is a fact that the stronger the internal colonialism, i.e. the greater the differences between the metropolis and its domestic colonies, the less opportunities there are for a true political alliance between workers and peasants.

Cardoso

Stavenhagen was here thinking of the experiences in Mexico which, in fact, were common to a number of Latin American countries. Brazil was, perhaps, the country in which the development optimism of the 1950s had found its most uninhibited expression. Everyone, right across the political spectrum, thought that Brazil was in the 'take-off stage', and that those most responsible for this condition were the growing number of 'entrepreneurs'. During this time sociologists in Sao Paolo established the Centre for Industrial Sociology where the various industries in the Sao Paolo area were studied in a Schumpeterian perspective. The results were not always as expected: the Brazilian businessmen did not turn out to be the backbone of the growing Latin American bourgeoisie; they were found to be totally devoid of initiative and energy, totally dependent on the government and foreign capital (Cardoso, 1967, pp 94-114). Doubt therefore arose about the Latin American bourgeoisie. The thought that it was incapable of fulfilling its historical mission – to release the productive powers and create a transition from feudalism to capitalism – turned out to be a most important aspect of the dependency theory.

Fernando Henrique Cardoso was among the sociologists who carried out the sociological studies of the 'entrepreneurs' in Sao Paolo, and later wrote a general critique of the current social sciences, particularly the 'theory of modernization' within the discipline of sociology (Cardoso and Faletto, 1969, pp 8-10). Cardoso and Faletto pointed out that the pattern 'from traditional to modern' was a reincarnation of the German sociologist Tönnies's old dichotomy of *Gemeinschaft* and *Gesellschaft*.

They raised two objections to this: firstly, neither concept is broad enough to cover all existing social situations, nor is it specific enough to distinguish the structures that determine the life-styles of various societies. Secondly, these concepts do not show how various stages of economic development are linked to the various types of social structure characterized as either 'traditional' or 'modern'.

> With this kind of characterization it continues to be impossible to explain the transition from one type of society to another. In fact, change in social structures, far from being only a cumulative process of incorporating new 'variables', involves a series of relations among social groups, forces, and classes, through which some of them try to impose their domination over society. (Ibid. p 10)

What they call the *historical-structural* method is the alternative to the prevailing, schematic and mechanical analysis:

> For us it is necessary to recognise from the beginning that social structures are the product of man's collective behaviour. Therefore, although enduring, social structures can be, and in fact are, continuously transformed by social movements. Consequently, our approach is both structural and historical: it emphasizes not just the structural conditioning of social life, but also the historical transformation of structures by conflict, social movements, and class struggles. Thus our methodology is historical-structural. (Ibid., p.x).

This criticism of the prevailing development theory and the search for alternative approaches was obviously an expression of a more widespread intellectual climate in Latin America in the mid-1960s.

Dos Santos

Theotonio Dos Santos, also a Brazilian, sums up the traditional ideas on development as follows (Dos Santos, 1968b [1973]):

– Development means advancement towards certain well-defined general objectives which correspond to the specific condition of man and society to be found in the most advanced societies of the modern world. The model is variously known as modern society, industrial society, mass society and so on.

– Underdeveloped countries will progress towards this model as soon as they have eliminated certain social, political, cultural and institutional obstacles. These obstacles are represented by 'traditional societies', 'feudal' systems, or 'feudal residues', depending on the particular school of thought.

– Certain economic, political and psychological processes can be singled out as allowing the most rational mobilization of national resources and these can be categorized for the use of economic planners.

– To all this is added the need to co-ordinate certain social and political forces in support of a development policy and to devise an ideological basis which organizes the will of various nations in the 'tasks' of development.

Once the conventional development theories have been proven to be indefensible, Dos Santos goes on to provide the basic prerequisites for a more solid theory of development:

– The theory of development must analyse the process of development in its various historical and concrete manifestations.

– It must extract, through such an historical analysis, the general laws of development of the societies it chooses to investigate.

– In formulating these laws, development theory must take into account the international contradictions of the process, abandoning any formalistic attempt to reduce it to a unilineal transition from one type of society to another. Rather the theory would have to show how through these very contradictions society as a whole can reach higher forms of organization. These forces, and the social forms they imply, are better described as social trends than as models of a future situation to which we should aspire.

Moving now from Brazil to Chile (and keeping in mind that both Cardoso and Dos Santos went to Chile after the Brazilian military coup in 1964) we find the same phenomenon: great dissatisfaction at the way in which the established social sciences explain the Latin American reality, and at their inability to provide guidelines for an adequate policy of development.

Sunkel

We have chosen the Chilean economist Osvaldo Sunkel (formerly with the ECLA) as an example of this dissatisfaction (see Sunkel, 1969 and 1971, as well as Sunkel and Paz, 1970). Sunkel claimed that the problem with the prevailing analysis of the development question was that it was based on conventional theories of growth and modernization. As claimed by other Latin Americans, to whom we have referred earlier, this theory saw the mature capitalist economy as the goal of all development efforts; the underdeveloped nations were analysed in terms of a previous and imperfect stage on the way to this goal. Sunkel believed that this idealized and mechanical vision ought to be replaced by a more historical method, the result of which would be a better understanding of the real nature of the underdeveloped nation's structure and its changes. The approach suggested by Sunkel simply meant that the characteristics of underdevelopment should be viewed as *normal* results of the functioning of a specific system. In the case of the underdeveloped nations these results are well known: low income, a slow rate of growth, regional imbalance, inequality, unemployment, dependency, monoculture and cultural, economic, social and political marginalization, etc. The conventional theory considered these symptoms to be deviations from the ideal pattern which, like children's diseases, would disappear with growth and modernization. It did not realize that behind this lay a system, the formal functioning of which produced these results, and that this would continue for as long as development policies attacked the symptoms of underdevelopment rather than the basic structural elements that had created underdevelopment.

According to Sunkel, once Latin America is seen in this perspective it becomes obvious that considerable influence was exercised by external ties; however, their importance should not cover up the existence of internal, structural problems. A realistic analysis of Latin American development should therefore be based on the assumption that the socioeconomic system has been shaped by two types of structural elements: external and internal. The former have been more important factors as far as Latin American development is concerned.

An adequate analytical scheme for the study of underdevelopment, and for the formulation of development strategies, must be based upon knowledge of the process, the structure and the system. Underdevelopment cannot be seen as a stage in the development of an economically, politically and culturally autonomous society. Underdevelopment should rather be thought of as part of the global historical process of development. Underdevelopment and development are two sides of the same universal process, i.e. they interact and are mutually conditional. Their geographic expression is manifested in two polarizations: first, the polarization of the world between the rich industrialized and developed nations on the one hand and the underdeveloped backward, poor, peripheral and dependent nations on the other; secondly, the internal polarization between advanced, modern industries and the so-called 'traditional sector'.

The concepts of development and underdevelopment must therefore be seen as partial yet mutually dependent structures forming *one single* system. One important characteristic which separates the two structures is that the developed system, mainly because of its ability to grow, to a great extent dominates while the underdeveloped system is dependent, partly because of the nature of its own dynamics. All of this can, of course, be used both *between* nations, as well as between regions *within* a country. This school of thought focused on two types of polarizing processes: one at the level of international relations, the other at the national level. So much for Sunkel.

Frank

As far as the group of scholars who were soon to be known as the *dependentistas* and their critique of the prevailing theory of development is concerned, it is difficult to ignore André Gunder Frank's influential paper 'The Sociology of Development and Underdevelopment of Sociology' from 1969. In it Frank criticized the Research Centre on Economic Development and Cultural Change and its periodical *Economic Development and Cultural Change* (the EDCC) to which Frank himself had been a contributor. Frank's Latin American experiences have obviously led him to question the 'paradigm' of which this periodical is the foremost representative. It should be noted that in it Frank acknowledges his debt to Rodolfo Stavenhagen, amongst others – and there are certain similarities between Frank's and Stavenhagen's critique; Frank's critique is, however, more theoretical while Stavenhagen's discussion, more concretely, is tied to Latin American, particularly Mexican, empirical studies. Frank's critique was also more directly aimed at specific scholars, particularly the group around the EDCC, e.g. Manning Nash, Bert F. Hoselitz, Marion Levy, Everett Hagen and David McClelland. Through his critique Frank wanted to show that the modernization perspective, as developed by the above-mentioned scholars was (1) empirically untenable, (2) theoretically insufficient and (3) practically incapable of stimulating a process of development in the Third World.

In view of the importance of his critique during the late 1960s it might be justified to quote Frank's arguments about these three points. However, we shall limit ourselves to an account of one of the variants of the paradigm of modernization, namely the one he calls 'the ideal-typical index method'. The idea of this method is to compare an underdeveloped country with a developed one by means of various indicators; the differences thus revealed are then established as the substance of development. This approach is manifested in two ways: by *pattern variables* and by *stages of growth.* As shown in Chapter 1 the tradition of pattern variables goes back as far as classical sociology, and was applied to the problems of underdevelopment by Bert Hoselitz. In that chapter we also dealt with the foremost representative of the school of 'stages', Walt Rostow.

Frank argues that many developed nations show strong particularistic tendencies, that ascribed status is widespread and that the structure of roles is not as functionally specific as our official ideology might have it. Similarly, traits of 'universalism', 'achievement' and 'specificity' might be found in the underdeveloped nations. After having destroyed the empirical basis of the pattern variable analysis on the problems of underdevelopment Frank goes on to question the theoretical bases for analysis:

> Hoselitz leaves far from clear just which is the social whole whose role patterns he would change from one set of variables to another in order to effect development. Here the theoretical inadequacy is even more glaring, for it contravenes the generally accepted rule of social and all scientific theory to look for and refer to the systemic whole in terms of which the reality (in this case underdevelopment) can be explained and changed. The social system which is today the determinant of underdevelopment certainly is not the family, tribe, community, a part of a dual society, or even, as I shall argue below, any underdeveloped country or countries taken by themselves.

As an example of the limitations of pattern variable analysis, Frank in terms of development policy mentions the fact that the growth of the middle-class groups in Latin America has not led to a higher level of development – quite the contrary.

Growth stages are a further development of the pattern variable analysis in the sense that the two idealized poles are united through a series of stages. As the reader might recall, Rostow mentions five such stages: (1) the traditional stage; (2) the pre-take-off stage; (3) the take-off; (4) the road to maturity; and (5) the mass consumption society. It is difficult to find these stages in reality.

> Rostow's stages and thesis are incorrect primarily because they do not correspond at all to the past or present reality of the underdeveloped countries whose development they are supposed to guide. It is explicit in Rostow, as it is implicit in Hoselitz, that underdevelopment is the original stage of what are supposedly traditional societies – that there

were no stages prior to the present stage of underdevelopment. It is further explicit in Rostow that the now developed societies were once underdeveloped. But all this is quite contrary to fact.

According to Frank, underdevelopment was not an original stage, but rather a created condition; to exemplify, he points to the British deindustrialization of India, the destructive effects of the slave trade on African societies and the obliteration of the Indian civilizations in Central and South America. The greatest problem in Rostow's analysis was, however, the fact that not all of the countries which according to him were ready for take-off, could manage the final jump.

The theoretical shortcoming of Rostow's analysis is primarily the fact that it is based on 'comparative statics' rather than being dynamic, and that the overall perspective is lost. In terms of development policy the approach is gravely compromised because of Rostow's political affiliation:

> As to the efficacy of the policy recommended by Rostow, it speaks for itself: no country, once underdeveloped, ever managed to develop by Rostow's stages. Is that why Rostow is now trying to help the people of Vietnam, the Congo, the Dominican Republic, and other underdeveloped countries to overcome the empirical, theoretical, and policy shortcomings of his manifestly non-communist intellectual aid to economic development and cultural change by bombs, napalm, chemical and biological weapons, and military occupation?

The tone of Frank's article is strongly polemic, which is illustrated by the above quotation; it is also typical of the intellectual climate at the universities of the metropoles during the late 1960s. During the so-called students' revolution of 1968 Frank was one of the main suppliers of arguments with which the students criticized their teachers for having used bourgeois propaganda in their teaching. In other words Frank played the role of 'popularizer' and intermediary in the critical, Latin American debate on the social sciences in the mid-1960s. As we shall show later, he played a similar role in disseminating the ideas of the dependency school.

Notes

1. As far as Marx's and Engels's evolutionist view of capitalist development is concerned, we ought to point out that their extensive writings, in fact, do contain attempts to analyse the problem in a more diversified manner. In their opinion Ireland was thrown back several centuries by the British invasion, instead of being set free by the more developed country's magic wand (which is what they thought would happen in India). We might also mention Lenin's growing insight into the complex and contradictory nature of the capitalist process of development.

2. See his letter to Engels (17/12, 1858) in Torr (1951) p 66.
3. On China, see references in note 2. Marx's comments on India are mainly found in Marx-Engels (1960).
4. See Hobsbawm's introduction to Marx (1964).
5. This does not imply that the Latin American Marxism did not exist in its 'pre-Soviet' form. The Argentinian socialist Juan B. Justo translated Marx's writings into Spanish, but rejected Marxism-Leninism (Aguilar, 1968, p 8).
6. The traditional alternative to the communist parties sanctioned by the Comintern was various Trotskyist groups, but they were not exactly in the centre of political activity either. It is not always easy to determine who reasonably might have been Trotskyists, since Trotskyism was the standard accusation following all those who were excluded from the Communist Party. The Trotskyist criticism of the Latin American communist parties was, however, fierce from time to time (Alexander, 1973).
7. 'Notes on Latin America', *Monthly Review* (February 1963).
8. Aidan Foster-Carter has dealt with the first relation in 'Neomarxist Approaches to Development and Underdevelopment' (Foster-Carter, 1973), and with the second one in 'From Rostow to Gunder Frank: Conflicting Paradigms in the Analysis of Underdevelopment' (Foster-Carter, 1976).
9. A.G. Frank defends himself by saying that he never claimed to be a Marxist (conversation in Gothenburg, Spring 1978).
10. It might be interesting to note that Foster-Carter was working as a sociologist in Dar-es-Salaam when he wrote this. As pointed out in Chapter 7, Dar-es-Salaam was one of the 'secondary centres' of the dependency school.
11. We thus view neo-Marxism as a *phase* rather than as a *school*. In what might be called 'Marxism in a theoretical context' there will always be one mainstream defending the integrity of Marxism. This mainstream has, during certain periods, had difficulties explaining reality by means of established theories. It might then be a question of analysing new problem areas (the problems of underdevelopment) by means of a theory which really was developed for use in a different social context, or accepting that reality has changed in a way that requires the introduction of new elements in the theory. We find an example of the latter during the early 20th Century when capitalism, in many ways, had become different from what Marx had analysed. The so-called 'second generation' of Marxists made numerous errors in their search for explanations of this. New hypotheses were put forward which were not always consistent with the views and methods of the mainstream. Eventually, the Marxist method (i.e. historical materialism) was refined to the point where it was capable of explaining the latest aspects of the development of world capitalism. The result was the theory of imperialism.

    During the period when the theory of imperialism was developed we might even speak of 'neo-Marxism' (Sweezy, 1972, pp 37 ff). When 'Marxist' theory was later adjusted to incorporate the new neo-Marxist traits with unchanged theoretical integrity, it returned to the mainstream.

We have chosen to call the mainstream 'Marxism', since the word 'orthodox' might contain a value judgement. Lukács provides an early example of attempts to define 'orthodox Marxism': according to Lukács, 'orthodox Marxism does not imply an uncritical acceptance of the results of Marx's research. In the Marxist context orthodoxy is purely a reference to method. It is the conviction that the true method of research is found in dialectic materialism, and that this method can be further developed, deepened and completed only in the spirit of its originator; all attempts to surpass or improve it have merely led to, and must lead to banality and eclecticism' (Lukács, 1923).

Our idea of 'Marxism' is obviously close to Lukács's 'orthodox Marxism'. However, one might question the true meaning of working in Marx's spirit: the dependency school has truly worked in that spirit without being Marxist for that reason (see e.g. Wallerstein's defence in Chapter 8). Secondly, it is often necessary to express some vague 'pre-understanding' in order to tackle a newly arisen problem. This book claims that the dependency school's attempts, even if they were not Marxist, eventually resulted in a vitalized, Marxist view of 'underdevelopment'.

There will always be dissenting voices in the development process of a theory. In the context of the new Marxist theory of development Bill Warren's voice has been heard the most (see Chapter 4). If we view Marxist theory before the dependency school as the thesis, the dependency school as the antithesis, and the current mainstream as the synthesis, we are forced to interpret Warren's contributions to the debate as a return to the thesis. The kind of Marxism Warren represents has strikingly been called 'neo-classical Marxism' by Dudley Seers (Seers, 1978). Although Warren explicitly starts from a Marxist position he nevertheless comes to much the same conclusion as do the neo-classical economists. This, according to Seers, is because both schools have their roots in the classics – Smith and Ricardo – and because both of them were developed in Europe during the 19th Century, thus having numerous common elements. 'Both doctrines assume competitive markets and the overriding importance of material incentives. They are both basically internationalist and also optimistic, technocratic and economistic. In particular, they both treat economic growth as 'development' and as due primarily to capital accumulation' (ibid.).

12. The positivist ideas date back to the sociological science of Auguste Comte (1798-1857). References to Comte are rare nowadays, and the connotation of *positivism* has changed and become more general; it might therefore be in order to explain Comte's positivism. His sociology centres around the tensions between that which is 'traditional' and that which is 'modern'. To Comte the former was *theological* and *military*, and the latter *scientific* and *industrial*. The process of modernization, which was inevitable and basically the same in all societies, also affected (and perhaps above all) human thinking, which developed from fetishism to 'positivism'. Positive thinking, marked by observation and accuracy, was developed by the natural sciences and later by the social sciences, whose origin was sociology. The purpose of sociology was to determine the stage reached by society, thus facilitating the creation of the modern

order. Comte's view of society was definitely deterministic, but political rulers could nevertheless facilitate the birth of the modern order by sociology. His political ideal was the administrating meritocracy.

His theories never gained any importance in Europe (except in French sociology, where certain elements remained). It is therefore paradoxical that the doctrine of positivism dominated Latin American philosophy. H.E. Davies says: 'In fact, in no other part of the modern world did positivism as a general pattern of thought achieve a stronger hold on the minds of a dominant elite than it seems to have achieved in Latin America' (Davies, 1972, p 99).

13. Prebisch's breadth and activity in other areas is seen by Di Marco's bibliography of his work (1972).
14. The interested reader will find an extensive analysis of the ideas of the ECLA in Rodriguez 1980. See also Hirschman (1961) and Cardoso (1977).
15. A survey of the Latin American debate on inflation between the monetarists and the structuralists may be found in Baer (1967) or Rodriguez (1980) Chap. 6.
16. The references in note 8 also contain a survey of the debate between the neo-classical economists and the ECLA school.
17. Sunkel applied these autobiographical notes during the SAREC Workshop on Development Theory (Västerhaninge, August 1977). See also Hettne and Wallensteen (1978).

3. The Latin American Dependency School

The Dependency Perspective Takes Shape

The economic stagnation in Latin America together with the lack of confidence in the prevailing development theories created a sense of great confusion. The intellectuals were groping for alternative explanatory models. There were certain limitations to the extent to which ECLA could provide assistance in this area: first, since ECLA focused its attention on purely economic problems, social and political problems were excluded from the analysis. Secondly, ECLA's dependence on conservative Latin American governments precluded the use of analyses and remedies that appeared too radical, such as land reforms. A group of economists who had earlier been associated with ECLA, as well as the younger generation of economists working for ECLA, together constituted one of the new currents. We begin this chapter by describing the radicalization of ECLA's approach; this is followed by a discussion of theorists who were influenced by Marxism or neo-Marxism.

The ECLA Analysis Radicalized: Furtado and Sunkel

One of the most influential of the more radical ECLA theorists was the Brazilian Celso Furtado.[1] He was originally a traditional economist in the sense that he strongly emphasized lack of capital in the underdeveloped countries. Like the others associated with ECLA he attributed this lack of capital mainly to external factors (i.e. the periphery exported raw materials and imported industrial goods), and also found the solution to the problem to be import substitution. After the rapid industrial growth in Brazil during the 1950s, he was optimistic about the future.

However, his views soon changed. As director of planning of the poorest regions of Brazil he experienced the developments leading up to the military take-over in 1964. In Furtado's analysis of this period we find a definition of development which indicates that he had abandoned the earlier emphasis on the growth of productivity.

> Economic development, being fundamentally a process of incorporating and diffusing new techniques, implies changes of a structural nature in both the systems of production and distribution of income. The way in

> which these changes take place depends, to a large extent, on the degree of flexibility of the institutional framework within which the economy operates.
> (Furtado, 1965, p 47)

Now, Furtado was also referring to differences between capitalist development in the centre and in the periphery in a way that was to become typical for the dependency school. The developed countries were characterized by the fact that there was an interdependent relationship between purchasing power and investment which, eventually, led to a general increase in the standard of living,[2] thus creating a basis for an industrial democracy in which various political forces could limit the power of the capital owners.

Furtado earlier assumed that the periphery would also develop along these lines, provided capitalist development could be started by means of import substitution. Now he claimed that the internal structure which colonialism had created in these countries was extremely rigid. The Great Depression, for example, had created an opportunity for Brazil to get rid of this structure, since the government, inadvertently, had followed a strict, Keynesian economic policy; it bought large quantities of coffee which were later destroyed. By 'using coffee as fuel for the locomotives' domestic employment was kept up, while the import possibilities were reduced. This was also an incentive for import substitution. However, the internal structure was not changed and the traditional sectors were not abolished, resulting in continued economic inefficiency and stagnation.

Furtado's earlier optimism had thus soon changed into pessimism. The ECLA strategy of industrialization had increased foreign dependence rather than reduced it. Imported consumption goods had merely been replaced by imported capital goods and intermediate products necessary to the industrial structure that had been created in Brazil. The dependence upon the export of primary products had also increased, since it alone was to pay for the imports.

From this growing interest in the internal social structure, Furtado came to the conclusion that it was obviously of great interest both to the foreign industries and to the domestic oligarchy to keep large groups of the population marginalized. In this way salaries could be kept down and profits up. Furtado described the social structure standing in the way of development in Brazil as follows:

> In short, the social structure . . . can be outlined as follows: at the top is a ruling class composed of various groups of interests, in many respects antagonistic to each other, therefore unable to form a plan for national developments, and holding the monopoly of power unchallenged; lower down we have a great mass of salaried urban workers employed in services, which forms a social strata [*sic*] rather than a proper class; beneath this is a class of industrial workers, which hardly represents one tenth of the active population of the country but

> constitutes its most homogenous sector; and finally the peasant masses. (Quoted in Brookfield, 1975, p 148)

From this point on, Furtado left his previously rather economistic analysis in favour of a broader approach in which the social structure played an important role. He now tried to combine certain parts of Marxism with Keynesian theory. According to Furtado, both had advantages and disadvantages. For Marxism it was a matter of isolating the structural insight from its unacceptable teleology; Keynes, on the other hand, had never put much emphasis on structural changes. His contribution consisted of a new and useful view of the government and its role in the economy.

It is interesting to see that Furtado had already touched on the problem of rigid social structures. As we shall later see, contemporary Marxists often dwell on this. Although Furtado never attempted to carry out an 'analysis of the modes of production', his approach nevertheless shows that there were dependency theorists who did not consider development in the periphery only as a reflection of what was going on in the centre – which is what the dependency school is usually accused of doing. Instead, he believed in some sort of interaction between external and internal factors, with the emphasis on the latter.

Furtado left Brazil after the 1964 coup, and moved to Paris, where he expanded his analysis to cover all of Latin America. His pessimistic 'aura' became more pronounced: the continent's only salvation, as he saw it, lay in increased self-reliance – which was brought out quite clearly in his book *Economic Development of Latin America* (Furtado, 1969). Here he says: 'A move towards the solution of these and other problems related to external relations would be inconceivable without a parallel effort to bring about structural reforms and create new forms of co-operation in the region' (p 302).

He particularly emphasized an increased public commitment. The government should strive to restructure the entire economy, so that modern technology could be disseminated to all sectors of production, thus also guaranteeing a more equitable distribution of income which, in turn, would put an end to social marginalization. It was also important that the Latin American countries gained a certain technological independence, and that the intra-regional trade expanded.

Furtado played an important role, not only in the Latin American debate, but, together with André Gunder Frank, as the most important proponent of the dependency perspective outside of Latin America. Most of his works have been translated into English, French and Spanish, and are thus read all over the world.

The Chilean Osvaldo Sunkel is also important in the context of the radicalization of the ECLA perspective. He started his professional career as an economist during the early 1950s and has thus, together with Furtado, worked within the framework of the established paradigm and contributed to its downfall during the 1960s.

As we have previously mentioned, Sunkel worked with ECLA during the early 1960s. He left this institution for a professor's chair at the University of Chile, where in 1966 he gave a lecture in which he dealt with the problem of dependency, noting how it had been neglected in Latin American social science.[3] He referred to the question of dependency 'as an area which until now has been taboo as far as serious analyses are concerned'. Sunkel pointed out that 'dependence' nevertheless had become a popular topic outside the lecture halls; he obviously intended to make this complex of problems academically respectable. He rejected the 'revolutionary' solution (which was diligently debated in radical circles): '. . . a radical, socialist revolution is, in my opinion, a highly improbable historical event in the immediate future of Latin America' (Sunkel, 1969, p 32).

His views on the Latin American bourgeoisie contain an entirely different air of optimism to those of the radicals, with whom we shall deal later. Sunkel than believed in the possibility of political alliances between certain middle-class groups and the poorer urban and rural strata:

> These new alliances (which ought not to be confused with the ones that have occurred in the past in Latin America) represent national collective interests and objectives in a better and different way from that which was the case in traditional dual societies. Nationalism, development, and organized mass participation are the ideological pillars of such alliances.
> (Ibid., p 27)

Certain Latin American countries (we assume that Sunkel primarily thought of Chile) should, on the basis of these alliances, be capable of carrying out a 'national policy of development', which Sunkel defined as follows:

> The nationalism of development is a force of national affirmation, an aspiration to self-determination and sovereignty, a desire to participate in the benefits and creation of modern and universal culture and science, the desire to attain liberty, democracy, equality of opportunities and well-being, which the more industrialized countries enjoy to a greater or lesser extent.
> (Ibid., p 32)

Unlike Raúl Prebisch, Sunkel emphasizes the internal factors: 'The possibilities of carrying out a national development policy basically depend on the domestic situation' (ibid., p 46). This is really the gist of the radicalization of the ECLA analysis. The ECLA had, as might be remembered, diplomatic reasons for not wanting to touch on the sensitive subjects of the Latin American countries' domestic affairs.

Compared to the dependency theorists who had been influenced by Marxism, Sunkel appears to be relatively moderate. He differs from them by being more eclectic. He does not reject Marxist theory, but works within a structuralist tradition developed by ECLA economists, to whose left wing

Sunkel and Pedro Paz, his collaborator in a classic development theoretical work, belonged (Sunkel and Paz, 1970).

Unlike the ECLA theorists, Sunkel and Paz chose a broader, interdisciplinary approach, while at the same time they spoke more openly about internal Latin American conditions, class contradictions, etc. Thus, Sunkel found the Marxist analysis of the historical development of imperialism to be acceptable, but argued that it had neglected to deal with that which happens *within* the countries subjected to imperialism. On this point he found the theory of the so-called 'backwash' effects of international trade (developed by Gunnar Myrdal and other structuralist oriented economists) to be at least a promising start. This theory was, however, incomplete in that it mainly dealt with the effects of trading in raw materials. Sunkel found a new form of the transnational corporations. He described the general tendency of the global system, in which both developed and underdeveloped countries formed integral parts in terms of *transnational integration and national disintegration* (see Figure 3.1).

Figure 3.1
Sunkel's Model of Global Dualism

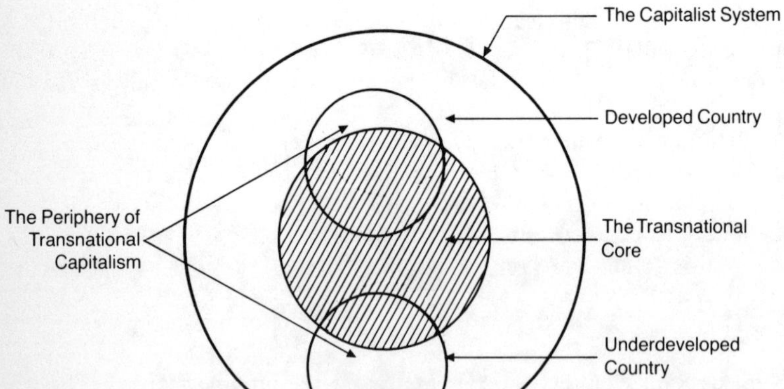

Obviously, the countries themselves are not the main components of this global system. According to Sunkel, the conventional theory of international trade makes a fundamental mistake by considering countries to be distinct units of an economic system, in which transactions between these units take place. The global system is, instead, characterized by two distinct but interacting structures: transnational capitalism represented by the economies of most of the industrialized countries (the centre) as well as the 'modern' sectors of the underdeveloped countries, and the regions that are peripheral to the centre as well as the much larger part of the underdeveloped countries which have been excluded from 'development' and remain in a state of stagnation and marginalization (the periphery). The relations between these two structures are, in turn, characterized by polarization, both at the international and the national level. Sunkel's global model is characterized by the fact that the substructures cut straight through the national boundaries. There exists a dynamic that determines the function of the whole system and the purpose of the analysis is to understand this process. The key institution in this analysis is the transnational corporation.

Sunkel's view about the long-term process of development was pessimistic: '. . . this transnational process of integration tends to intensify the process of cultural, political, social and economic underdevelopment in the peripheral nations, where it, at the same time, increases dependence and precipitates domestic disintegration'.

After the military coup in Chile, Sunkel continued his work on 'transnational capitalism and national disintegration' at the University of Sussex in England. Sunkel's later thoughts on development and dependence may be found among his various writings in connection with this project. Since they, within the framework of the structuralist school, may be said to form part of the current development debate, we shall return to them in Chapter 8.

Marxist Influences: Cardoso and Faletto

Some of the views did not emanate directly from the ECLA, but should instead be seen in the light of the Latin American Marxist tradition. Let us first examine the more traditional Marxist influences. They originated in a 'sociological annex' to the ECLA, i.e. the *Latin American Institute for Social and Economic Planning* (ILPES). After the military coup in Brazil in 1964, Fernando Henrique Cardoso moved to Chile and joined the ILPES.[4] Here Cardoso and the Chilean historian Enzo Faletto conducted sociological and historical studies of various cases of *dependencia*, a concept which quickly gained support among the social scientists at the ECLA and at the universities in Santiago.

The fact that social scientists from various parts of Latin America could discuss and compare experiences from different countries was, no doubt, important to the further development of the dependency perspective. Thus it is hardly correct to tie the new ideas to one or two names alone.[5] However, a mimeographed manuscript entitled *Dependencia y Desarrollo en América Latina* (Dependency and Development in Latin America) by Cardoso and

Faletto did circulate during 1967. This work (published as a book in 1969) is now considered to be one of the classics of the dependency theory (Cardoso and Faletto, 1969).

In contrast to the ECLA analyses, Cardoso and Faletto focused on the sociopolitical aspects of dependency. 'Only a study of the conditions of the decision making will enable us to explain why a change of economic conditions will benefit some countries but not others.' In other words, they saw economic development as an expression of various combinations of class interest that vary from one historical situation to another. The way in which a dependent economy was linked to the world market was crucial; the linkage as well as the local response might vary. Thus, the dependency situation constituted an historically changing pattern, the complexity of which precluded all general laws of development – particularly those claiming that all countries go through certain predetermined stages of development.

However, it is possible roughly to identify certain stages of development in countries placed in similar historical circumstances, e.g. the Latin American countries. After they gained independence (from Spain or Portugal), political power was based on an alliance between the modern, commercial agrarian sector and the old hacienda economy. The new commercial elite dominated this alliance and the economic-political result was what in Latin America is called *desarrollo hacia afuera*, an export-oriented development, based on the production of raw materials. This phase principally lasted until the Great Depression in the 1930s, which, conventionally, is considered to be the starting point of a more differentiated and introverted type of economic development in Latin America, or *desarrollo hacia adentro*.

From their sociopolitical perspective, Cardoso and Faletto claimed that this type of development actually started much earlier (the time varied from country to country) because of the rise of a new middle class which was gradually absorbed by the various national power structures; thus, the emphasis was on the power political base rather than on the external impetus, which was the same for most of the Latin American countries. However, the *response* changed from country to country, depending on the way in which the class alliances were made up.

The regime of Getúlio Vargas in Brazil (1930) was, for instance, based on a compromise between the oligarchy made up of sugar and coffee producers and the new urban bourgeoisie. Vargas's policies provided an incentive, while the coffee economy at the same time was kept alive by heavy subsidies.[6]

Colombia presented a contrasting situation. The urban interests did not succeed in acquiring any power from the traditional oligarchy, so the positive response to the new economic opportunities consequently failed to appear. The so-called banana republics (the Central American mini-states) on the other hand lacked the prerequisites for a more independent economic policy; the effects of the Great Depression were therefore purely negative. The peasants revolted in reaction to their deteriorating situation, and were put down by military force.

Some of the larger Latin American countries continued their line of industrialization after the Second World War. As mentioned earlier, the ECLA provided the necessary arguments, but in international banking circles the policy of import substitution was considered to be inappropriate. However, the rationale for carrying out this policy was, according to Cardoso, totally irrelevant since it was determined primarily by the nature of the class alliances in the Latin American countries. When, for reasons mentioned above, this policy had had its day and economic stagnation ensued, these alliances collapsed, as did the typical 'populist alliance' between the bourgeoisie and organized labour – a fragile arrangement that served as the basis of Latin American democracy. When that could no longer be maintained, military dictatorships followed one after the other. Typical of them all was the fall of the Goulart regime in Brazil in 1964. Concomitant with a new political situation were, of course, new economic strategies and development trends.

From this account it is quite obvious that Cardoso and Faletto represented an approach which was mainly characterized by its orientation towards concrete studies of dependency. Cardoso explicitly refrained from the formulation of a new theory, and rejected, on several occasions, after the dependency perspective's definite breakthrough, the idea that the dependency theory should be thought of as a theory independent of the Marxist theory of imperialism. Instead, Cardoso maintained that: 'The theory of imperialist capitalism, as is well known, has so far attained its most significant treatment in Lenin's works' (Cardoso, 1972, p 83).

However, if it was not for a relatively revisionistic attitude to basic tenets of Leninism, Cardoso would not have been considered a true dependency theorist:

> In spite of the accuracy of Lenin's insights as measured against historical events during the first half of the century in many parts of the world, some important recent changes have deeply affected the pattern of relationship between imperialist and dependent nations. These changes demand a reappraisal of emergent structures and their main tendencies. Even if these modifications are not so deep as the shift that enabled Lenin to characterize a new stage of capitalism during the period of imperialist expansion, they are marked enough to warrant a major modification of the established analyses of capitalism and imperialism. Nevertheless, contemporary international capitalist expansion and control of dependent economies undoubtedly prove that this new pattern of economic relationships among nations remains imperialist. However, the main points of Lenin's characterization of imperialism and capitalism are no longer fully adequate to describe and explain the present forms of capital accumulation and external expansion.

It is interesting to note that Cardoso considers Baran's and Sweezy's analyses of monopoly capitalism as a further refinement of the Marxist theory. In his opinion a similar refinement is required to tackle the consequences of monopoly capitalism in the dependent economies. Here Baran again provides important ideas (in his *Political Economy of Growth*), to which Cardoso, nevertheless, has some objections (Cardoso, 1977, p 23). The important thing, as far as Cardoso is concerned, is that he never sees development and dependence as completely incompatible.

'Development of underdevelopment' (in A.G. Frank) sums up another misconception. The fact is that the assumption of a structural 'lack of dynamics' in the dependent economies (caused by imperialism) is a misrepresentation of the true nature of the economic view of the situation. 'It is necessary to understand that in specific situations it is possible to expect *development* and *dependency*' (Cardoso, 1972, p 94). We shall show later that an 'extreme' dependency position considers development and underdevelopment to be two sides of the same coin, and sees dependence as the ultimate cause of underdevelopment.

Neo-Marxist Influences: Dos Santos and Marini

Another Brazilian, Theotonio Dos Santos, had also moved to Santiago de Chile after the military coup in Brazil. In 1966 he published the first results of his research in Chile: *Crisis Económica y Crisis Política*.[7] In *El Nuevo Carácter de la Dependencia*, which was published the following year, Dos Santos introduced the term 'the New Dependence' in an attempt to explain the failure of the policy of import substitution.[8] 'The New Dependence' was characterized by the fact that North American investment in Latin America had increased as well as changed orientation. The emphasis was shifted away from raw materials to industry, from which the most advanced and dynamic sectors, such as electronics, were selected (Dos Santos, 1978).

According to Dos Santos, this seemed to indicate that a new international division of labour was about to be established, in which the periphery was no longer made up of raw material exporting enclave economies. The modern sector of the entire periphery was now incorporated in the imperialist system; but the development remained partial and with no dynamics of its own because of the dependency relations.

In an article from 1968 (Dos Santos, 1968b [1973]) Dos Santos not only criticized the established development theories, but also offered the dependency approach as an alternative. This article also contained the following, frequently-quoted definition of the concept of dependency:

> By dependence we mean a situation in which the economy of certain countries is conditioned by the development and expansion of another economy to which the former is subjected. The relation of interdependence between two or more economies, and between these and world trade, assumes the form of dependence when some countries (the dominant ones) can expand and can be self-sustaining, while other countries (the dependent ones) can do this only as a reflection of that expansion, which can have either a positive or a negative effect on their immediate development.

This definition is also found in an article published in the *American Economic Review* in 1970: 'The Structure of Dependence', which principally sums up Dos Santos's views *vis-à-vis* the widening debate during the 1970s. We shall return to this subject in a later chapter.

The Latin American societies could, in Dos Santos's opinion, only be studied if allowances were made for the fact that they were an integral part of the world capitalist system. To analyse the problem of development from an historical point of view, he identified three different forms of dependence: (1) colonial dependence; (2) financial-industrial dependence; and (3) technological-industrial dependence. The first one was characterized by trade monopolies complemented by colonial monopolies of land, mines and labour in the colonized countries. The second form of dependence occurred during the latter part of the 19th Century, and was characterized by large concentrations of capital in the centres, and by investments in the production of raw materials and agricultural products in the periphery. The countries belonging to the latter developed into export economies, the structure of which was marked by their position of dependence. The third form of dependence came into existence after the Second World War and was characterized by multinational corporations establishing industries that were linked to the dependent countries' domestic markets. Dos Santos's writings are primarily related to this third form which constitutes 'the New Dependence'.

'The New Dependence' was essentially an answer to the ECLA policy of import substitution as well as an attempt to show the limitations of this kind of policy. The industrialization resulting from the policy of import substitution was doomed to stagnation after a short while because of the restrictions placed on the expansion of the domestic market by dependence. These restrictions were: the working class was heavily exploited, which limited its purchasing power. Secondly, the technology was capital intensive, which created relatively few jobs. Thirdly, the repatriation of profits led to an extremely limited domestic surplus. Dos Santos came to the conclusion that the alleged backwardness of these economies was not caused by a lack of integration with capitalism, but rather that the most serious obstacles to their overall development were due to the international system and its laws of development (Dos Santos, 1968b [1973]). The solutions proposed by organizations such as the ECLA and UNCTAD were therefore insufficient. The only alternatives were, according to Dos Santos, military regimes which opened the door to fascism (Brazil), or revolutionary regimes which laid the foundation of socialism (Chile). This tendency towards a polarized view – fascism or socialism – which was in no way peculiar to Dos Santos, was presumably a result of the fact that most of the dependency theorists came from either Brazil or Chile.

According to Dos Santos, the concept of 'dependence' could not be formulated outside the boundaries of the theory of imperialism, but should be seen as a complement to the term imperialism, since 'dependency is the internal face of imperialism in our Latin American countries' (Dos Santos, 1977a). A dependency theory was therefore needed as a complement to the theory of imperialism. The latter should analyse the factors behind the internationalization of capitalism, while the former should show the effects of this process in the relevant countries.

Dos Santos later abandoned the above-mentioned definition of dependence and attached greater importance to the internal structures. He emphasized the fact that the internal factors, determined (*determina*) social changes. However, dependence created the prerequisites for the development of internal structures, and the relation between the external and the internal factors was considered as dialectic (Dos Santos, 1977a, 1977b and 1978).

Another well-known dependency theorist, Ruy Mauro Marini, was also a member of the group of Brazilians working in Chile. He was primarily engaged in the formulation of a model that could explain how capitalism, at a global level, could simultaneously generate development in one part of the world and underdevelopment in another. Marini made a strong distinction between 'dependent' or 'peripheral capitalism' and the form of capitalism found in the centres. The development of the former was conditioned by that of the latter. This form of dependence led to a transfer of surplus from the peripheral countries to the centre. (See Marini 1969a and b; 1972a and b.)

The peripheral economies were according to Marini dominated by foreign capital, the production of which was primarily intended for export. This implied that, in these countries, the firms' realization of profits was basically independent of the domestic demand (primarily determined by the workers' wages). Thus, the workers' role was limited to that of producing as cheaply as possible, which, in turn, meant that their wages could be pressed down. However, the firms must be able to realize their profits somewhere – and this was done in the centre, where wages had been able to rise more than they would have done without the relations with the periphery. According to Marini, both workers and capital owners in the centre had a common interest in maintaining their contacts with the periphery in a way that enabled them to continue 'exploiting' the economic surplus.[9]

Marini introduced the concept of *superexploitation* in order to explain the process of exploitation in the periphery which was made possible by the fact that domestic demand was of little importance to the firms' realization of their profits. The low wages led to the eventual stagnation of the small domestic market, with an economic crisis as the inevitable result.

When Marini analysed the development in Brazil by means of this model (see e.g. Marini, 1972a), he developed another concept which became central to the dependency school – namely that of subimperialism. Marini used this term in an attempt to translate Lenin's definition of imperialism to a 'dependent capitalism'. Thus, subimperialism was supposed to be 'the highest stage of dependent capitalism'.[10]

The Crystallized Theory of Dependence: Frank

André Gunder Frank joined the circle of Latin American *dependentistas* during the mid-1960s, and he soon became one of the driving forces behind the early development of the dependency school. He became internationally known for his critique of the established development theory, which we have discussed in the previous chapter; at the same time he served as a link between the Latin American debate and the English-speaking academic world by publishing most of his works in English. At this point it should be mentioned that outside Latin America the dependency school has been more or less identified with Frank.

Frank was one of the first in Latin America to work with an alternative theory of the Latin American economic development. The earliest results from this attempt were presented in a book entitled *Capitalism and Underdevelopment in Latin America*, published in 1967. In this book, which was an analysis of the economic history of Brazil and Chile, he came to the conclusion that 'development and underdevelopment are two sides of the same coin'. Thus, according to Frank, it was the incorporation into the world capitalist system that led to development in some areas and underdevelopment in others.

Following Baran, Frank stressed that it was the utilization of the economic surplus that had caused development and underdevelopment. Frank's analysis accentuated the monopolistic structure of capitalism and its effects on the real and the potential surplus. The world capitalist system was characterized by a *metropolis-satellite* structure, where the metropolis exploited the satellite. While this had facilitated the expropriation of large portions of the underdeveloped countries' actual surplus, it had also prevented these countries from realizing their potential surplus. The monopoly structure was found at all levels, i.e. the international, the national and the local level, and created a situation of exploitation which, in turn, caused the 'chain-like' flow of the surplus from the remotest Latin American village to Wall Street in New York.

> The monopoly capitalist structure and the surplus expropriation/appropriation contradiction run through the entire Chilean economy, past and present. Indeed, it is this exploitative relation which in chain-like fashion extends the capitalist link between the capitalist world and national metropolises to the regional centers (part of whose surplus they appropriate), and from these to local centers, and so on to large landowners or merchants who expropriate surplus from small peasants or tenants, and sometimes even from these latter to landless laborers exploited by them in turn. At each step along the way, the relatively few capitalists above exercise monopoly power over the many below, expropriating some or all of their economic surplus and, to the extent that they are not expropriated in turn by the still fewer above them, appropriating it for their own use. Thus at each point, the international, national and local capitalist system generates economic development for the few and underdevelopment for the many.
> (Ibid., pp 7-8)

The satellite tended to be increasingly dominated by the metropolis as well as increasingly dependent upon it. The strength of this dependency relation might, however, vary from time to time. A weakening might occur when the metropolis experiences crises, such as depressions or wars. Some development had also begun in the satellites during such periods, which was why Frank asserted that the weaker of the metropolis-satellite relations, the better the development prospects of the satellites.

There was another important contradiction of capitalism, according to Frank – the contradiction of continuity in change. Here he argued that the basic structure of capitalism had remained unchanged since the 16th Century, despite all changes. The 'development of underdevelopment' that had taken place in the periphery had continuously accentuated the fundamental contradiction. This was why development strategies such as those formulated by the ECLA were totally meaningless.

Frank's theory may be summarized as in Figure 3.2. The metropolis-satellite relations, which are found at all levels of world capitalism, are shown by the lines drawn between the circles. A split circle shows that an agent may act as both a metropolis and a satellite, depending on the perspective from which you look at the circle. The process of exploitation starts at the bottom of the figure, where the landless labourers (satellites) are exploited by the small landowners. In this relation the small landowners act as 'agents' of the metropolis, and can thus appropriate part of the surplus. However, they cannot keep all of it. Some of it 'flows' up through the system, since the small landowners are exploited by the large landowners and traders, and in this relation assume the role of satellites. New metropoles are found at higher levels in the hierarchy; they, in turn, exploit the large landowners and the traders, who now become satellites. Thus the economic surplus flows upward in the system in a chain-like fashion until it eventually reaches the world metropolis (M).

In other words, a comprehensive view of world capitalism and the fact that the world capitalist system embraces the *entire* economy of each member country were, according to Frank, important prerequisites. He thereby also rejected the notion of 'dualism', an economy consisting of two separate, unconnected sectors – one modern and one traditional. He even went so far as to deny that feudal production relations have ever prevailed in Latin America during its colonial history. Instead, he assumed that an all-embracing, integrated world capitalist system existed even during the mercantilist phase of capitalism. This was explained by the fact that the primary purpose of the economy founded in Latin America by the newly-arrived Spaniards and Portuguese was to produce goods for export – which, in Frank's opinion, did not constitute a feudal economy.

The implications of this view are important for the political strategy. Since there were no feudal, semi-feudal, or other pre-capitalist modes of production present in Latin America, there was no reason for organizations of the left to support a 'bourgeois democratic revolution'. All efforts should instead be directed towards a 'socialist revolution'.

It may be argued that Frank's writings gave 'the dependency theory' a

Figure 3.2
Frank's Metropolis-Satellite Model

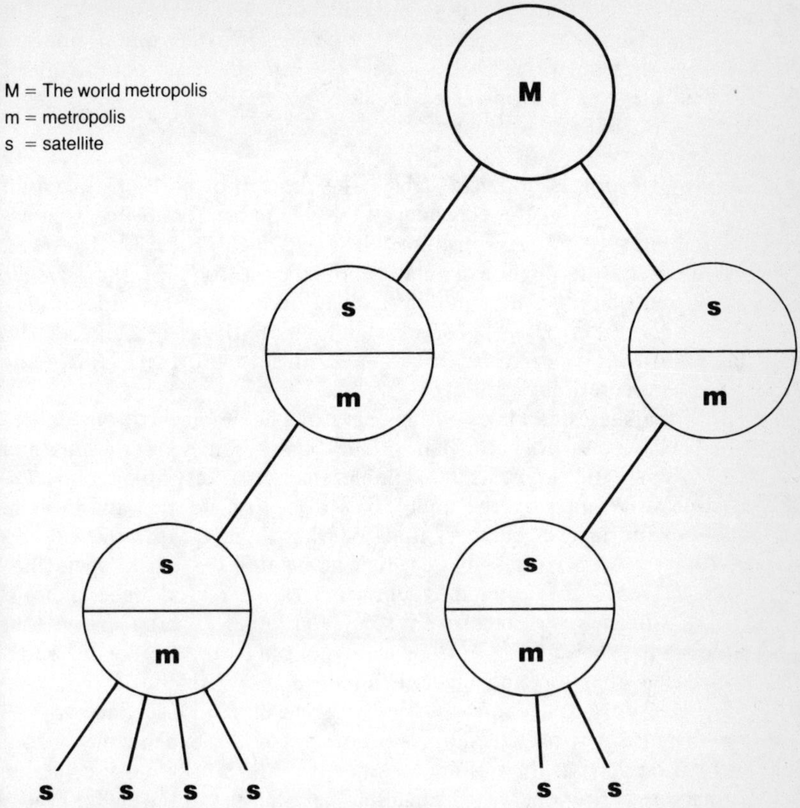

paradigmatic form, if by the latter we mean that the theory could now be expressed in a small number of theses that were contrary to established ideas while at the same time they seemed to be in better agreement with the reality of the Third World than was the prevailing orthodoxy in development theory.

The Essence of the Dependency Perspective

There is a great deal of confusion about what the dependency school[11] actually represented and about what it really said about the concrete effects of dependence, the relative importance of external and internal factors, etc. Consequently, the critique of the dependency school, to which we shall return in the next chapter, has often been sweeping and unfair. It is quite natural for the object of the critique to react by not recognizing himself and by considering it to be a caricature. The following, discontented observation by Cardoso is one example of this kind of reaction:

> The most general and formal of Gunder Frank's works are received as though they were his best, the formal definition of dependency furnished by Theotonio dos Santos is appended, the problematic of subimperialism, and marginality is sometimes inserted, one or another of my works or of Sunkel is footnoted, and the result is a theory of dependency – a strawman easy to destroy.
> (Cardoso, 1976, p 13)

Cardoso's reaction is understandable. The theoretical positions taken up by the representatives of the dependency school are far from being as homogeneous and unequivocal as the critique might lead one to believe.[12] However, after a relatively thorough examination of the majority of the school's theoretical contributions, it is not difficult to understand the critics either. Since the various advocates of the school group themselves differently, depending on the issue, it is almost impossible to provide a systematic account of its theoretical positions.

Most of the suggested classifications have one common flaw: one-dimensionality. Let us use Richard Bath's and Dilmus James's ambitious and generally sympathetic survey as an example: their classification of *dependentistas* is primarily based on the importance placed on external and internal factors. They distinguish between the following three groups: the 'conservatives' (inner reform is meaningful); the 'moderates' (external dependence limits the efficacy of economic-political measures); and the 'radicals' (external dependence must be broken) (Bath and James, 1976). It is true that the authors use other criteria in their discussion, but they are not used as a basis for the classification, and appear in a more *ad hoc* fashion.

Other classification attempts are similarly one-dimensional. Sanjaya Lall has, for instance, written an important critique of the dependency school (see Chapter 4): he uses the various assessments of the possibility of capitalist development as a criterion, and distinguishes between the following: (1) those who believe that dependence always leads to poverty; (2) those who believe that growth is limited by market restrictions, and that it therefore, sooner or later, turns into stagnation; and finally (3) those who believe that growth is possible, but always subordinate to that of the centre (Lall, 1975).

A third attempt at classification, that of Gabriel Palma, distinguishes between (1) dependence as a theory of Latin American underdevelopment, (2) dependence as an elaboration and a reformulation of the ECLA analyses of Latin American development problems, and (3) dependence as a method of analysing concrete cases of underdevelopment in the Third World (Palma, 1978). Palma makes the interesting observation that the view of the first category is similar to that of the so-called Narodniks during the latter part of the 19th Century, i.e. that capitalist development in Russia was impossible because of various structural constraints (see Chapter 1).[13] He then compares Lenin's critique of the Narodniks' view with the Marxist critique of the dependency school (with which he sympathizes). Palma is therefore more positively inclined towards the scholars in the third category, who have no theoretical ambitions of their own, but who often consider their work to be a complement to the Marxist theory of imperialism.[14] It is obvious that the classification has a polemic purpose, i.e. to reject the dependency school as an independent theoretical tradition, and to facilitate the fusion of certain branches of the school and Marxism.

Although all these approaches are relevant in their own ways, a comparison between them shows that different criteria of classification may lead to quite different conclusions about the role of dependency theory. It is therefore necessary to construct a multidimensional scheme in which the various criteria are made explicit. We shall use six dimensions which enable us to sum up the various views of dependency theorists in a more nuanced way.

Holism v. Particularism

Along this dimension we locate authors who produce global models, the dynamics of which are determined by the system in its entirety, rather than by processes in the various parts of the system; others construe an overall perspective from the constituent parts.

In his critique of the modernization perspective (see Chapter 2) A.G. Frank used the concept of *holism* as a scientific criterion by means of which he rejected the 'bourgeois' theory of development. Frank stressed that underdevelopment in a particular country can only be understood when it is seen as an effect of that country's position and function in the larger system (of which it is an integral part). This holistic ambition eventually leads to an analysis of the *global accumulation of capital* of the type carried out by Frank and Samir Amin (see Chapter 7). Sunkel's model of transnational capitalism is characterized by a similar holistic ambition. Here we also find a dynamic which determines the way in which the whole system works. We might call it structural dualism at the global level.

Other dependency theorists have narrowed down their analysis to the dependent societies, and refrained from global approaches. We are referring to Dos Santos and Marini, who both tried to develop a special theory about peripheral capitalism, and to Cardoso and Faletto, who saw the dependency approach as a method of a concrete analysis of the periphery. We shall later argue in favour of regarding the 'world system theorists' as a breakaway group of the dependency school and the establishment of a distinct theoretical tradition. In summary, we might therefore say that an attraction towards holism, i.e. an accentuation of the whole, was characteristic of the dependency school even though its analysis primarily concerned the periphery.

External v. Internal

Here it is a question of what really governs development in a peripheral economy; external or internal factors. External factors lie outside the domain of the national economy; internal ones refer to domestic causal relations.

It is a popular misconception that the dependency school explained underdevelopment by the external factor only, i.e. the imperialist-capitalist penetration. Theoretically figuring out how external and internal conditions interact has, in fact, been one of the school's main problems, to which a number of more or less elegant solutions have been found. The notion of external conditions mechanically determining internal ones is tied to Frank's earlier writings, above all to the controversial metropolis-satellite model in which dependency traces a path from Wall Street to the remotest Indian villages. The concept of 'satellite' suggests a total lack of own dynamics. It is significant that the use of this concept has been limited, and that the more neutral conceptual pair centre-periphery has been used instead.[15]

Although Frank occasionally warned against a mechanical-externalistic interpretation of the model, that trap is difficult to avoid because of the structure of the model. However, it should be remembered that during the mid-1960s the dependency approach had a sharp polemic sting directed at the then prevailing evolutionist theory of development which disregarded international relations and claimed that the development of the national economy was basically internally determined. The polemic exaggerations were soon abandoned; in Dos Santos's writings we find a tendency towards seeing the interaction between external and internal factors, although the former are dominant. In a controversy with Frank, Dos Santos says about underdevelopment that it 'rather than being one of satellization is a case of the formation of a certain type of internal structure conditioned by international relations of dependence' (Dos Santos, 1968b [1973], p 76). In a later article (Dos Santos, 1977b), he goes one step further, and provides a distinction between 'conditioning' (external factors) and 'determining' (internal factors). This distinction may not be particularly informative, but it does suggest that the emphasis has been shifted from the external to the internal factors.

Sunkel also tries to steer clear of Scylla and Charybdis, and sees a *dialectic* relation between the external and the internal. However, as in the case of Dos Santos's distinction, it is doubtful whether the concept of 'dialectics' leads us one step closer to a distinct idea of the relationship between the external and the internal.

Cardoso is obviously more inclined to emphasize internal factors. In his and Faletto's analysis the response to the external impulse varied because the class alliances varied from country to country. Furtado's point of view is quite similar. He accentuates the rigid colonial structures in his explanation of Brazil's failure to achieve a self-generating growth.

Augustin Cueva offers the most 'internalistic' view:

> dependency theory holds that the nature of our social formations is dependent on how they are integrated with the world capitalist system. But is it not more correct to state the inverse? Is it not the nature of our societies that determines its links with the capitalist world?
> (Cueva, 1974 [1976])

This statement places Cueva firmly in the Marxist camp rather than in the dependency school. It was thus characteristic of the latter to place a greater or lesser amount of importance on the external factors.

Economic v. Sociopolitical Analysis

Certain authors of the dependency school work exclusively with economic analysis, whereas others emphasize social and political conditions. Normally, this difference can be explained by the author's disciplinary origin. The difference is nevertheless important to the result of the analysis.

The early dependency analyses were mostly carried out by economists, while the contributions from other branches of the social sciences were relatively few. This explains the strong economic orientation which was particularly pronounced in the earlier ECLA studies. Prebisch, for example, never really abandoned the purely economic analysis. Sunkel wanted to, but never managed it. In this context, Furtado is interesting. From having been a 'conventional' ECLA economist, he gradually began to emphasize sociopolitical aspects.

Frank's and Dos Santos's formulations of the problems of dependence are based on the interaction between different *economies*; they dutifully include some references to class structure and political conditions. In true neo-Marxist spirit they analyse development and underdevelopment as a consequence of the flow of the economic surplus in the metropolis-satellite model. Their view of political alternatives is rather simplified: socialism or fascism. This is partly, in turn, due to the fact that the dependency theorists are mostly Brazilians or Chileans, and partly because Brazil and Chile symbolized the alternatives of socialism and fascism during a strategic period in the history of the dependency school.

The *dependentistas* are often accused of neglecting class analysis, which might not only be due to their thinking in terms of models, but also to a certain bias towards economics. The use of concepts such as 'class', 'class consciousness' and 'class struggle' (which is quite common) does not constitute an analysis of the political dynamics of a dependent structure. Although Cardoso and Faletto do emphasize both social structure and political conditions, their approach is limited by the fact that their interest is mainly in the government and the political process of decision-making, and not so much in the great mass of Latin Americans who are the real victims of underdevelopment. Cardoso later acknowledged this flaw:

> To me what is important is to try to understand and encourage social forces to counterbalance the power of private enterprise and the political presence of the armies in countries where the armies are politically important. I am thinking of popular movements and grass-roots kinds of reaction. What kind of party or movement can mobilize people in this kind of society? The problem of development in our days cannot remain restricted to a discussion about import substitution, not even to a debate on different strategies for growth, in terms of export or non-export policies, internal or external markets, orien-

tation of the economy, etc. The main issue is people's movements and consciousness of their own interests.
(Hettne and Wallensteen, 1978, p 32)

In other words, Cardoso uses a broad, interdisciplinary approach, an historical-structural analysis (as he calls it) which considers both structural determination and historical change. Even if underdevelopment *is* determined by a given structure, the process is, in his opinion, not mechanical but dialectic, containing dynamics, changes and alternatives.

Sectoral/Regional Contradictions v. Class Contradictions

While some authors accentuate the fact that a regional or sectoral polarization occurs in the total system, both at the international and at the national level, others base their analysis on the fact that the fundamental conflict is found in class contradictions. In other words, these authors seek the dynamics in the class struggle.

Marxists often criticize the dependency school for its lack of class analysis. The contradictions in Frank's metropole-satellite model were primarily *regional*. Despite several attempts at modification (e.g. Frank, 1972), the impression of regions opposing each other in some kind of exploitative relationship remains. In Frank's opinion, the Latin American bourgeoisie is incapable of starting a process of accumulation and unconscious of its own needs and interests. This 'class analysis' is, furthermore, restricted to the bourgeoisie (the lumpenbourgeoisie) which, from a Marxist point of view disqualifies it, since 'class' must be thought of as a concept that implies relations. We shall deal with the Marxist critique in greater detail later.

Marini's analysis also rests on regional contradictions. He claims that capitalists and workers *jointly* exploit the periphery. Looking at Sunkel's approach, we find that he emphasizes the sectoral contradictions between the transnational sector and the underdeveloped economy. This contradiction is dominant, with an inhibitive effect on class consciousness and class struggle.

Cardoso does try to carry out a class analysis, but in a rather complicated and diffuse fashion, which seems to annoy those who are used to the primary contradiction between labour and capital. Cardoso claims that the class structure which developed in Western Europe is basically different from that which developed in Brazil, and that *a priori* it is impossible to say which is 'progressive' and which is 'reactionary'. The components of his analysis are not the 'classes', but the structural relationships between various social groups.

Underdevelopment v. Development

'Dependency theory' is often used synonymously with 'theory of underdevelopment', and to certain representatives of the dependency school, development is totally incompatible with any kind of dependence. Here again we find Frank representing the most extreme view ('development of underdevelopment'), while the opposite view is held by those who are close to classical Marxism.

It should be pointed out that by development in this context we mean capitalist development. The question then is: is capitalism possible in the periphery? To Marx and Engels this was a matter of course – almost equivalent to a natural law – a position from which a Marxist can only stray with some difficulty: Cardoso claims that capitalist development in the periphery is possible, but limited to what he calls 'dependent capitalist development' or 'associated dependent development'. We have already mentioned that Cardoso's 'historical structuralism' implied a dialectic view of development as a process containing changes and alternatives.

Somewhere in the middle of this spectrum we find authors like Sunkel and Dos Santos. The latter rejects Frank's theory of 'development of underdevelopment' and claims that it is necessary to realize that development *and* dependence might, in certain situations, be expected. We might call Sunkel's approach 'pessimistic' in the sense that he sees underdevelopment as a long, inevitable process that threatens large parts of the periphery with marginalization and stagnation. However, it should be pointed out that it is certain structural segments of the countries of the periphery that are being underdeveloped, not the countries *per se*. As opposed to the centre, these peripheral segments are of such a magnitude that they affect the entire 'national economies'.

Voluntarism v. Determinism

The various representatives of the dependency school have all taken great care to keep their analyses politically relevant, and the majority of them are all advocates of a rather loosely defined socialist revolution. The popularity of the dependency school can partly be explained by the growing impatience with the defeatism of the Latin American communist parties. As already mentioned, the official Marxist analysis stated that the Latin American countries must develop from feudalism to capitalism. Consequently the communist parties' strategy consisted in supporting progressive bourgeois parties striving for a national, industrial-capitalist development and in fighting the alliances between feudal and imperialist forces.

The neo-Marxist views which claimed that Latin America was already capitalist, but doomed to underdevelopment, provided an entirely different basis for a political strategy. 'Revolution Now!' was the typical attitude, and the Cuban Revolution had led the way. The early dependency school, primarily Frank, is thus associated with a 'voluntarist' line which was sharply contrasted with the communist parties' determinism. Other *dependentistas*, like Cardoso, are found somewhere between the extremes. Cardoso accuses the Latin American Marxists of 'determinism', and Debray and Guevara of voluntarism. However, this differentiated view elicits a political ambiguity which is annoying to some (Myer, 1975). Further down the deterministic line we find Sunkel, whose markedly structuralist approach rarely reaches the actual social groups and their political situation. Politically, he has advocated a reformism which is close to social democracy.

From this discussion it should be possible to construct an *ideal-typical* dependency position which, whatever relevance it might have in reality, does express a certain internal consistency. For example a typical dependency position in terms of methodology would stress holism, external factors, sociopolitical analysis, regional contradictions, polarization between development and underdevelopment and the role of subjective factors in history. Generally, we might say that those who are consistently identified with the left antipole of the scheme assume a typical dependency position. Such a position can be summarized in the following:

– The most important obstacles to development were not lack of capital or entrepreneurial skills, but were to be found in the international division of labour. In short, they were external to the underdeveloped economy – not internal.
– The international division of labour was analysed in terms of relations between regions of which two kinds – centre and periphery – assumed particular importance, since a transfer of surplus took place from the latter to the former regions.
– Due to the fact that the periphery was deprived of its surplus, which the centre could utilize instead for development purposes, development in the centre somehow implied underdevelopment in the periphery. Thus development and underdevelopment could be described as two aspects of a single global process. All regions participating in this process were consequently considered as capitalist, although a distinction was made between central and peripheral capitalism.
– Since the periphery was doomed to underdevelopment because of its linkage to the centre, it was considered necessary for a country to disassociate itself from the world market and strive for self-reliance. To make this possible a more or less revolutionary political transformation was necessary. As soon as the external obstacles had been removed, development as a more or less automatic and inherent process was taken for granted.

Notes

1. The discussion of Furtado is partly based on Brookfield (1975) Chap. 5.
2. A more extensive explanation of this reasoning is found in our discussion of Samir Amin's model of global accumulation of capital. Amin's analysis of 'pure' capitalism is reminiscent of that of Furtado. See also Ruy Mauro Marini, below.
3. This lecture was later published as *National Development Policy and External Dependence in Latin America* (Sunkel, 1969).
4. The best introduction to the writings of Cardoso is found in Kahl (1976).
5. Apropos this, Cardoso says: 'Every new paradigm procedes from a complex discussion among persons, institutions and groups, which in the

modern world are located in different countries. With time the discussion becomes more complex, it is enriched and provokes internal controversies' (Cardoso, 1976). The concept of *dependencia*, in the sense which it later had among dependency theorists, was introduced in a paper published by Cardoso in 1965: *El Proceso de Desarollo en América Latina: Hipótesis para una Interpretación Sociológica* (Cardoso, 1965).

6. This was a case of 'inadvertent Keynesianism', as we have pointed out earlier. The purchasing power was kept up by 'running the locomotives on coffee' during the Great Depression, leaving Brazil relatively strengthened.
7. This was later published as: *Socialismo o Fascismo: Dilema de América Latina* (PLA, Santiago, 1968).
8. Both of these books were later issued in one volume, entitled *Socialismo o Fascismo: El Nuevo Carácter de la Dependencia y el Dilema Latinamericano* (Chile, 1971). Revised edition, Consejo Editorial, México, 1978.
9. The model of 'peripheral capitalism' with which Marini was working is largely based on Rosa Luxemburg's book *The Accumulation of Capital* (Luxemburg, 1913). Since the model has been further developed and made more sophisticated by Samir Amin, we have chosen to provide a more detailed examination of this type of dependency theoretical work in connection with our discussion of him in Chapter 7. This is why we have dealt so perfunctorily with Marini at this point.
10. This is how we interpret Marini when he says: 'Subimperialism – the form which dependent capitalism assumes upon reaching the stage of monopolies and finance capital' (Marini, 1972a, p 15).
11. In other words, the object of our analysis is the *dependency school*, a concept that appears together with the *dependency theory* and the *dependency paradigm*. We shall use 'dependency school' because it appears to be the most neutral term. The concept of 'theory' is unsuitable, since a number of different dependency theorists have received their theoretical impulses from different sources. When the dependency school was at its peak during the late 1960s and the early 1970s a number of authors wanted to develop a distinct theory, but this idea has now been abandoned. As far as the paradigm concept is concerned, we might say that the dependency perspective was born during a paradigm crisis – the dependency school's first task was to tear up the prevailing ideas about development and underdevelopment – but there are different opinions about the dependency school having replaced the old paradigm with a new. An analysis of the dependency school's paradigmatic breakthrough may be found in Foster-Carter (1976) and Roxborough (1976). To avoid a controversy about the terminology, we shall use 'school' by which we mean a group of authors who are united by a common perspective, but who may not necessarily agree on all details.
12. Leys (1977) is an example of a highly generalized, and therefore often unfair, critique.
13. A detailed analysis may be found in Walicki (1969).
14. When he wrote this article, Palma was directly influenced by Cardoso who was in England at that time (interview with Palma in London, May 1980).

15. Wallerstein, who most consistently has continued along Frank's line of thought, uses the concepts of 'core'-'periphery', and the term 'external arena' to describe the areas which have not as yet been incorporated into the global capitalist system (see Chapter 8).

4. Criticism and Disintegration

The enthusiasm about the new ideas of the 1960s subsided gradually during the early 1970s. The dependency school was now criticized by those who had previously supported it. At the beginning, the critique was directed at isolated errors and misunderstandings in the dependency analysis. As a general approach, dependency had been accepted, and was left alone – for the time being.

The ensuing debate was a more or less internal dispute between various Marxists. This controversy turned out to be of great importance to the future of the dependency school. It might, however, be interesting to see how neo-classical economists viewed the dependency school before we examine the Marxist critique. We conclude this chapter with a summary of the Latin American contributions to this debate.

The Neo-classical Reaction

It would be misleading to speak of a real debate between conventional economists and the dependency school. It was more of a long poignant pause. Foster-Carter has provided a striking description of this by referring to the way in which André Gunder Frank's writings were received by the advocates of the modernization paradigm (Foster-Carter, 1976). Frank's works were reviewed in only a few of the well-known journals, and all of them took a more or less unappreciative attitude. Alec Nove, for example, intimated that he would hardly have passed a student who had produced a paper similar in quality to that of Frank (Nove, 1974).

This lack of communication and sympathy can only be explained by the fact that, as already mentioned, it was a matter of two completely different paradigms. The neo-classical economists did not consider the dependency school's analyses to be 'scientific'. They claimed – often correctly – that the dependency theorists had little knowledge of neo-classical economic theory. It can of course hardly be denied that their knowledge in this particular area was often far from perfect. Some of the major dependency works opened with a critical summary of neo-classical theory to which no self-respecting neo-classical economist would put his name (see, e.g. Amin, 1970).

The first serious discussion of the school by a non-Marxist economist came in 1975 when Sanjaya Lall tried to penetrate the dependency theory, and to provide an evaluation of it, based on its own assumptions (Lall, 1975). Not only was he confused by the fact that the Latin American dependency school held so many varying views of dependency, but also by the fact that the concept of dependence was used by most of those who were in some way involved in the problems of the Third World, regardless of ideological colour. Lall therefore wondered if 'dependence' really was a useful concept in the analysis of underdevelopment. In order for the term 'dependence' to be of any use in a theory of underdevelopment, Lall required two criteria to be met:

1) It must lay down certain characteristics of dependent economies which are not found in non-dependent ones.
2) These characteristics must be shown to affect adversely the course and pattern of development of the dependent countries.

To see whether the first criterion had been met, Lall went through a number of aspects, both sociopolitical and economic, which were characteristic of dependent countries, and examined if they were present in non-dependent countries. This he found to be the case. The dominance of foreign capital – one of the most important aspects of dependence – is a good example. 'Canada and Belgium are more "dependent" on foreign investments than are e.g. India or Pakistan, and yet the former two cannot be categorized as "dependent countries".' It was therefore, in Lall's opinion, impossible to distinguish between dependent and non-dependent countries on the basis of static criteria. This does not mean that Lall denied the existence of the characteristics used by the dependency school to describe dependent countries. He merely wanted to show that they were not special expressions of a 'dependent capitalism', but rather typical expressions of capitalist development in general. 'Both dominance and dependence exist, but they are as commonplace in the Centre as they are in the Periphery' (ibid., p 802).

Lall's second criterion concerned the question of whether a 'dependency theory' could be constructed in accordance with these static characteristics. He found no causal connection between the static characteristics and underdevelopment, however, and thus no basis for a 'theory of Latin American underdevelopment'. In Lall's opinion, one might call it a catalogue of social, economic, political and cultural factors, which nevertheless are unable to help us explain the dynamics of Latin American underdevelopment.[1] Lall therefore pointed out that 'when reading the literature, you often get the impression that "dependence" is defined by circular reasoning: less developed countries are poor because they are dependent, and they show all the characteristics of dependence.'

Although there was no debate between neo-classical economists and dependency theorists on the dependency theory as such, one important aspect of the latter was, however, discussed: the *theory of unequal exchange*.

As we have already mentioned, Prebisch had stressed that one cause of underdevelopment was exploitation through trade. Since the beginning of the 20th Century, Marxists had dealt with this question as part of the theory of unequal exchange (Bauer, 1907), but had never given it a high priority. Stimulated by Prebisch's analysis, the Marxists revived the question, which eventually came into its own in Arrighi Emmanuel's book *L'echange inégal* (Emmanuel, 1969).

The theory of unequal exchange deals with the mechanisms of value transfers between countries. It attempts to construct a theory of foreign trade based on the Marxian theory of value. Briefly, the principle of unequal exchange is this: a commodity's price is determined by the market; an exchange between two commodites is always made on the basis of these price equivalents. On the other hand, a commodity also has an 'objective' value. In order to determine this objective value, Marx used the number of hours worked by labour as his system of reference. Since 'price' and 'value' have different systems of reference, they need not coincide. An exchange of commodities might therefore be unequal in terms of value, despite equal commodity prices, thus causing a transfer of value.

The development of a theory of unequal exchange was therefore not directly linked to the Latin American dependency school, although a number of Latin Americans also worked on this question (see Braun, 1973, and Caputo and Pizarro, 1974). The dependency theorists saw trade as one of several ways in which the centre exploited the periphery; they therefore considered the theory of unequal exchange only as part of the theory of underdevelopment.

The reason why the neo-classical economists even bothered to criticize the theory of unequal exchange was that, apart from being important to development theoretical issues, it influenced the entire neo-classical theory of trade. Metcalfe and Steedman showed that the Heckscher-Ohlin conclusion about the tendency towards an international equalization of factor prices was not general. This started a debate in economic journals in which even Paul Samuelson participated.[2] However, the most severe critics of the theory of unequal exchange were Marxist, not neo-classical economists.

Development v. Underdevelopment: The Marxist Critique

The Marxists remained rather passive during the initial stages of debate started by the dependency school. The school's critique of Marx's universal scheme of development, as described in the Communist Manifesto for example, could hardly be considered open to objections. Nor could objections be raised against the conclusion that the use of the concept of an 'Asiatic mode of production' for the purpose of explaining the relative stagnation in a number of non-European countries had been unsuccessful.[3]

The silence was broken during the early 1970s, not for the purpose of belittling the efforts of the dependency school, but rather to lead it on to the 'right track'. The critique was primarily directed at the way in which the dependency school dealt with class relations. Without a class analysis, the 'theory of dependence' appeared as an 'eclectic combination of orthodox economic theory and revolutionary phrases' (Kay, 1975, p 103).

Frank was particularly singled out for criticism. It was, from a Marxist point of view, totally unsatisfactory to explain underdevelopment by the centre's exploitation of the periphery's economic surplus. The transfer of the economic surplus was, of course, one important aspect of underdevelopment, but the latter must be explained by deeper underlying factors, which, in turn, also explained the transfer of the economic surplus.

How was this to be accomplished? The only way was to use Marx's own method of historic analysis, historical materialism. As we have already seen, an analysis of the history of a given society must, according to Marx, start from the structure of social relations. Such an analysis therefore requires a study of the basic class relations in a society. Different modes of production create different class relations. Thus, in order to explain the Marxist criticism of Frank as well as the 'Marxist alternative' to the dependency analysis (with which we shall deal more thoroughly in Chapter 8), it is necessary to examine the different views of the modes of production in the periphery, since they, in turn, implicitly contain views on the causes of underdevelopment.

In this context an article by Ernesto Laclau (Laclau, 1971) is often referred to.[4] Laclau was opposed to Frank's theory that capitalism has pervaded Latin America since the Spanish conquest, and questioned what Frank really meant by capitalism. Since no explicit definition was provided, Laclau was forced to look for characteristics that, according to Frank, indicated the capitalist mode of production:

1) A system of production for the market, in which
2) profit constitutes the motive of production, and
3) this profit is realized for the benefit of someone other than the direct producer.

Feudalism, on the other hand, was in Frank's opinion a closed subsistence economy. This implied that the crucial difference between capitalism and feudalism was the existence of a substantial market. Thus, Frank did not consider the free labour market prerequisite to the capitalist mode of production, and studied only what in Marxist terminology is called the 'sphere of circulation', or the 'sphere of exchange'. Quoting Laclau:

> Only by abstracting them [the production relations] can he (Frank) arrive at a sufficiently wide notion of capitalism to include the different exploitative situations suffered by the indigenous Peruvian peasantry, the Chilean inquilinos, the Equadorian huasipungueros, the slaves of the West Indies sugar plantations or textile workers of Manchester.
> (Laclau, 1971, p 25)

Laclau, on the other hand, followed Marx when he defined a mode of production. What then really separated the capitalist mode of production from the pre-capitalist one was the fact that the worker was free to sell his labour. Marx used this condition to prove the uniqueness of capitalism *per se*, as well as to allow a definition of capitalism as a unique mode of production. In fact, the market had been characteristic of several pre-capitalist modes of production, which proved that a definition based on the 'sphere of exchange' was insufficient. The production sphere must be considered as well. Laclau carried the matter to an extreme by saying that Frank's definition implied that 'capitalism has reigned supreme since the Neolithic Age'.

Laclau went on to discuss the possibility of different modes of production coexisting. As opposed to Frank, he considered it likely that a given economic system might be a combination of coexisting modes of production. Within such a combination, one mode of production will assume a dominating position. In this way Laclau was able to show the coexistence of, amongst other things, slave economy and capitalism without having to neglect the dominating role played by the latter. However, this should not be interpreted as an acceptance of the theory of the dualist thesis:

> To affirm the feudal character of relations of production in the agrarian sector does not necessarily involve maintaining a dualist thesis. Dualism implies that no connections exist between the 'modern' or 'progressive' sector and the 'closed' or 'traditional' sector. Yet we have argued that, on the contrary, servile exploitation was accentuated and consolidated by the very tendency of entrepreneurs – presumably 'modern' in type – to maximize profits; the apparent lack of communication between the two sectors herewith disappears.
> (Laclau, 1971, p 31)

Laclau's analytical objective was met by basing the definition of an economic system on the relations of production, and by viewing the former as a structured and diversified entity. He was then able to prove that there had been, and still were, feudal elements in Latin America. Most important of all, these feudal elements did not exist independently of capitalism, nor as something which would automatically disappear with the introduction of capitalism, but rather as an inherent and structured part of a larger system. The feudal mode of production was therefore not only able to survive in Latin America, but was strengthened by foreign penetration during certain periods.

With these different views of the mode of production in mind we may now consider the causes of underdevelopment. Frank and Laclau were in agreement on the fact that a transfer of the surplus from the periphery to the centre did, in fact, take place. Frank, however, believed that this surplus transfer was the true *cause* of underdevelopment, whereas Laclau claimed that it was merely an *expression* of more basic relations. To answer as required to the question of what causes underdevelopment, we need therefore to answer the questions of *how* and *why* this transfer of surplus has taken place as well. In Laclau's opinion, Frank has been unsuccessful in doing so, mainly because of his 'broad' definition of capitalism. How was he to distinguish between the contradictions of 16th Century 'capitalism' and those peculiar to 20th Century capitalism?

> If Cortez, Pizarro, Clive and Cecil Rhodes are all one and the same, there is no way of tracing the nature and origins of economic dependence in relation of production. If, on the other hand, we cease to regard capitalism as a Deus ex Machina whose omnipresence frees us from all explanatory problems, and try instead to trace the origins of dependence in concrete modes to renounce all talk of a single unique contradiction. Because relationships of dependence have always existed on the margins of the existence of capitalism.
> (Laclau, 1971, p 34)

The difference between Frank and the Marxists concerning the causes of underdevelopment becomes more obvious when Frank claims that the root of underdevelopment is to be found in the periphery's contacts with the centre – contacts marked by the periphery's role as a producer and exporter of primary products.[5] Marxists, on the other hand, point out that a number of now developed countries have also played this role; but since their class structures were completely different, the end results were also different. The search for a satisfactory answer to this question must be based on the class structure associated with material production.

There are some who claim that this question (i.e. whether internal conditions or external penetration was the cause of underdevelopment) is totally meaningless, and that the polarization is an obstacle to the proper understanding of the real causes of underdevelopment. 'How would you decide which of the heart or the stomach was 'basic'? The question is meaningless' (Foster-Carter, 1978). Since both of the components are important, neither can be excluded.

However, this contribution to the debate reveals a possible misunderstanding: Marxists do not neglect the importance of external factors in the process of underdevelopment when they claim that internal factors are most important. External factors are certainly capable of influencing the internal class structures to the extent that a change of the system is made possible; it is just that all historical analysis must be based on the process of production, i.e. the prevailing forces and relations of production in a society. The contradiction between the latter is the driving force behind the development of each class society. It also creates a class conflict which, regardless of whether the class structure is changed by internal or external factors, remains 'the motor of history'.

A frequently occurring example will serve as an illustration of this point: the slave economy in the New World. In the words of John Weeks and Elizabeth Dore:

> This was a system wholly 'imposed' or created by external force; it did not exist prior to the spread of mercantile capitalism: indeed, the class of direct producers was forcibly created through warfare fostered or exploited by mercantile capital in Africa, and then the captives were transported to the New World. But once the slave society was created, its further evolution was primarily determined by the class struggle internal to it, between slave and master.
> (Weeks and Dore, 1979, p 78)

Nor is that question meaningless, since the choice of approach depends on how causal relations are viewed. The effects of this on further analysis may be illustrated by the political and strategic aspects.

There is no feudalism in Latin America according to Frank's definition of the modes of production. He therefore reaches the conclusion that the only way to break the 'development of underdevelopment' is to break with capitalism and introduce socialism. In Marxist eyes, this 'theory of revolution' is more of a 'nationalist ideology', since it neglects class conflicts and legitimates 'class collaborations'.

> Socialism has become then, something which is 'chosen' for its superiority over capitalism, rather than an outcome dictated by the balance of class forces and the dynamic of class struggle. The arguments centre on why it is necessary, not on whether it is immediately possible. And consequently, detailed analyses of the nature and focus of existing class struggles are few and far between, while analyses of the relationships between national and international capital are in abundant supply.
> (Phillips, 1977, p 20)

According to the Marxist critics of the dependency school, the logical consequence of Frank's 'theory' would be autarky rather than socialism (Brenner, 1977, p 91).

Laclau's analysis, however, also showed that Marx had been too optimistic in predicting that the development of the periphery would be a 'mirror-like reflection' of that of the centre. The capitalist penetration of the periphery did not cause the disintegration of the pre-capitalist social formations. The latter not only survived, but were periodically strengthened. Thus, to blame underdevelopment on the capitalist penetration, as Frank had done, was to misunderstand the entire problem. Since the pre-capitalist elements had not disintegrated, it was rather a question of *insufficient* capitalist penetration.

It is interesting to see that the early Marxist critique of the dependency school actually came from Latin America (Laclau is Argentinian), where a more 'orthodox' Marxist group immediately took up the challenge. Although this group is rarely mentioned, which is quite natural in view of the popularity enjoyed by the dependency school, it continued its severe critique of the dependency theorists throughout the 1970s. This is illustrated by the conference on Latin America's modes of production in Mexico City in 1974.

A number of original contributions were presented, which were all critical of the dependency school.[6] However, this will be discussed in greater detail in the next section when we deal with the debate among the *dependentistas*.

The theoretical critique also resulted in a number of empirical studies, which proved the hypothesis of 'the development of underdevelopment' to be questionable. Bill Warren's study is presumably the best known of these (Warren, 1973). He found that the prospects for a successful, capitalist development (which in his opinion, meant industrialization) were relatively good in many underdeveloped countries; that a considerable capitalist development had already taken place in the Third World, particularly since the Second World War; that potential obstacles to this development were not to be sought among the external factors (imperialism), but rather among the internal contradictions; that imperialism facilitated the industrialization of the Third World; and, finally, that the Third World's dependence on the developed nations has decreased and will continue to do so, resulting in a shift of power within the capitalist world.

Thus, Warren made a frontal assault on the thesis that imperialism was standing in the way of an internal, capitalist development in the periphery. He claimed that the opposite was the case: imperialism had accelerated this development by breaking down the traditional and static societies, and thus paving the way for the industrial society.

Warren also claimed that the rapid industrialization of the periphery after the Second World War was a result of its political independence, combined with certain changes in the world economy.

> Independence has been a direct cause (not just a permissive condition) of industrial advance by giving the underdeveloped countries a degree of manoeuvre and initiative which, over time, must inevitably come into play, and which is conducive to economic advance.
> (Ibid., pp 11-12)

> What has been crucial is the combination of political independence with certain objective conditions in the post-war period. Specifically East-West rivalries and inter-imperialist rivalries, which have been the major external influence, have linked with internal forces, especially the rise of new ruling groups and the increase in popular, often petty bourgeois mobilization.
> (Ibid., p 13)

Returning to Laclau for a moment, we have already mentioned the fact that his analysis was not only meant as a critique of Frank and the rest of the *dependentistas*, but also as a critique of Marx's optimistic view of the future of the 'backward' countries. In this context, Warren had no objection to Marx. His views on imperialism were, in many respects, similar to Marx's views on colonialism. Like Marx, he saw imperialism as a transitory stage – as a system which 'declines as capitalism grows' (ibid., p 41). This 'return to the master' was, of course, soon challenged; however, we shall save the debate around Warren's article for the chapter on current trends in the theory of development.

Although Frank was the one who was most criticized by the Marxists, the critique was also directed at other dependency theorists whose works were based on neo-Marxist ideas (we, of course, exclude Furtado, Sunkel and others who never claimed that they were 'Marxists'). We have already mentioned that Dos Santos attempted to abandon neo-Marxism; he criticized Frank's view that underdevelopment was a question of external exploitation. Instead, he emphasized that the Latin American underdevelopment was a result of certain internal structure, which, in turn, were determined by international relations of dependence. He continued to identify the types of dependence which, in turn determined the different internal structures, and emphasized the fact that not only was there a contradiction between the internal and the external structure, but that this very contradiction was the root of underdevelopment.

In his concrete analyses of underdevelopment Dos Santos, however, abandoned this view and let regional contradictions and the transfer of the economic surplus play the key roles, along with the now dominant external factors. In doing so, he returned to Frank's position, and was thus immediately exposed to Marxist criticism.

At this point it might be convenient to mention the most important aspects of the Marxist critique of Emmanuel's theory of unequal exchange. Of course, Marxists did not deny the existence of unequal exchange, which, after all, was one of the ways in which the surplus might be transferred from the periphery to the centre. Their critique was aimed at Emmanuel's analysis, because it was incapable of showing that this really was so. In Emmanuel's opinion, the basic contradiction was the one between 'rich' and 'poor' countries. The developed countries exploited the underdeveloped ones – which implied that even the workers in the developed countries were responsible for the exploitation of the Third World. To a Marxist this notion is absurd. Like Frank and Dos Santos, Emmanuel based his definition of classes on the 'sphere of circulation', and was therefore also singled out for the above critique.[7]

Dos Santos's difficulties in ridding himself of his neo-Marxist heritage are revealed in his definition of dependence. Like many other dependency theorists he distinguished between two types of capitalism: 'normal' and 'dependent' – of which the former was capable of achieving a 'self-generating growth', and the latter merely of developing as 'a reflection of the former'. This view is, according to Marxism, nothing but a 'romantic notion' of the true nature of capitalism (Bernstein, 1979), as well as a reflection of a 'nostalgic longing for a frustrated, autonomous capitalist development' (Cueva, 1974).

> Underdevelopment theory cannot have it both ways. If the field of analysis is world economy, if the centre needs the periphery for modes

> of exploitation that off-set the tendency of the rate of profit to fall, if the circuit of capital in general is realized on the international plane, then there is *no* capitalist formation whose development can be regionally autonomous, self-generating or self-perpetuating. 'Development' cannot be conceptualized by its self-centred nature and lack of dependence, nor 'underdevelopment' by its dependence and lack of autonomy.
> (Bernstein, 1979, p 92)

Dependency theorists who analysed peripheral capitalism in this fashion were described by certain Marxists as 'Narodniks' because their 'moral' critique of capitalism was quite similar to that expressed by the original bearers of the name (Palma, 1978). The severity of the Narodniks' claim that no capitalist development was possible in Russia was echoed in certain dependency theorists' claim that no capitalist development was possible in the periphery, partly because of the late start of the industrialization. Therefore, the Marxists needed only refer to Lenin's writings for suitable counter arguments in their debate with the current 'Narodniks'. As mentioned in Chapter 1, Lenin primarily dealt with these questions in his *Development of Capitalism in Russia*, in which he discussed the effects of the links between external and internal structures on the development of backward regions. There Lenin argued that what the Narodniks believed to be the reason for the lack of capitalist development in Russia in reality was a result of it.

Cardoso is perhaps closest to Lenin's work and the one who most consistently has tried to elaborate on the approach used by Lenin in his analysis of the capitalist development in Russia. Consequently, he never regarded the notion of dependence as a universally valid concept upon which a 'theory of dependency' can be constructed (Cardoso, 1970). In his opinion, a theory of capitalism was already available – the Marxist theory. The purpose of the notion was rather to be used in concrete analyses of how external and internal factors affect development in the periphery. Cardoso pointed out that it was incorrect mechanically to draw a dividing line between external and internal factors in such a study, and that it was instead a matter of a dialectic interplay, in which the internal factors ultimately determined the concrete manifestations in the periphery of a change in the world capitalist system.

Cardoso has consistently claimed that capitalist development *is* taking place in Latin America, although it is of a rather special kind. Furthermore, he cannot be criticized for ignoring the internal structures and the class struggle in his analyses; on the contrary – the internal structures are crucial in a development process. Cardoso has, however, objected to the orthodox Marxist view of classes, according to which all classes are rooted in the process of material production. To him, this view is too narrow, if the functioning of the peripheral societies is to be understood; they are, in his opinion, too complex for an analysis that follows Marx's universal scheme. The class concept must contain structural and institutional factors, races, ethnic groups, religions, etc., all of which may be included in a dependence analysis, since the purpose of such an analysis is merely to study concrete situations in the periphery.

Cardoso's view of classes has, of course, been subjected to Marxist critique. John Myer has accused Cardoso of engaging in 'Marxist and Leninist phraseology' (Myer, 1975; see also O'Brien, 1973). Since Cardoso does not base his definition of 'class' on the way in which different groups are related in the area of production, he cannot be considered to be a 'Marxist'. However, it is difficult to deny the importance of the structural relations which Cardoso has identified, even though Marxists have been doing so for a long time. In fact, Myer did not succeed in showing how these factors were to be incorporated into a Marxist theory.

In this context, it might be interesting to look at the critique of Foster-Carter's distinction between Marxism and neo-Marxism which we, with certain reservations (see Chapter 2), have also adopted. The reader might recall that the concept of neo-Marxism covered a Marxist-inspired, but relatively independent, theoretical tradition with which one associates names such as Baran, Sweezy and Frank. It was of great significance as a source of inspiration to the dependency school. The dismissal of this distinction is of great importance to Marxists who are concerned about the integrity of Marxism. Taylor accomplishes this by calling it a 'sociological phantasy' (Taylor, 1974). His main argument is that Foster-Carter erroneously assumes that the *space* allowed to a specific problem by a certain theoretical tradition is a measure of the latter's ability to analyse the problem theoretically. Consequently, he admits that Marxism, as compared to neo-Marxism, has devoted relatively little attention to the conditions in the Third World; but this does not mean that classical Marxism is theoretically less equipped to tackle this problem, and that it is therefore necessary to abandon fundamental Marxian concepts. In line with the above-mentioned critique, Taylor emphasizes the fact that concepts such as 'surplus', 'dependence', 'underdevelopment', etc., tend to obscure important issues that might be dealt with more effectively by the 'traditional' Marxist analysis – even if the conceptual apparatus of the latter might require some clarification. Thus, at the same time as he evaluates both 'schools' (in the process of which he reduces neo-Marxism to Baran and Frank), he dismisses the idea that they should be seen as competing theoretical alternatives:

> Foster-Carter is perhaps on his weakest ground when he argues that there do, in fact, exist two such unities as 'Marxism' and 'Neo-Marxism'. How can we possibly group together the works of Emmanuel and Bettelheim, or perhaps, more questioningly, Jalée and Amin? Foster-Carter's answer is, quite simply, that they are all concerned with analysing the same real object, namely imperialist penetration and its effects upon an 'underdeveloped' society. This, however, is really equivalent to making such a broad generalisation as that the biological sciences take nature as their real object; and it doesn't help us at all

> in assessing the relative value of one problematic as against another. (Taylor, op. cit.)

Supporters of law and order, or the ideological cops, in the Marxist camp have greeted this attack with loud cheers. Henry Bernstein, for example, claims that 'John Taylor's critique has totally demolished Foster-Carter's celebration of neo-Marxism' (Bernstein, 1979, p 102). The concept is, nevertheless, being used sporadically – not because of its lucidity, but simply because it is needed. Our use of the concept is based on this heuristic function. As dealt with in more detail in Chapter 2, we see neo-Marxism as a *phase* in the theoretical development of Marxism – not as a distinct school.

Probably the most important non-Latin American contribution to the Marxist critique of the dependency approach was Colin Leys's article 'Underdevelopment and Dependency: Critical Notes' (Leys, 1977). For several years, Leys was the most prominent dependency theorist in Kenya, so when he turned his back on the dependency school, he also repudiated the result of ten years of his own work.[8] Leys claimed that the dependency theory was no longer applicable, and that it somehow had to be transcended. There were several reasons for this. First, it was repetitious and theoretically stagnant. Secondly, it was incapable of providing a solution to, as well as a formulation of, certain problems. Finally, it lacked realism. Leys's more theoretical objections to the dependency theory were:

- The meaning of 'development' is obscure. In contrast to Asia and Africa there seem to be few original ideas in Latin America about the positive content of development.
- It is unclear whether it is the underdeveloped countries or the masses in these countries that suffer from exploitation. The obvious answer is of course 'both' but the emphasis of analysis has theoretical implications.
- Concepts like 'centre' and 'periphery' are primitive and nothing but polemical inversions of the simplistic pairings of 'bourgeois' development theory (traditional-modern etc.).
- The theory tends to be economistic in the sense that social classes, the state, politics, ideology get very little attention.
- The ultimate causes of underdevelopment are not identified apart from the thesis that they originate in a 'centre'.

(Leys, op. cit.)

Leys's article was the go-ahead for the new, Marxist view of development (note that contrary to the neo-Marxists, Marxists speak of 'development' rather than of 'underdevelopment') to which we shall return in Chapter 8. The rest of this chapter is devoted to the internal, Latin American debate.

At The Crossroads: The Debate among the Dependentistas

The military coup in Chile on 11 September 1973 constituted a turning point in the Latin American debate on underdevelopment and dependence. Until then the dependency school had had a fair wind – mainly because of the rise of a number of popular regimes in Latin America during the late 1960s and the early 1970s. These regimes (i.e. Argentina, Bolivia, Chile and Peru) were greatly influenced by the dependency school's arguments which was particularly obvious in Velasco's Peru and Allende's Chile. The 'enemy' was often identified with US imperialism, resulting in a number of nationalizations and other measures directed against foreign capital.

With a slight exaggeration it might be said that there were as many 'dependency theories' as there were dependency theorists; a multiplicity which was already present in Chile. A debate among the *dependentistas* was therefore only to be expected, but this debate was certainly kept in a positive vein. We have already mentioned the Latin American critique of André Gunder Frank. His much too mechanical interpretation of dependence was rejected – and Frank replied with a 'mea culpa' (Frank, 1972).

Vania Bambirra's *El capitalismo dependiente en América Latina* (Bambirra, 1972) is also representative of the positive critique of that period. In the second chapter of this book Bambirra, who worked together with Dos Santos, evaluated Cardoso's and Faletto's analysis of development as 'one of the most relevant analyses'. The relatively kind critique that followed dealt with three problems which were closely associated with the authors' 'much too sociological view':

The method adopted. The economic aspect was included only as a loosely defined structure, upon which the authors had built a mainly sociological analysis. The economic factor was thus of importance only to the definition of the structural parameters; the study then went on to analyse the behaviour of various social groups from a sociological point of view. Bambirra claimed that the behaviour of social groups and classes must be derived from their objective economic interests, and from the way in which the latter change over time. Thus, the economic factor will appear to be static when the economic and the sociological analyses are not performed concurrently.

The way in which the development of various Latin American socioeconomic structures was analysed: Cardoso and Faletto did not provide a thorough discussion about the structural changes in Latin America from the mid 19th Century onward. They ought to have provided an analysis of how structural changes in the developed, capitalist societies also led to changes in the dependent countries.

The classification of countries: As a result of what was mentioned above, Bambirra felt that the authors' way of classifying the countries in the study was inappropriate. Two types of countries had been used for the historical analysis: those which had managed to gain national control of the process of production, and enclave economies. Accordingly, both Mexico and Chile were characterized as enclave economies which, in Bambirra's opinion, was unrealistic. Both countries actually belonged somewhere between the two prototypes.

Despite important exceptions, such as Cardoso, the prevailing view among the development theorists in Chile during this period was that a 'theory of dependence' could be constructed, and that the work on this had only just begun. The critique was therefore, in reality, quite constructive and positive. However, there were some critical voices objecting to the 'project' of constructing a theory of dependence. We have already discussed the Argentinian Laclau. The importance of his comments was, however, not realized until later.[9]

The dependency school was also criticized by a number of structuralists, who, based on empirical studies, found a number of flaws in its underdevelopment perspective. The ECLA economists Anibal Pinto and Jan Kñákel showed that although a polarization between the centre and the periphery had, in fact, taken place during the 1960s, it was not primarily the result of structural links between the two regions (Pinto and Kñákal, 1972). The polarization was caused by an exceptionally rapid growth in the centre, which could only be explained by the internal factors in that region:

> It seems necessary to recall that colonial or neo-colonial 'exactions' constitute a subordinate aspect of the Center's dynamization in that period although they might have been significant for certain peripheral countries. The best evidence for this, which contradicts known arguments, may be found in the extraordinary development of those Center areas lacking colonial bases.
> (Ibid., p 117)

The dependency theorists were also proved wrong in certain more narrowly defined areas, one of which was the effects of 'technological dependence'. Technological dependence was generally considered to be a crucial element in the overall dependence. Among other things, the dependency theorists claimed that since those who controlled the generation of technology (i.e. the centre) also have the capacity to control its exploitation, this would lead to the permanence of technological dependency. The possibilities for a generation of domestic technology were therefore excluded (see e.g. Merhav, 1969). Empirical studies in Latin America found, however, that this was not the case, particularly in the 'semi-industrialized' countries. Argentina, which is representative of this type of country, had, for instance, during the 1970s shown a relatively rapid development of domestic technology. Successive adaptations to local conditions of imported technology had resulted in new technological assets that were markedly different from those imported, and with a commercial value of their own. Argentina had thus managed to *export* technology. This type of export was generally by domestic firms, and it was limited to other Latin American countries, i.e. countries with a number of structural similarities.[10]

The same kind of development was also under way in Mexico – a fact that has been corroborated by a study of the industries in the Monterrey area. This study reaches the following conclusion:

> Not only are established Mexican firms in a broad range of industries performing comparably with foreign firms in terms of profitability, growth and exports, but they appear to be at least as innovative in the sense of introducing new products and productive processes. Perhaps even more important, they appear to be relying substantially on domestic institutions, and particularly resources internal to the firm, to generate the new technology. To say the least, a national industrial base, not subordinated to foreign competition, appears to be alive and well and living in Monterrey.
> (Fairchild, 1977, p 30)

The emergence of technology generation by indigenous enterprises in underdeveloped countries raised new questions concerning the role of technology imports in general, and of direct investment of multinational corporations in particular, since these firms are the most important actors in the generation, application and international transfer of modern technology. In the dependency literature the dynamic aspects of technology as well as the possible 'spillover' effects of foreign investment were totally ignored. Evidence from the Mexican manufacturing industry showed, however, that foreign investment could give rise to indirect gains (or spillovers) to the host economy through the realization of external economies (Blomström and Persson, 1983). Regarding the most important sources of spillover efficiency, another study suggests that foreign entry promotes greater efficiency in Mexican firms by increasing competition. In that way foreign firms force domestically owned ones to adopt more efficient methods of production (Blomström, 1983)

After the military take-over in Chile, Mexico City subsequently assumed the role as Latin America's new theoretical centre.[11] As such, it received a number of prominent development theorists who had been forced to leave Chile. However, it might be appropriate to give a short description of Mexico's unique position in Latin America before we discuss the debate initiated by these expatriate scholars.[12]

Mexico is, in many ways, different from the rest of Latin America. Apart from being a big country with a relatively developed economy, it is also politically more stable. Also the Mexican culture is, in many respects, unique and quite different from that of the other Latin American countries. The Mexican identity is asserted at many levels (art, music, literature, etc.). For our purposes, it is particularly interesting to note that the Marxist tradition in Mexico is different. It is quite obvious that so-called neo-Marxism has had relatively little effect upon the Mexican Marxists, and that the more traditional type of Marxism has prevailed. Compared to Chile, where neo-Marxism had a greater influence in the universities, Mexican Marxism was far less visionary, with a greater tendency towards determinism. Although an analysis of the reasons for this difference is beyond the scope of this book, one important reason might be the influence on Mexican intellectual life of the exiled Spanish opponents of the Franco regime.

Thus, it is no mere coincidence that the ideas of the dependency school were developed in the southern parts of the Latin American continent, or that they ran into stiff opposition in Mexico. (We have already mentioned that some Mexican social scientists, such as Rodolfo Stavenhagen, did not join the dependency school because of their Mexican roots – although they started out along similar lines (see Chapter 2).) In addition to the concrete, political set-backs which the dependency school had suffered – first in Chile in 1973 and later across the entire southern part of the continent – it now also faced a completely different Marxist tradition. The ensuing debate not only influenced the dependency theorists' views, but also revitalized the Marxist debate in Mexico.

Augustine Cueva provided an important contribution to the Marxist critique by further elaborating on that of Laclau.[13] His writings (see particularly Cueva, 1974 and 1977) contain only a few references to the Marxist critique in Europe, although the latter was basically similar. This is quite natural since Marx's method is now being used to answer the questions originally posed by the *dependentistas*.

The dependency school's response was off-hand. The critique was dismissed by a simple reference to the fact that the critics had neither understood the dependency theory nor provided any viable alternatives. The following is an excerpt from Vania Bambirra's reply to Cueva: 'It is difficult to follow Cueva's line of argument, since he starts with Gunder Frank, jumps to Dos Santos, returns to Frank, continues on to Cardoso and Faletto – then to Marini – Frank again, Cardoso and Faletto again, Frank, Marini, Frank . . .' (Bambirra, 1978, p 71). Dos Santos used similar arguments (Dos Santos, 1978). On top of it all, he did 'not even consider it justified to respond to the critique', since the critics were not at all versed in the dependency theory. Thus, his 'reply' consisted of a restatement of his idea of a dependency theory.

Bambirra's reply to the Marxists' critique also contained references to Ruy Mauro Marini's writings on peripheral capitalism. In her opinion, they were an elaboration on the Marxist theory – a fact which the critics quite obviously had missed. 'To be a Marxist is to create, not just to repeat texts; it is important to know how to use the dialectic method when analyzing a concrete situation' (Bambirra, 1978, p 69).

It should be obvious that Marini's theoretical constructs about peripheral capitalism and orthodox Marxian tradition, are in many ways incompatible. It is all very well that the dependency theorists 'have filled pages with class analyses' (ibid., p 57), but using these in the theories is an entirely different matter.

One of Cardoso's articles (Cardoso, 1976) contained an interesting contribution to the Latin American dependency debate. In it he shows that the *dependentistas* were never a homogeneous group. Using the same method that Stavenhagen had used ten years before to criticize the traditional theory of development (see Chapter 2), Cardoso now criticized 'Dependency Theory'. In other words, he constructed a number of fallacies, and then proceeded to analyse them:

Capitalist development at the periphery is not viable. Certain structural obstacles, as well as the lack of dynamic capital, prevent the development of an entirely capitalist system. In Cardoso's opinion, it is wrong to claim that this *must* be so; i.e. that this is the result of the workings of some 'natural' law. Contradictions do not stand in the way of capitalist development, but constitute a natural part of it.

Dependent capitalism is based on extensive exploitation of labour and is tied to the necessity of underpaying labour. This notion points out the problem of limited and stagnant domestic markets, which, in turn, is an important factor in the explanation of 'subimperialism'. This view is much too mechanical and ignores the dynamic aspects of (even peripheral) capitalism.

Local bourgeoisies no longer exist as an active social force. The proponents of this view claim that the local bourgeoisie in the periphery is parasitic (lumpenbourgeoisie). It is neither capable of achieving a normal, rational accumulation of capital, nor is it able to realize its own true 'interests' (cf. Frank). This view, still quoting Cardoso, confuses the unsuccessful ideology of national populism and the true interests of the local, industrial bourgeoisie.

The penetration by multinational firms leads local states to pursue an expansionist policy, typically 'subimperialist'. Like the rest of these theses this one exaggerates the local capitalists' incompetence. It is incorrect to say that the increase in export activity has favoured only the multinational corporations.

The periphery's only alternatives are socialism or fascism. The ruling classes in Latin America have, undoubtedly, become increasingly militarized; but that does not necessarily imply a fascist political organization.

Thus, Cardoso dismissed all of these theses, claiming that they were created merely to support each other:

> Theoretical and analytical efforts to show what is specific and new in the current forms of dependency seem to have dissipated into images full of easy but misleading abstractions: 'development of underdevelopment', 'sub-imperialism', 'lumpen-bourgeoisie', 'revolutions of the marginals' etc. Although such ideas sometimes point to important aspects of the specificity of the industrialization process at the peri-

phery, and to the forms of domination which accompany it, they also lead to distorted analyses.
(Ibid., p 1)

Marini answered this critique by accusing Cardoso of 'sociologism'.[14] He defended his thesis that 'dependent capitalism' was, in essence, different from capitalism in the advanced countries. Therefore, the basis for a dependency theory was still there. Marini's opinion is, however, an exception in Latin America today. Although many of the questions raised by the dependency theorists have played (and will play) an important role in the Latin American debate on underdevelopment (as well as in the rest of the world), only a few today would answer these with a 'dependency theory'. Before taking up the current trends in development theory, we shall, however, account for the development debate related to the issue of dependence in other Third World contexts (the Caribbean, Asia and Africa).

Notes

1. Lall's conclusions were tested empirically by Thomas Weisskopf, who found them to be correct (Weisskopf, 1976).
2. A summary of the debate is found in Evans (1980).
3. Sofri (1969) contains an excellent survey of the debate on the Asiatic mode of production.
4. An earlier attempt to provide a Marxist analysis of the Latin American mode of production is found in Marinéz-Alliér (1967). However, Laclau's article 'Feudalism and Capitalism in Latin America' (Laclau, 1971) attracted much more attention. Thus, Laclau's article might be said to have extended this debate to include the causes of underdevelopment. The question then, as now, was whether to emphasize the *exchange relations*, or the *relations of production*. During the 1950s Sweezy, who represented the former view, argued with Dobb, who represented the latter. In the debate on underdevelopment, Frank and Wallerstein held the former view, while Bernstein, Brenner, Laclau, among others, held the latter. A thorough critique of the so-called Neo-Smithian Marxism may be found in the above-mentioned article by Brenner, in Weeks and Dore (1979) and in Taylor (1974 and 1979). Replies are found in Wallerstein (1979).
5. Brenner offers the following comments about Frank's attempts to extend his theory of underdevelopment by a class analysis: 'Frank continues to regard class as a phenomenon of the market . . . Although he now does focus on class, Frank continues to treat it as a derivative phenomenon, arising directly from the needs of profit maximization' (Brenner, 1977, p 86).
6. Some of the papers presented at this conference are published in *Historia y Sociedad*, No. 5, 1975.
7. The first Marxist critique of Emmanuel was written by Bettelheim, who

was Emmanuel's faculty adviser, and was published as an appendix to Emmanuel's book.

8. Leys's analysis of African problems in this perspective is examined in Chapter 7.
9. The Latin American opposition to Laclau's arguments are dealt with in Leaver (1977). Leaver points out that 'Frank initially came out of this debate with Laclau as a loser' (p 198).
10. These were the findings of the research project *El Programa BID/CEPAL de Investigaciones en Temas Ciencia y Tecnologia*, led by Jorge Katz. More details may be found in e.g. Katz (1978); Katz and Ablin (1978); and Ablin (1979). Sanjaya Lall has obtained similar results for India (see e.g. Lall, 1978).
11. Mexico City is still a dominating development theoretical centre in Latin America, although Brazil has taken over part of this role.
12. Pedro Paz has pointed out that one of the reasons why the Mexican critique was particularly severe was this country's unique position in Latin America (conversation in Mexico City, October 1980).
13. There was also more ideologically influenced critique in Mexico. This critique came from the Mexican Communist Party (PCM). See e.g. Semo (1975).
14. In fact, Marini answered another article of Cardoso (written jointly with José Serra), which was directly addressed to Marini, but Cardoso's main arguments are the same as in Cardoso (1976). The exchange of views is found in *Revista Mexicana de Sociología*, Ano XL/Vol XL, Número extraordinario, 1978.

5. Dependency Theory in Action: Caribbean Approaches in Underdevelopment

In the Caribbean the debate about the problem of dependence was in many respects similar to the Latin American one. The reason is not difficult to find. The 'plantation systems' established in the Caribbean during the 17th Century were artificial communities based on European capital and African labour, the sole purpose of which was to produce sugar (Beckford, 1972; Patterson, 1967). The abolition of slavery modified, but did not change this social structure in any significant way (Smith, 1965). Thus, the various Caribbean economies can hardly be said to possess any dynamics of their own, but must be seen as subsystems of the capitalist world economy. Since the dependency perspective provides an obvious angle of approach, the ensuing discussion about underdevelopment and dependence, which may be seen as a parallel to the Latin American one, is therefore not surprising.

The Idea of Dependency in a Caribbean Context

Jamaica's current economic problems must be seen in the light of the island's historical role as a plantation system, totally dependent upon the development of the world economy. Until 1838, Jamaica was a pure plantation economy. After the abolition of slavery, when a number of ex-slaves refused to work at the plantations, the Jamaican economy became 'dualistic', i.e. a self-supporting peasant economy existed side by side with the plantation economy. The fall in sugar production was at the same time compensated for by a shift to and a concentration on banana-growing. The 1930s revealed Jamaica's dependence upon a small number of agricultural export commodities, and its negative economic, social and political consequences. Several investigation commissions were appointed during the 1940s, but they went no further than to point out that the costs of production had risen faster than world market prices. Dependence was accepted almost as a natural state. The ambitious economic policies of the 1950s and the 1960s were based on the strategy of 'industrialization by invitation'; but like the Latin American strategy of import substitution, this strategy proved incapable of solving Jamaica's development problems.

It is thus obvious that one of the important reasons for the lively development debate in the Caribbean was that region's experience of dependence as an historical situation; however, the relative advancement of the academic infrastructure was also an important factor.

The University College of the West Indies was founded in 1946. A British committee of higher education in the Colonies called special attention to the social sciences in its report:

> The West Indies provide abundant opportunity for economic, historical, and sociological research in the widest sense. The territories show great variety in their political and racial histories while they sometimes present the same general problems with interesting local differences . . . We find it difficult to resist the temptation to enlarge upon the intellectual adventures that are awaiting in this field.
> (Quoted from ISER, Research Programme and Progress Report, University College of the West Indies, Jamaica, 1955, p 1)

The attitude of the report is unmistakably colonial. The Caribbean was seen as a laboratory for the social sciences. New empirical knowledge was needed – not new theories:

> Fundamental research in the West Indian context must be empirical in its bias. It must seek at once to establish a body of knowledge, a systematic accumulation of data. It is the factual equipment of the Caribbean economist or sociologist that is most lacking. The concepts already shaped in the world at large can usually be adapted to his purposes without special difficulty provided there is an adequate basis of local knowledge.
> (Ibid.)

This was the spirit in which the first generation of Caribbean social scientists were trained.

Industrialization by Invitation: W.A. Lewis

The origins of the Latin American and the Caribbean debates were quite similar: the former was based on Raúl Prebisch's strategy of industrialization, and the latter on W.A. Lewis's well-known arguments for an industrialization of the Caribbean (Lewis, 1949 and 1950). Like Prebisch in Latin America, Lewis found that the production of raw materials for the world market alone could not raise the material standard of the Caribbean countries, mainly because they were threatened by overpopulation.[1] In 1938 Lewis had already pointed out that 'no other policy appears to provide as many permanent jobs as that of developing the domestic industry' (Lewis, 1938 [1977]). During the 1940s he followed the Puerto Rican *Industrial Development Company* and its policy of industrialization with great interest, essentially sharing its views. It was important to build up a pattern of industrialization that could bring out the comparative advantages of cheap labour, for example. Since industrial capitalists are rarely tempted by regions that are totally devoid of industry, the government must, to begin with, set a good example and build some itself; private initiative can then be stimulated at a later stage.[2] This Puerto Rican model was extremely important to Lewis's general strategy for Caribbean industrialization, known as the strategy of *industrialization by invitation.* A strategy of import substitution was obviously inadequate in the Caribbean case: 'Most industries must export or die.'[3]

To Lewis the threat of overpopulation was the most decisive argument in favour of industrialization; hence the opening statement of his famous article 'The Industrialization of the British West Indies':

> The case for rapid industrialization in the West Indies rests chiefly on over-population. The islands already carry a larger population than agriculture can absorb, and populations are growing at rates of 1.5 to 2.0 per cent per annum. It is, therefore, urgent to create new opportunities for employment off the land.
> (Lewis, 1950, p 1)

Agriculture could not feed the population, and had not been able to do so for several decades,[4] partly because of the growth of the population, and partly because of the mechanization of the plantation sector. The decreasing number of women employed and the increase in the number of unproductive occupations were, in Lewis's opinion, indications of over-population. The tourist industry and emigration relieved the situation marginally; the conclusion, that it would be necessary to concentrate on industrialization, was therefore inevitable. However, it was not a matter of choosing between industry or agriculture. Both were necessary:

> If agriculture is to give a higher standard of living, then industry must be developed. But equally, if industry is to be developed, then agriculture must give a higher standard of living, in order to provide a demand for manufactures. The agricultural and the industrial revolutions thus reinforce each other, and neither can go very far unless the other is occurring at the same time.
> (Ibid., p 16)

Lewis also believed that export industries were necessary. The domestic market was too small to support a strategy of import substitution. There is, in other words, an important difference between the approaches of Lewis and Prebisch. In Lewis's opinion, the West Indian islands (with the exception of Trinidad) lacked resources and should follow a development model which concentrated on exporting industrial goods and importing food and raw materials.

Although Lewis today is considered to be a relatively conventional economist, and has been severely criticized as such by his younger West Indian colleagues, it is interesting to note that his recommendations, at that time, were highly unorthodox. The British colonial administration had never really considered the possibility of industrializing the West Indies. Lewis claimed that their *laissez-faire* policy constituted the most important obstacle to industrialization:

> These views were never accepted outside England by persons responsible for the government of countries that were industrializing. Neither were they accepted by England herself in the long centuries from 1400 to 1850 when she was laying the foundations of her industrial greatness on the basis of vigorous fostering of new industries behind monopolistic grants, patents, subsidies and protective barriers. They have never been accepted by the rulers of any nation at the time when it was in its early throes of industrialization, whether by England, or the United States, or Germany, or Japan, or Russia, or any other country. It is only when England had become the leading manufacturing country in the world that she embraced *laissez-faire* views, and sought, unsuccessfully, to sell them to other nations. Independent nations, including the self-governing dominions, refused to buy them, but India and the rest of the dependent Empire were allowed no option. It has been the misfortune of the West Indies to be caught in the trap of these ideas.
> (Ibid., pp 34-5)

It is therefore not quite correct to call Lewis a 'lackey of imperialism', which radical West Indian social scientists have tended to do. Of course, this does not mean that Lewis's strategy did not have other weaknesses, such as the 'sheep-herd' or 'snowball theory' of industrial development:

> Industries are like sheep; they like to move together. In consequence, a place which has no industries is unattractive to new industries; while a place which has plenty of industries attracts still more. The analogy of the snowball is even better than that of the sheep. For, once the snowball starts to move downhill, it will move of its own momentum, and will get bigger and bigger as it goes along. So it is with industry. Once an industrial centre is established and begins to grown, it will go on growing. But the big problem is, how do we get started? A place which has no industries is unattractive; if it had some, it would get more; but without some it doesn't get any. You have, as it were, to begin by rolling your snowball up the mountain. Once you get it there, the rest is easy, but you cannot get it there without first making an initial effort.
> (Ibid., p 36)

This theory obviously ignored a number of complications which would eventually surface during the various industrialization attempts, but apart from that, how was a government to proceed in order to achieve Lewis's so-called 'snowball effect'? Lewis assumed that active and rational measures by the government were required to compensate for the fact that the market system was incapable of initiating the process of industrialization. It would be necessary to create a 'special agency' for industrialization, as well as special incentives to overcome the initial difficulties.

Lewis's argument assumed the existence of a customs union. In reality, he did not believe that industrialization of the West Indies would be possible without a federal, Caribbean government. As far as the incentives were concerned, he primarily suggested low wages and suitable factories, or preferably complete industrial areas ('trading estates') with buildings, energy and transport facilities.

> There is not much point in simply scheduling an area for industrial development, as the Jamaica government has done. What the industrialist is looking for is a factory building, well planned, with public utility services laid on; he is not impressed by an empty piece of ground. (Ibid., pp 46-7)

In other words, during the difficult initial stage (and until the snowball has started to roll) the government may start businesses on its own initiative, i.e. primarily industries producing for the domestic market. 'The export industries are best suited for persons who already are established on the export market.' Since the government's financial resources are often limited, as is the number of businesses it can start, it is advisable to offer some of these businesses to private interests as a means of acquiring funds for the starting up of new businesses. Lewis also suggested subsidies, limited tax exemption and continued service to the established business as possible incentives.

> The new arrival should feel free to cast on to the shoulders of the corporation any difficulty that crops up. All this costs money, but it pays a wonderful dividend. For if the new arrival writes home to say that all is well, it will not be long before others come after him.
> (Ibid., p 53)

The term 'industrialization by invitation' is therefore an adequate description of Lewis's industrialization strategy. The various arguments which we have discussed are found in a more general form in his classic essay 'Economic Development with Unlimited Supply of Labour' (Lewis, 1954). Here Lewis assumes that the economy in the Third World is dual, i.e. that it consists of two sectors, one modern, industrial and capitalist and one traditional, agricultural and self-supporting. The productivity in the two sectors differs greatly and the marginal productivity of labour in the traditional sector is zero, i.e. it is possible to remove labour from this sector without reducing its output.

In Lewis's model the role of the traditional sector is to supply the modern sector with an unlimited quantity of labour at stable wages. The expansion of the modern sector, combined with the flow of labour from the traditional sector (at stable, low wages) leads to increasing profits, which, in turn, are ploughed back into the businesses, thus leading to further expansion.

Lewis's model has been the subject of numerous discussions, and subjected to much criticism. First, some doubt has been thrown on the low marginal productivity of traditional agriculture; it has furthermore been pointed out that so-called underemployment in agriculture is institutional. It is indeed true that labour might be utilized more efficiently, but the basis of this assumption must also be studied from a sociological and a socio-anthropological point of view.[5] Secondly, Lewis's model has been accused of being unrealistic because it assumes a stable political regime and an effective administration. A process which involves the transfer of large parts of the population from the primary sector to the secondary sector imposes fundamental changes on the social structure, which, in turn, expose the political system to great strain.

The discussions about Lewis's famous model rarely include its actual background; that is why we have found it appropriate to provide a relatively thorough account of those of Lewis's earlier writings which deal explicitly with the West Indies, although they did not escape criticism either. We shall now return to the specifically Caribbean part of the debate, particularly the dependency debate, which generally may be seen as a reaction to Lewis – just as the Latin American dependency debate may be seen as a reaction to Prebisch. Of course, it was not only, or primarily, a question of intellectual dialectics. The various West Indian governments applied the strategy recommended by Lewis more or less consistently during the 1950s and the 1960s. The result, however, was not industrialization and full employment (although the industrial sector did, in fact, grow considerably), but, in the words of the dependency theorists, 'dependence' and 'structural underdevelopment'. According to Girvan, this happened during the first half of the 1960s. The new ideas came from a group of economists who called themselves the *New World Group*.

The New World Group

Towards the end of 1962 the New World Group was founded in Georgetown, Guyana. The actual reason for this was the growing racial conflict (between Indians and Africans), which had been brought to a peak by Guyana's economic difficulties. The group also started a periodical, the *New World Quarterly* (NWQ), the purpose of which was to lead the way towards an analysis of Guyana's more basic conflicts.

> The editor of this magazine firmly believes that many of the existing disputes are more apparent than real and that the areas of difference

> could at least be clarified by serious and objective discussion. All those interested in Guyana are faced with the same problems. The real need is to give a correct description of the problems and an indication of what can be done. There is, at present, too much posturing and too little thought.[6]

The first issue of the NWQ (with a poem by Aimé-Césaire on its front page) was mainly devoted to a long-term economic, social and cultural programme for Guyana.[7] *Dependence* appeared as a leading theme in the analysis of the problems of Guyana:

> Socially, the society is stratified with low but growing mobility. Culturally it is dependent, borrowing its values and preferred behaviour from the metropolitan power, from Europe and from outside generally. The social and cultural boundaries tend to be the same as the racial (and geographical) boundaries and (allowing for the inevitable effects of lags) are not very different from the economic boundaries. The stability of this order is threatened by the breakdown of the old imperial system which brings the social and cultural kin of Europe under heavy fire. In so far as the whole society has been largely Europeanised, a cultural basis for Independence has yet to be defined. In so far as there has been differential Europeanisation, those of closer kin (cultural as well as racial) feel more vulnerable.
> (Girvan and Jefferson, 1971, p 242)

The problems of the rest of the West Indies differed little from those of Guyana, although the industrialization policies of the 1950s in Jamaica and Trinidad and Tobago had, in fact, resulted in an increase of the industrial sector. In spite of this, unemployment remained high (Jamaica, 1967: 18 per cent; Trinidad and Tobago, 1966: 14 per cent). To the younger generation of economists, Lewis's strategy now appeared doubtful. Among those were Norman Girvan and Owen Jefferson, whose doctoral theses had dealt with the economic development of Jamaica.[8] Girvan and Jefferson became editors of the NWQ, when for practical reasons it moved to Kingston, Jamaica. Other radical economists, such as Lloyd Best, George Beckford, Havelock Brewster, Alister McIntyre and Clive Thomas were also associated with NWQ.

The group was now called the New World Associates and is described by Girvan as 'a loosely knit group of Caribbean intellectuals whose aim is to develop an indigenous view of the region'.[9] How, then, did this 'indigenous view' manifest itself? In addition to the general dependence perspective there were certain specifically Caribbean problems which arose as a result of the *smallness* and the *plantation background* of these economies. Orlando Patterson and George Beckford had dealt with the latter aspect in a socio-historical perspective,[10] while Lloyd Best had dealt with the economic aspects (Best, 1968).

The *plantation economy* is by definition a dependent economy. In this case, it was a result of Caribbean land, African labour and European capital. Best identified the following stages in the development of this dependent economic subsystem:

1) The pure plantation economy (1600-1838)
2) The modified plantation economy (1839-1938)
3) The further modified plantation economy (1939-)

The first stage coincided with the period of slavery, and there was no other economic activity besides the plantations. Slavery was abolished during the second stage, and a marginal peasant economy then developed alongside the plantations. An even more diversified economy developed during the third stage, when new staples, such as oil and bauxite, and a modest industrialization in accordance with W.A. Lewis's prescription were developed. However, the heritage from the pure plantation economy continued to paralyse economic 'development'.

Beckford has set up a number of concrete mechanisms through which the plantation economy generated underdevelopment:

1) Domestic food production is restricted because of the land requirements of the plantation production.
2) The terms-of-trade deteriorate because of *inter alia* rationalizations of plantation production, which lower the export prices.
3) The so-called link and spread effects of plantation production are insignificant. This in turn, impedes the inner dynamics of the economy.
4) The plantation labourers' low level of education.
5) The general unwieldiness of the plantation economy makes it difficult to adjust to the fluctuations of the world economy.

The enclave economies specializing in mineral exports (oil and bauxite) which later developed in the Caribbean displayed similar structural problems (Girvan, 1970). These examples clearly show that Caribbean social scientists considered the *structural approach* proposed by the ECLA to be important.

And now to the problem of 'size'. The classical work in this field is William G. Demas's *The Economics of Development in Small Countries with Special Reference to the Caribbean* (Demas, 1965). Demas saw development as a process of *structural transformation*, which was difficult to accomplish in a *small* economy because of a biased allocation of resources, the need for specialization (in order to take advantage of the economies of scale), the dependence on the world market, and the limited internal market. Regional integration was, to Demas, the only way out of this dilemma. The extensive debate about regional integration of the Caribbean is merely a logical consequence of the discussions about the problem of 'size'. The failure of CARIFTA (Caribbean Free Trade Association) clearly indicated the problems of dependence.[11] Economic integration turned out to be incompatible with the policy of 'Industrialization by invitation', because the initiative came from outside, i.e. primarily from the multinational corporations, and was not based on planning for common needs and the utilization of the internal market. Through the integration process the larger (Jamaica, Trinidad), or the more 'hospitable' (Barbados) islands would merely act as bases for the penetration of foreign capital into the smaller islands.

The Caribbean economic situation is obviously characterized by unique historical conditions which, in turn, have affected the theoretical debate. A certain degree – or rather a certain type – of dependence was inevitable in the Caribbean. In an article from 1964, Alister McIntyre made a distinction between:

> *Structural dependence* – the dependence that arises because of the size and structure of the economy and cannot be helped, and *functional dependence* – the dependence that arises as a result of the particular policies chosen and can therefore be avoided if alternative policies are pursued.
> (McIntyre, from Girvan-Jefferson, 1971, pp 165-83)

It is interesting to note that Havelock Brewster, in an attempt to provide a purely conceptual expression of the phenomenon of dependence, based his definition on the *internal* situation:

> Economic dependence may be defined as a lack of capacity to manipulate the operative elements of an economic system. Such a situation is characterised by an absence of inter-dependence between the economic functions of a system. This lack of inter-dependence implies that the system has no internal dynamic which could enable it to function as an independent, autonomous, entity.
> (Brewster, 1973, p 91)

This approach is remarkable in that it avoided the Latin American *dependentistas'* preoccupation with the external relations. By observing the economy's internal *modus operandi* instead, he was able to identify a qualitative difference between the external dependence of an economy like the British and for example that of Trinidad. When compared with the majority of the Latin American economies, the Caribbean ones appear to be extremes in terms of structural dependence, which might explain Brewster's choice of approach.

There are, however, interesting differences between the Latin American and the Caribbean debates on development. It has often been pointed out that the Latin American debate has provided few ideas about the substance of development. How would development manifest itself after the paralysing hold of dependence had been broken? Few dependency theorists saw the Indian tradition as the cultural 'counterpoint' which eventually would give the Latin American process of development its genuinely Latin American contents. Such ideas were only found among writers and artists. The cultural heritage from Europe is considerably more superficial in the Caribbean. The great majority of the Jamaican population is black, and only a small elite is saturated with Western ideas. Certain elements of African culture are still alive in the rural areas and the slums of Kingston, in for example religious movements (Rastafari) and music (reggae). A spontaneous ideology of self-reliance has been developed within this cultural tradition emphasizing collectivism and creativity, and rejecting Western materialism (Babylon). A number of radical social scientists accentuate the connection between Rastafari and an alternative strategy of development.[12] George Beckford says in an interview:

> We have been having a cultural revolution preceding the political revolution. My interpretation of the culture of 'dread' is one that is based on the concrete alienation of the sub-proletariat in Jamaica. This is based on an ideology of the rejection of Babylon i.e. the western capitalist system. The manifestations of that cultural revolution can be found in the music, in the manner of speech, dress, food, communal patterns of production etc. This to my mind reflects a major development in terms of not just cultural rejection of capitalism but the embryonic advances towards an indigenous social living. That is what I describe as the 'politics of dread'. It is not just Rastafarian culture as such but basically the politics of the ghetto.
> (Interview with Beckford)

So far we have tried to give an indication of the intellectual substance of the radical debate between the members of the New World Group during the 1960s. The conservative Jamaican Labour Party (JLP) was in power, which meant that the group, in reality, also played the role of political opposition. The political conflict came to a head in 1968 – and, as in the rest of the world, the storm-centre was at the university. The so-called 'Rodney Riots' in October of 1968 were the immediate result of the Jamaican government's expulsion of Walter Rodney, a radical dependency theorist and university teacher.

Black Power: Walter Rodney

Rodney originally came from Guyana, but received his university education in Jamaica. At the time of the founding of the New World Group (towards the end of 1962) he moved to England to complete his postgraduate studies. In 1966 he received a PhD at the School of Oriental and African Studies for his thesis 'A History of the Upper Guinea Coast, 1545-1800'. As an expert on African history he was offered a position at the University College in Tanzania, but was invited to return to the University of the West Indies, where, in January of 1968, he introduced a new course in African history. However, in the autumn of the same year he was prevented from returning to the University after a visit to a writers' congress in Canada.

A small digression is required to explain how Rodney managed to become *persona non grata* in Jamaica so quickly. The island became independent in 1962 and got its national anthem, its national bird and its national flower. What it did not get was a feeling of national identity. The dominating culture was white middle class of which the black Jamaican majority had no part. There was, however, also a black culture with traditions from the days of slavery, which for decades had manifested itself in the Rastafari movement. This was a millenaristic religion based on the Bible, but suitably adapted to oppressed Africans abroad, who hoped to return to their native soil by divine intervention. The growth of the Rastafari movement created a great demand for knowledge about Africa, about which the blacks of Jamaica had a rather diffuse idea. This is the background to Rodney's brief but dramatic career at the University of the West Indies.

News travelled fast about the young, radical and dynamic university teacher who could spellbind his audience, and 'knew all about Africa'. The dependency theorists at the university had just started an intensive public campaign and Rodney became the most sought-after lecturer at black, middle-class gatherings as well as at Rasta meetings in the slums of Kingston. He was dangerous, primarily because he described the dependence *problematique* in racial terms – a subject which had never been brought up in the Latin American debate:

> There are two basic sections in the imperialist world – one that is dominated and one that is dominant. Every country in the dominant metropolitan area has a large majority of whites – USA, Britain, France, etc. Every country in the dominated colonial areas has an overwhelming majority of non-whites, as in most of Asia, Africa and the West Indies. Power, therefore, resides in the white countries and is exercised over blacks!
> (Rodney, 1975, p 18)

In other words, dependence was not only a matter of relations between national states and between social classes, but also of relations between races. The solution was therefore to be found in Black Power. Rodney's famous lectures on African history were therefore just as much lectures on the history of white oppression:

> The white capitalist cannibal has always fed on the world's black peoples. White capitalist imperialist society is profoundly and unmistakably racist.
>
> The West Indies have always been a part of white capitalist society. We have been the most oppressed section because we were a slave society and the legacy of slavery still rests heavily upon the West Indian black man.
> (Ibid., p 25)

Emancipation was to Rodney not so much a matter of economic rights as it was the right to a cultural identity; in this context, his thoughts are more reminiscent of African ideas, of *African personality* and *Négritude*, than of Latin American dependency theory. Consequently, his contacts with the Rastafari movement were well developed, which, in turn, the government considered to be a greater political danger than communist agitators.

After his expulsion from Jamaica, Rodney moved back to Tanzania, where he stayed for seven years as a professor of history. He eventually played an important role in the East African dependence debate, to which we shall return in Chapter 7.[13]

The Disintegration of the New World Group

After 1968, a political polarization indirectly led to the disintegration of the New World Group, since leading members, like Lloyd Best, wanted to avoid a more activist orientation:

> The individuals in the Group may, if they so wish, decide to work 'in the field'. But then their jobs in the intellectual system will only have to be done by others. What is more, when they go into the field, there is no guarantee that the various political organisations they will found will all go the same way. The achievement of New World will then be to have spawned a number of political movements with some common consciousness of the Caribbean condition; but groups like New World will still be needed to defend the community against the new orthodoxy.
> (Best, 1967, pp 5-6)

The radical initiative was eventually absorbed in a new political current – a combination of Marxism and Black Power with the weekly *Abeng* (1969) as its mouthpiece. At that time the PNP (People's National Party), the alternative to the JLP, shifted its orientation towards the New World Group's views. The dependence perspective, combined with economic nationalism, turned into party politics. The balance of political power shifted. The government had, for some time, based its economic policies on W.A. Lewis's industrialization strategies, and Lewis's position was still unchallenged during the mid-1960s. In 1964 he wrote the following in Jamaica's largest daily: '. . . Foreign investment is better than none, since it raises Jamaican incomes too. But Jamaican investment is better, if the money can be saved at home' (*Daily Gleaner*, 12 Sept 1964). By 1972, Lewis's strategy had lost some of its credibility and was attacked by leading economists from the University of Kingston. Lewis, who was then chief of the Caribbean Development Bank, replied in a series of articles in the *Daily Gleaner*, 3 May 1972:

> Why is our economy not able to provide full employment? The simple answer is because our money costs of production are too high in relation to world prices. The man in the street has instead been taught to put all the blame on foreign devils. On the contrary . . . if there were

fewer foreigners we would have even more unemployment.

Lewis's economic strategy was, in reality, unchanged. He saw no way for Jamaica, or the other Caribbean states, to manage without foreign capital. In his opinion the four most important remedies were: (1) devaluation; (2) export incentives; (3) various measures to increase productivity; and (4) an income policy which would keep down wages. This orthodox recipe was soon challenged by one of the economists in the New World Group, Owen Jefferson (Jefferson, 1972b). In his opinion it was remarkable that Lewis's analysis of the high costs of production did not contain any references to excess profits, inflated land prices and the low efficiency of the management of a number of companies – factors which most probably also affected the costs of production. A devaluation would affect the 60 per cent of the population who controlled only 20 per cent of the national income. The importance of foreign capital was, in reality, a myth:

> A very large share of the surpluses generated in the economy accrue to foreign firms which have invested in some of the most profitable sectors. Such surpluses tend to be exported, but even if reinvested paved the way for even greater outflows in the future. The major foreign sectors can only be bought out by the profits of those same sectors. Between 1959 and 1969 the amount of foreign capital flowing into Jamaica was approximately J$375,8 million, while the amount of profits flowing out was about J$398,8 million.
> (*Daily Gleaner*, 18 May 1972)

A radical theoretical bastion had been established in Kingston, and in 1972 its defenders felt strong enough to attack Sir Arthur himself. What was needed, according to Jefferson, was not more foreign capital, but radical structural reforms.

> The carrying out of fundamental changes in the economy is almost certain to lead to some amount of economic dislocation in the short run. The crucial question is whether Commonwealth Caribbean societies now have the necessary social and political cohesion to stand the inevitable strain arising from such a situation.
> (*Daily Gleaner*, 18 May 1972)

The subsequent political development supplied an answer to Jefferson's question. Unfortunately that answer was, as we shall see, negative. Manley's People's National Party (the PNP) won the parliamentary election in 1972. The influence exercised by the dependency theorists reached new heights, and culminated when some of them were absorbed in the new power structure as economic experts.

The Struggle for Self-reliance

As far as the Caribbean political debate is concerned, there is a clear dividing line between the countries who follow a strategy of international co-operation and those who follow a strategy of self-reliance based on socialist principles. Puerto Rico, which is about to be incorporated in the United States, Trinidad and Tobago, and Barbados are typical representatives of the former group, while Cuba leads the latter, for a time followed by Jamaica until the 1980 election, and Grenada until the 1983 invasion. The political radicalization in the Caribbean is, with the exception of Cuba, a fairly recent phenomenon. Although Michael Manley's PNP assumed power in 1972, Jamaican policy did not depart too much from the normal path until after the 1976 election.

It is obvious that the small Caribbean economies are incapable of achieving a substantial degree of self-reliance – a fact that has provided the opponents of the dependency theory and the strategy of self-reliance with excellent arguments, which Lewis, in fact, had already formulated. The problem of size might be overcome by economic integration; however, that approach is counteracted by the islands' overlapping production policies, by the fact that some islands are bigger and more powerful than others, and, finally, by the fact that the dichotomy between 'collaborators' and 'rebels' created a lack of confidence between the various Caribbean countries. To this contradiction must be added the effects of another, namely the rapidly growing internal political polarization which is the inevitable result of efforts at socialist transformation.

Manley's Jamaica

We have already touched upon the economic history of Jamaica in our discussion of the Caribbean dependency debate. The reader might recall that the industrialization strategy of the 1960s did little to change the extremely high level of unemployment and the social misery in the rural districts and the slums of Kingston. The socially and politically explosive situation during the latter part of the 1960s and the early 1970s prepared the ground for Manley's victory in the 1972 election. The policies of the Jamaican Labour Party (the JLP) had lost credibility, and the new government was in desperate need of new, radical ideas. The following excerpt from the PNP's 1972 election manifesto illustrates the view of the opposition:

> The state of the country today represents a bitter contrast to what was expected and hoped for in 1962. Unemployment has soared to such new and frightening levels that the Government dare not publish the figures, but reliable estimates put it at over 20 per cent – more than one-fifth of our labour force. Housing conditions remain deplorable for the majority of our people . . . The state of our roads, particularly in rural areas, is a national disgrace . . . Parish councils have been starved of funds needed to repair existing roads and to build new roads for farmers to get their crops to market. While the JLP boast of the

> number of school buildings that have been erected, the quality of education has deteriorated at every level and the teaching profession is frustrated and demoralised. And so it goes in every Department and Sector – loud boasts – big promises – little performance. Overshadowing all these is the spectre of violent and organised crime that haunts every sector of our society. But most ominous of all from the long term point of view is the fact that the people are losing faith in the democratic process itself.
> (*Daily Gleaner*, 24 Feb 1972)

A different approach had to be tried and interesting new ideas came from the dependency theorists at the University of the West Indies, of whom several were to assume government positions: Norman Girvan became head of planning, Owen Jefferson joined the management of the Central Bank, and Rex Nettleford, who had dealt primarily with questions of *cultural* dependence, became the Prime Minister's special adviser on cultural affairs. Manley himself was an intellectually oriented politician, who enjoyed elaborating on the philosophical basis of his now defunct development strategy both verbally and in writing. This is not to say that the new government as a whole embraced the ideology of self-reliance. In fact the Manley regime was split between moderate and radical factions whose relative positions in the power structure were affected by the outcome of the development process. This not only meant that the economic policy was contradictory from the start but also that it was carried out with decreasing determination as the economic and social problems accumulated.

In addition to the fact that Manley's choice of staff was an obvious reflection of his ideology of self-reliance, his thoughts on foreign and domestic policies have been extensively documented. His books *The Politics of Change: A Jamaican Testament* (1974) and *A Voice at the Workplace: Reflections on Colonialism and the Jamaican Worker* (1975) deal mainly with his thoughts on development. In *The Politics of Change* he speaks of Jamaica as a part of the Third World, a notion which was truly appalling to the members of the white Jamaican upper class.

> Jamaica is a part of the Third World. By the Third World one means that entire range of countries, mainly tropical, that were the scene of the great colonial explosion which reached its crescendo in the latter part of the nineteenth and the first part of the twentieth centuries. All of these territories stretching as they do through the Caribbean, Africa, India and the Near and Far East were used as sources of raw materials and primary agricultural products destined for the great manufacturing countries which were mainly concentrated in Europe. After the Second World War a reverse political process commenced led by India and quickly to be followed in the Caribbean, Africa and the rest of the colonial world. In short order all the former colonies had attained political independence. However, without exception, these

territories entered upon political independence suffering from enormous economic disabilities.
(Manley, 1974, p 12)

The by then rather widely accepted dependency theory is presented in the same instructive and straightforward manner:

As is now well understood, all the newly independent territories have found themselves trapped in an economic dilemma. Their trade is established in traditional patterns with the metropolitan powers. In these patterns, the former colonies supply the basic materials which attract the smallest share of the 'value added' of the total economic process. These are exported to our metropolitan partners and in return we import the manufactured goods and the products of heavy industry which represent the lion's share of the 'value added' of the total process. To begin with there is this disequilibrium between what the former colonies have to offer and what our metropolitan partners supply. To make matters worse the prices of raw materials and primary agricultural products show an historic tendency to instability around general levels that do not tend to rise. On the other hand, the prices of manufactured goods in world trade tend to be consistent within a pattern of steady increases. As a consequence, and as is well documented, it takes more and more tons of Jamaican sugar to purchase an American or British tractor as the years pass. Hence, the terms of trade which are inherently against us to begin with, tend to move increasingly against us.
(Manley, 1974, p 124-5)

As may be seen from this quotation, Manley advocated a softer, 'Prebischian' theory of dependency. The most important changes in Jamaican foreign policy during the Manley regime were the swing towards the non-aligned movement and the 'fraternal' relations with Cuba. Both were clearly expressed in his speech at the meeting of the non-aligned nations in Havana, in September of 1979:

As many have said, and, we trust, all sincerely believe, the Non-Aligned Movement begins with the struggle against imperialism. No area of the world has had a more extended exposure to experience of, nor proximity to imperialism than Latin America and the Caribbean. We have seen forces of progress extinguished in Guatemala, snuffed out like a candle in the Domincan Republic, undermined and finally overwhelmed in Chile; I dare to assert that, despite these tragic reversals, the forces committed to the struggle against imperialism are stronger today than ever before. We believe that this is so because our hemisphere has had a Movement and a Man: a catalyst and a rock: and the Movement is the Cuban Revolution, and the Man is Fidel Castro.

Thus, between 1972 and 1980 the Prime Minister of Jamaica was one of the leading politicians in the Third World who had made the dependency theory his ideology. The setbacks suffered during his first term of office merely drove him further down the chosen path. The majority of the Jamaican population showed renewed confidence in Manley in the 1976 election; but, by 1980 its patience had finally come to an end.

The critique was primarily of a more practical-political kind. It was, of course, facilitated by the fact that the PNP's development strategy, which was heavily influenced by the dependency theory, had provided few, if any, immediate solutions to the problems in Jamaica. The situation had actually deteriorated in a way reminiscent of Chile and the Allende Popular Front regime.

The economic development of Jamaica proves two things: one, that the economy has changed a great deal, i.e. from being a pure plantation economy to being considerably more diversified; and two, that the policy of diversification has not succeeded in changing Jamaica's basic position of dependence. It is therefore not surprising that the Manley regime's new economic policy led to difficult problems of adjustment, particularly since it challenged strong foreign interests. The bauxite industry, which had developed during the 1950s and the 1960s, is a good example of this.

In 1974, the government imposed an excise tax on the production of bauxite amounting to 7.5 per cent of the aluminium price. Since the export of bauxite provided the greater part of Jamaica's export income, the government expected a neat addition to its annual receipts – provided the five multinational aluminium companies went along with the tax. They were, however, able to increase their production in other countries, the result of which was a 38 per cent drop in Jamaican bauxite and aluminium oxide production between 1974 and 1976. The Jamaican share of total aluminium oxide production dropped from 9.4 per cent to 6 per cent (*Economist*, 21 June 1980). Manley was consequently forced to undertake a tax reduction which eventually mollified the multinationals.

However, bauxite was not Jamaica's only problem. The dependency theorists also criticized the dependence on tourism as a source of income, a practice which, in their opinion, merely emphasized Jamaica's role as an object of exploitation and intensified its already extreme *cultural* dependence. The tourist traffic was drastically reduced as a result of a campaign in the North American media, in which the island in the sun was portrayed as an orgy of violence. Hotel occupancy went down to 30 per cent during 1977, while the so-called Dollar Tourist Belt in the North assumed a ghost-like character.

Agriculture also faced problems: sugar production dropped by 20 per cent during the 1970s, while banana production declined drastically after 1977. The reasons for these setbacks were partly flooding, and partly a new, poorly-planned land reform which primarily affected the sugar plantations.

All of this tended to increase Jamaica's *financial* dependence. After several rounds of negotiation with the IMF in 1976 and 1977, and following a severe conflict within PNP, the government, in 1978, accepted the IMF's conditions, which in effect put an end to 'self-reliance' and 'democratic socialism'. Jamaica was granted a loan of 250 million dollars on condition that necessary steps were taken to reduce both the inflation and the budget deficit. The agreement also stipulated that an IMF delegation was to visit Jamaica during December of 1979 to ascertain whether or not these steps had been taken, and the extent to which they had had the intended effect. As it turned out, Jamaica did not pass the 'IMF Test'.

Jamaica was thus gradually pushed into a severe economic, social and political crisis by a combination of the inherent adjustment problems of a new development strategy, the destabilizing policies to which foreign capital interests always tend to resort when a dependent country embarks upon a new, 'hostile' political course, and the JLP's merciless campaign which was facilitated by the traditional fear of communism. It is quite probable that the exaggerated confidence placed in the strategy of self-reliance helped prepare the ground for the economic failure which eventually forced the Manley government into a politically unviable situation. The JLP and its leader, Seaga, naturally accused the Manley government of being incompetent and irresponsible. Seaga claimed that Jamaica's problems were a result of 'Cubanization', and held up Puerto Rico as a model in the following statement:

> The Puerto Rican model of economic development was more relevant to Caribbean life-style and objectives than that of Cuba . . . the Caribbean was near the world's richest continent – the United States – and that was its greatest asset . . . the Caribbean was ideal not for its bauxite, oil or tourism, but as a base for reexporting goods to the North American market.
> (*Daily Gleaner*, 9 Dec 1979)

Political sallies of this type were accompanied by increasing violence, caused by social misery. The government was deeply shaken, and found itself in a difficult political crisis just before Christmas in 1979. In spite of this, the course was unaltered. In a radio speech on 2 December, D.K. Duncan, the secretary general of the PNP and the leader of the leftist faction, stated:

> We are now working against the background of our experience of the last two years. And what is that experience? A fall in the standard of living for the majority. A decline in our health services and other vital services all born out of the worst economic conditions we have ever experienced and the bitter medicine of the IMF agreement. Having lived in the valley for such a long time we of the PNP are determined to press forward now. The mood of the National Executive Meeting was: Action Now . . . This was no ordinary NEC-meeting. Hours and hours were spent studying our economy, the problems, the world economy and the obstacles in the way to increasing production and providing

> more jobs. As a party committed to socialism we have been conducting a program of education at all levels of the party about how our economy works, and with the exhaustive analysis of the economy at the NEC meeting itself comrades were well armed with information and education. We examined the performance of the economy in all the key sectors: agriculture, tourism, bauxite and alumina and small business production . . . We saw the role of foreign domination and control of our resources as the main obstacles to the development of our country and progress of our people . . . We affirmed that there was only one way forward: to struggle relentlessly against imperialism. The NEC was particularly concerned that we should continue our efforts to reconstruct our economy on a self-reliant footing, decreasing dependence on the outside world.
> (Taped from radio)

However, Jamaica was in a deep economic, social and political crisis and the majority of its people was now reluctant to follow the tortuous road of self-reliance. The 1980 election put an end to Manley's rule. The return to power of the JLP led to rather dramatic shifts in Jamaica's policies of development and foreign affairs. Edward Seaga's first official act on taking office was to expel the Cuban ambassador, and the first anniversary of the JLP government was celebrated by a diplomatic break with Cuba. Instead a 'Puerto Rican connection' is being established.

There are indications that the USA was aware of Jamaica's break with Cuba two days in advance. Jamaica's willingness to follow US wishes must be understood in relation to its 'new' development strategy, which can be described as dependent capitalist development, Puerto Rican style. Seaga's policy, thus, is export-led development in close connection with Puerto Rican business and tagged on to the North American market. Jamaica has been subject to special treatment in Reagan's Caribbean Basin Initiative (CBI). Significantly this programme excluded Cuba, Nicaragua and Grenada, the three enemies selected to illustrate the new US firmness in dealing with its security problems. Some Caribbean leaders did not however see in Grenada the kind of threat that Reagan was making out of it. Not without some justification they conceive the CBI as a programme particularly addressed to client states such as Jamaica and El Salvador. As Reagan's showcase of 'freedom in action', Jamaica cannot be allowed to fail. The economic scene has not become much brighter and the IMF is as unhappy with Seaga's Jamaica as it was with Manley's. However, pressed by Reagan, the IMF now takes an attitude of understanding and benevolence that is quite unusual in the light of its past record.

The Debate at the University

We have already mentioned that Manley's victory in 1972 led to a number of radical intellectuals being given political positions; this, in turn, left an intellectual vacuum in the social sciences. The university – conveniently hidden halfway up Jamaica's Blue Mountain – returned to the apathy of the days before the student revolt. The dependency theorists had, during their struggle for power, managed to force out several of those who represented more conventional views. Their departure for various government positions meant that the field was now open to a more orthodox type of Marxism, which naturally gave voice to the current Marxist critique described in Chapter 4.

Similar tones were also heard from other quarters. Carl Stone, social scientist and political commentator on the largest daily paper, claimed that although the dependency theory had to some extent managed to diagnose the Jamaican *malaise*, it had precious little to say about the cure. The effects of the intellectual fusion of dependency theorists and the Manley regime after 1972 were catastrophic. The question of how external and internal factors were linked together was, in Stone's opinion, extremely complicated. The external environment determined domestic policies to the extent that it provided the framework. An unrealistic view of the limitations posed by the internal factors would most certainly lead to failure. Stone did not exclude the possiblity of Jamaica having been subjected to a deliberate destabilization campaign from abroad, but a large part of the domestic violence after 1976 was due to internal polarization. Both the JLP and the PNP had organized groups of hoodlums who fought each other during the 1976 election; these groups subsequently abandoned their political objectives in favour of purely criminal ones.

How did those dependency theorists who shared the political responsibility react to the economic chaos which culminated during Christmas of 1979, when it became obvious that Jamaica was not going to pass the IMF test? Owen Jefferson, who had been one of the leading critics of W.A. Lewis, and was deputy chairman of the Bank of Jamaica under Manley, gave this reply when asked whether, after his practical experiences, he had changed his theoretical views:

> The question is a bit early because I have only been in the practical work for a little more than a year. I don't think it has changed my view of the way in which the system actually operates with regard to the dependency syndrome but what it has certainly impressed with me is the difficulty of breaking out of it . . . One of our assumptions was that ownership of resources does in fact constitute control, which is not really true because of the very important technology factor and the fact that the market is very impredictable (Interview, Kingston, 1979.)

Jefferson pointed out that it took a while even for the OPEC to reach its present strength, despite the fact that oil was a special case as far as the effective building of cartels was concerned. The IBA (the International Bauxite Association) had, on the other hand, been in existence for only a short while. So far it had been extremely difficult to create any basis for effective cooperation between the countries involved. Foreign capital usually considered any attempt to reduce the dependence of an economy as an unfriendly act. It was also important to balance the implementation of various economic policies in order to avoid total chaos. The fact that the problems turned out to be bigger than expected did not, in Jefferson's opinion, mean that the diagnosis was wrong. Jefferson claimed that the underdeveloped countries' policy of self-reliance must be a joint effort. The building up of this kind of co-operation was necessarily a long process which was frequently slowed down by problems, like the 1973 oil price increases. The possibility of making structural changes, in Jefferson's opinion, became more and more difficult, once the economy started to deteriorate. According to Jefferson, there is nothing wrong with the dependence theory. 'What we need now is a theory on how to break dependence – without breaking your neck in the process.'

The Independence of the Caribbean Debate

We may, in conclusion, ask whether the Caribbean dependency debate was an entirely independent process of intellectual development? It is difficult to give a definite answer. Considering the geographical proximity to Latin America, it is almost preposterous to think of the Caribbean as some kind of intellectual enclave in which ideas are autonomously generated – which is more or less what Norman Girvan claimed it to be. Most of what we have said so far has supported Girvan's theory. The Caribbean *academic infrastructure* was relatively well developed, because the University of the West Indies, and especially economic research, was quite advanced. The political radicalization of the 1960s certainly displayed a dynamic of its own. Dependence as a social reality was obvious, and historians and sociologists began to base their interpretations of the development in the islands on the notion of a distinctly Caribbean social structure: the plantation community. We have also pointed out certain peculiarities in the way in which dependence was formulated and defined. However, care must be taken not to exaggerate the autonomy of the development of ideas in the Caribbean. The English economist G.E. Cumper, who worked at the university in Kingston during the period when the Caribbean dependence school, the New World Group, came into being, criticized Girvan's thesis of autonomy. Cumper emphasized the importance of the role played by the Cuban Revolution and the radical Cuban intellectuals, an observation which is confirmed by the early issues of the *New World Quarterly*.

> If . . . we accept that the Cuban revolution influenced the Caribbean dependence economists, we must accept also that the Caribbean school did not grow up in isolation from the Latin American tradition, not only is Cuba culturally part of Latin America, but there are very specific links between the economic policies of the revolution and the Santiago structuralists.
> (Cumper, 1974, p 468)

However, Cuba may not be the best example of Latin American influence. After all, Cuba belongs to the Caribbean region, but may possibly be thought of as a bridge between Latin America and the Caribbean.

In the economist Dudley Seers, whom we met in Chapter 1 as one of the early structuralists, Cumper found a source of inspiration and a link between separate intellectuals' streams:

> I turn now to Girvan's omission of mention of Seers, who would appear to be a key figure in defining the relationship between Caribbean, Latin American and 'Western' writers on development both through his writing and his personal influence. Over a period which on Girvan's analysis is crucial for the emergence of the Caribbean school – say, from 1958 to 1968, Seers published a number of articles which incorporate almost all the points which have come to be presented as characteristic of that school.[14] One of these was expressly intended to bring to the attention of English-speaking economists the work of the Latin American structuralists. In his personal influence Seers provided a link between institutions and events which, on Girvan's showing, should have represented separate intellectual streams; E.C.L.A., economists and governments in Jamaica and Barbados, English economists working on development problems (particularly at Oxford), and the Yale Economic Growth Centres. (At E.C.L.A. he was friendly with Boti, who subsequently became an influential economist in the early stages of the Cuban revolution.) I do not see how anyone who reads Seers' articles can accept Girvan's implication that the Caribbean school arose independently of Latin America and of Western development economics.
> (Ibid., pp 466-7)

The right person to clear up this matter is obviously Seers himself. When asked whether Cumper's claim was correct or not, Seers answered 'With some truth.'[15] He was, nevertheless, inclined to emphasize the 'independence' of the Caribbean school *as compared to other* secondary centres dealt with in this book: e.g. Tanzania and Senegal (= IDEP). The contributors to the Tanzanian debate were, at least in the beginning, mainly English or West Indian, whereas the IDEP in Senegal was represented by no one but Samir Amin himself. In other words, Seers agrees with Cumper's claim that Girvan overestimated the autonomy of the Caribbean dependence school, but he nevertheless considers it to be relatively independent and original.

Notes

1. These thoughts were also reflected in Lewis's *Labour in the West Indies. The Birth of a Workers' Movement* (1938, reprinted 1977).
2. Lewis (1949) p 154 cf., 'The Company is taking the initiative in trying to persuade manufacturers to come to Puerto Rico. It is, of course, equally anxious that local capital should be invested in industry, and some local capital is coming forward. But most local capitalists are shy of industry. They have not the "know-how", and even more important (since "know-how" can be hired), they have not the market connections which are essential to profit. Success on a big scale therefore depends on persuading established US manufacturers to come to Puerto Rico.'
3. Lewis (1949). Already in the Puerto Rico article, Lewis draws conclusions concerning the British West Indies: 'If the British islands were to follow the Puerto Rican example, they would be given much less emphasis than they do at present to local markets, local capitalists and local raw materials, and would be concentrating on trying to persuade some of those UK manufacturers who are already supplying markets in Latin America, in the USA, or in Canada, to establish factories in the British West Indies, and to supply their American markets from the islands. Local markets are so small that it is only if the islands can build up a large export of manufacturers that industrialization will be able to contribute substantially to employment.'
4. The figures concerning the Jamaican agricultural population are 1881: 209,000, 1891: 271,000, 1911: 271,000, 1921: 286,000, 1943: 228,000. As can be seen, the absorption capacity was reached during the 1920s.
5. A thorough discussion on the problem of labour utilization is found in Myrdal (1968) pp 959 f.
6. 'Statement by the Editor', *New World Quarterly*, vol. 1, no. 1 (March) 1963.
7. See also Girvan and Jefferson (1971 [1977]).
8. Jefferson defended his doctoral thesis 'The Economic Development of Jamaica 1950-61' at Oxford in 1964. It was later published as *The Post-War Economic Development of Jamaica* (ISER, 1972); Girvan defended his thesis, entitled 'Foreign Investment and Economic Development in Jamaica since World War II', at the London School of Economics in 1965. It was eventually published under the somewhat bolder title of *Foreign Capital and Economic Underdevelopment in Jamaica* (ISER, 1971).
9. Girvan (1971) p 27 (Note 7). A large part of the group's production is found in Girvan and Jefferson (1971).
10. Patterson (1967) and George L. Beckford, *Persistent Poverty: Underdevelopment in Plantation Economies of the Third World* (1972). As indicated by the subtitle, Beckford's work concerns plantation economies in general.
11. An excellent analysis of economic integration in a dependence situation is found in Axline (1979) pp 15-22.
12. Interviews with George Beckford, Carl Stone and Rex Nettleford, Kingston, December 1979.
13. Walter Rodney resumed his political activities after having returned to

his native Guyana. He was assassinated in the summer of 1980.

14. The articles by Dudley Seers to which Cumper is referring are: 'An Approach to the Short-Period Analysis of Primary Producing Economies', *Oxford Economic Papers*, February 1959; 'A Model of Comparative Rates of Growth in the World Economy', *Economic Journal*, March 1962; 'A Theory of Inflation and Growth in Underdeveloped Economies Based on the Experience of Latin America', *Oxford Economic Papers*, June 1962; 'The Limitations of the Special Case', *Yale University Economic Growth Center, Paper No 28*, 1963; 'The Mechanism of an Open Petroleum Economy', *Social and Economic Studies*, vol. 13, no. 2, 1964.
15. Conversation in Brighton, June 1980.

6. The Development of Capitalism in Asia

The Idea of Dependence in an Asian Context

In Paul Baran's *Political Economy of Growth*, which was dealt with in an earlier chapter, it is Asia rather than Latin America that plays the leading role in the analysis of how the utilization of surplus leads to development in the centre and to underdevelopment in the periphery. The conspicuous case of underdevelopment is India, whereas Japan provides proof of the fact that the ability to avoid colonial exploitation was the most important prerequisite for an indigenous capitalist development process. On this Baran says:

> Indeed, there can be no doubt that had the amount of economic surplus that Britain has torn from India been *invested in India*, India's economic development to date would have borne little similarity to the actual somber record. It is idle to speculate whether India by now would have reached a level of economic advancement commensurate with its fabulous natural resources and with the potentialities of its people. In any case the fate of the successive Indian generations would not have resembled even remotely the chronic catastrophe of the last two centuries.
> (Baran, 1957, p 148)

Apart from transferring a substantial economic surplus from India, the British actively underdeveloped India:

> Thus the British administration of India systematically destroyed all the fibres and foundations of Indian society. Its land and taxation policy ruined India's village economy and substituted for it the parasitic landowner and moneylender. Its commercial policy destroyed the Indian artisan and created the infamous slums of the Indian cities filled with millions of starving and diseased paupers. Its economic policy broke down whatever beginnings there were of an indigenous industrial development and promoted the proliferations of speculators, petty businessmen, agents, and sharks of all descriptions eking out a sterile and precarious livelihood in the meshes of a decaying society.
> (Ibid., p 149)

On this basis, one would have expected that India, rather than Latin America, had been the centre of a debate on dependence. It was not – at least not of the kind of debate we know from Latin America. However, there was in fact during the latter part of the 19th Century a contribution reminiscent of the Latin American discussion during its early stages. We are, of course, referring to Dadabhai Naoroji's famous *Drain Theory*.

The Drain Theory

The drain theory should be seen as an integral part of the coming of age of an Indian national consciousness during the latter part of the 19th Century (Chandra, 1975, p 114). It was argued that England exacted an annual 'tribute' of enormous proportions. The empirical estimations have shown different results, but the actual size of it is less important in this context. The 'drain' was exercised not only in British India but also in the princely states, of which Mysore bore a particularly heavy burden (Hettne, 1978, p 85). The critics of the 'drain' claimed that this transfer of capital deprived India of development opportunities in the form of infrastructural investments, education, etc. The similarity with Baran's surplus theory is striking, and it is not surprising that he refers to this 19th Century debate, which so much centred on the problem of drain, rather than to more recent historical accounts. It is almost as if this early Indian 'dependency debate', via Baran, has influenced the Latin American debate. In the current Indian development debate, dependence is, as we shall see, a rather marginal phenomenon.

Naoroji, the central figure in the Indian 'drain' debate, worked mostly in London. His most important work was *Poverty and Un-British Rule in India*, published in England in 1901. The 'drain' issue was first brought up in 1866; a tentative version of his theory was completed the following year. Indian economists have pointed out the similarity between Naoroji's theory and the considerably younger Prebisch-Singer thesis, which we discussed in an earlier chapter (Minocha, 1970, p 37).[1] However, this similarity is far from perfect. The exploitation of India was due to its subordinate position in the British Empire, not the forces of the free market. Naoroji was a good liberal and admirer of the British way of life. The problem, as he saw it, was that the British rule in India was 'un-British'. A true liberal policy which did not favour India at Britain's expense would, in accordance with the then current economic ideas, permit India to develop economically:

> Hitherto England has to some extent made herself rich by plundering India in diverse subtle and ingenious ways. But what I desire and maintain is that England can become far richer by dealing justly and honourably with India, and thereby England will not only be a blessing to India and itself, but will be a lesson and a blessing to mankind.
> (Naoroji, 1901 [1962], p ix)

Gandhi

Naoroji did not advance a theory of dependence as we know it from Latin

America. His analysis was mainly concerned with the devastating effects on the Indian economy of a unilateral and unjust economic relation. It never crossed Naoroji's mind that free trade might also carry with it some disadvantages as a result of the nature of the exchange and the structural conditions in the two countries. It is therefore hardly correct to see Naoroji as an Indian Prebisch. However, *it is* correct to say that he laid the foundations of an economic nationalism: the *Swadeshi* movement of 1905 was a reflection of this sentiment. The movement's objective was to stimulate Indian production by campaigns for domestically produced goods. *Swadeshi* was the first expression of an Indian strategy for self-reliance; the concept later became one of the cornerstones in Gandhi's philosophy. Gandhi himself defines *Swadeshi* as follows:

> After much thinking I have arrived at a definition of *Swadeshi* that perhaps best illustrates my meaning. *Swadeshi* is that spirit in us which restricts us to the use and service of our immediate surroundings to the exclusion of the more remote. Thus as for religion, I must restrict myself to my ancestral religion. That is the use of my immediate religious surrounding. If I find it defective I should serve it by purging it of the indigenous institutions and serve them by curing them of their proved defects. In that of economics I should use only the things that are produced by my immediate neighbours and serve those industries by making them efficient and complete where they might be found wanting.
> (Gandhi, n.d., p 177)

Thus, to Gandhi *Swadeshi* was a comprehensive restoration of Indian society and culture, the development of which had been hampered and distorted by the ties with Great Britain. Dependence as a general idea, and the strategy of self-reliance as its natural opposite, are therefore basic understandings of the Indian politicians and intellectuals, particularly those holding 'Gandhian' views.

Gandhi's ideas on economic development were not derived exclusively (or perhaps in this case not even primarily) from the Hindu tradition; he was in fact heavily influenced by the Western, especially Russian populist tradition. Like the economics of populism, Gandhian economic thought can only be understood as a *counter-theory* to Western economics. From Tolstoy, Gandhi borrowed the concepts of egalitarianism, simplicity and asceticism (the last two, of course, having their Hindu parallels), from Ruskin the emphasis on ethics in economic development, and from Kropotkin a hatred of economic centralization and bureaucracy. Thus, the ideal for Gandhi was the rural economy. He visualized the society as being built up of circles of self-supporting and self-contained units, exchanging only necessary commodities with other villages, where they were not locally producible. Agriculture and handicraft based strictly on subsistence, in place of an economy of surplus, would be the foundations. Land should be communal property, and the implements and tools of a cottage industry should belong to the family traditionally engaged in it. Since, in this society, owners of the means of production would also be labourers, exploitation based on individual property would be impossible. Thus, Gandhi's way out of dependence on the West was basically the reinforcement of Indian tradition, a solution that from a Marxist point of view was the opposite to 'progress'.

On the eve of Indian independence in 1947 the problem of planning had already been discussed for many years. The issue was: what kind of planning and planning for whom? The power structure of India was very complex since the liberation movement had, for various reasons, kept together highly diverse segments of Indian society. Some years before independence three different plans were produced representing different economic and social interests. The Bombay Plan was sponsored by leading industrialists and favoured a kind of state capitalist system, in which the activities of the state should make it easier for big business to prosper and grow. The People's Plan emanated from labour organizations and advocated comprehensive state planning with the aim of socialism inspired by the Soviet model of development. The Gandhian Plan was put together by pupils of Gandhi and his emphasis on rural development and the building of a society based on Indian values played a prominent part in this plan. These various interests were related to particular segments of the Indian power structure and have constituted three different societal forces that may be called 'capitalism', 'socialism' and 'Gandhiism' respectively. On the whole, Indian development has been influenced by the first two, whereas Gandhiism has played a more ritual role.

The JP movement, which started in early 1974 in Bihar, provided the first serious challenge that the Congress regime had faced since independence. It represented among other things a resurgence of Gandhian political activism after more than 25 years of passivity. This passivity was caused by the particular interpretation of Gandhiism made by Vinoba Bhave, but in the early 1970s many Sarvodayites, led by Jayaprakash Narayan, challenged Bhave's views. The 'constructive approach' was, they felt, not sufficient. Political struggle was also necessary.

The Sarvodaya organization was, however, too weak (except perhaps in Bihar) to carry out JP's 'total revolution', and therefore JP made use of the organized political opposition to attain the necessary infrastructure. The Gandhian element in the JP movement became more and more diluted as the movement was elevated from its original Bihar context and transformed into an all-India movement. In spite of this the political establishment was alarmed, and on 26 June 1975 the President of India declared a state of national emergency due to 'internal disturbances'. The 1977 election destroyed the Indian dominant party, which in itself was a most remarkable outcome. A 'new' party emerged to take over government responsibility. This organization, the Janata Party, was a most unusual and peculiar political configuration, and the most unbelievable thing about it was perhaps that a Gandhian economic programme was announced by the new government.

Janata's election manifesto had spoken out against 'elitism, consumerism, and urbanism'. Light industry was preferred to heavy industry and rural to urban. It was, furthermore, necessary to steer away from both capitalism and socialism and strive for self-reliance.

However, after the election the Janata government's economic declarations turned out to be much more vague. The bold programme of self-reliance incontrovertibly implied a fundamental change in the development strategy. The heavy odds against its implementation stemmed not only from the lack of unity within the government but also from various structural constraints.

It is obvious that the Gandhian image of the Janata government to a very large extent was a concession to the role played by JP in the struggle against Indira Gandhi.

Even if the government had wanted to implement a Gandhian economic programme it was too paralysed by internal conflicts to accomplish much. In the midst of this unprecedented political disintegration JP died, physically broken by his term in prison during the Emergency and psychologically broken by disillusionment from watching the performance of what had been mainly his creation, the Janata Party. Was that the end of a self-reliant and indigenous approach to India's economic and social ills?

M.N. Roy and Indian Marxism

Indian dependence has, however, also been subjected to a Marxist analysis. In Chapter 2 we discussed Marx's views on the non-European world, and stressed that he was particularly interested in India and China, which he analysed in terms of a particular 'Asian' mode of production. We also pointed out that this mode of production was denied its own dynamics, which, in a sense, *legitimized* colonialism as the basis for modern development. In relation to classical Marxism, or even more so, in relation to the tactically determined diagnoses of the Communist International, Indian Marxists were more inclined to blame Indian underdevelopment on imperialism and capitalism. Like Naoroji, the Indian Marxist, M.N. Roy, viewed India as a nation in chains, with a distorted 'natural' development. To Roy, the cause was 'colonial capitalism', as he called it.

> The introduction of higher means of production in cotton manufacture marked an era of social and economic progress in England, but it had a retrograde effect upon India. The forces that helped to build so many industrial centres in the former, were used for the destruction of prosperous towns and urban industrial centres in the latter. The reason of this diametrically opposite effect of the same course was that India as well as English society came under a more developed method of exploitation, but the improved means of production which made this new method of exploitation possible, remained the property of the bourgeoisie of one country, which became the political ruler of the other.
> (Roy, 1921 (1971), pp 67-8)

India had been subjected to capitalist exploitation without being allowed to reap the fruits of capitalist development. Bastiann Wielenga has observed that Roy's comment is very close to the neo-Marxist idea of the 'development of underdevelopment' (Wielenga, 1976, p 67).

Thus, if Dadobhai Naoroji can be seen as an early Indian counterpart to Prebisch, then it is equally justified to claim that M.N. Roy is André Gunder Frank's predecessor. It is of relatively minor importance that these analogies are far from perfect. What, in this context, is really interesting is that they are occasionally made by Indian intellectuals, and that the similarities indicate an awareness of the problem of 'dependency' which is at least as old as the Latin American one. The Latin American theory of dependency can hardly have been sensational to the Indian intellectuals; and, as we shall see, the Indian critique was more negative than positive.

The Attitude Towards Dependency Theory

Thus both the *notion* of dependence as well as dependence as *an historical experience* have been clearly identifiable in the Indian intellectual and political debate for quite some time. Simplistic explanations of how India's economic problems were mainly caused by external factors were, however, subsequently abandoned, since a monocausal theory was insufficient. In this context, it should also be remembered that the ratio of the British population to the total population of India was marginal during the colonial period. It is, of course, an indisputable fact that colonialism played an important part in the development of Indian society. However, it would be an exaggeration to claim that it had been fundamentally structured by the expansion of world capitalism. The role of the caste system in the Indian class structure indicates the importance of internal factors. Furthermore, Indian foreign policy has been considerably more independent than has been the case in the majority of the Latin American countries, even though maintaining this independence in times of economic and financial hardship has been difficult.

In this context it is also noteworthy that, of all the countries in the Third World, India possesses the most developed academic infrastructure. The proportion of imported theories and methods is, of course, considerable, particularly in the area of social science, but they originate in Europe and the United States, rather than in other countries in the Third World. It would probably be alien to Indian self-esteem to import a Latin American theory. While preparing this book, we visited a great number of Indian social science research institutes, where interviews with various researchers soon revealed that hardly any work was based on the ideas of the dependency school.[2] Indian social scientists have, on the whole, assumed a rather sceptical attitude towards Latin American dependency theory. In the words of Rajni Kothari: 'The dependency theory is very relevant but it becomes an alibi for lack of self-development. You can always put the blame on the door of the exploiters but the exploitation that takes place in your own society is not questioned' (Interview, 10 April 1976).

Similar, but stronger sentiments are voiced in the following excerpt from the *Economic and Political Weekly* 23 April 1977, p 666): 'There could be no greater slur inflicted on our capabilities: we are nincompoops, we are unable to ensure a local supply of exploiters, the process of exploitation has to be initiated elsewhere . . . This itself is neo-colonialism of a sort.'

The reasons for this attitude can only be guessed at; some of them have already been mentioned, e.g. the incongruity of seeing the complex Indian social structure, with its enormous development problems, as a result of the penetration of international capital. Another reason might be that the comparative breadth and depth of the Indian Marxist tradition have prevented neo-Marxist ideas from gaining a foothold. The strength of the Indian Marxist tradition of analysis became particularly noticeable in the extensive debate about the capitalist mode of production and Indian agriculture during the early 1970s.[3]

The Indian Mode of Production Debate

Although we are able to provide only a brief summary of this debate, it is relevant because it is an interesting parallel to the previously mentioned theoretical conflict between Frank and Laclau.[4] The key questions in the debate were:

1) To what extent is it possible to claim that Indian agriculture is characterized by a capitalist mode of production?
2) If it is not capitalist, how should it then be described in terms of modes of production?
3) If it is capitalist what, then, was the nature of the pre-capitalist mode of production?
4) Can Indian agriculture – and the Indian social formation as a whole – be described as an articulation of several modes of production, and if so, which?
5) Is there a specific mode of production – neither capitalist nor semi-feudal – in India?

This debate – which in theoretical richness and wealth of empirical data brought forward can only be compared to the Latin American dependency debate – in fact covered many more issues, such as an identification of the principal rural classes, the main contradictions in rural India, peasant movements and implications regarding political strategy for the left parties (Thorner, 1982).

The debate about the capitalist nature of Indian agriculture began at the empirical level, and its purpose was primarily to identify the capitalist farmers; eventually, it took up conceptual problems (the criteria of 'capitalism'), methodological questions (levels of analysis), and theoretical perspectives (the transition from feudalism to capitalism). We shall concentrate upon the questions that are relevant to the dependency school and the critique of it.

Utsa Patnaik has analysed the development of capitalism in Indian agriculture in several of her contributions, and objected to Frank's idea of the satellite automatically becoming capitalist as a result of imperialist penetration (Patnaik, 1972). Frank dismissed her conclusion, since it implies that Indian agriculture is feudal:

> to say that extended reproduction and accumulation is a criterion of capitalism is one thing and to say that because the surplus is not invested in agriculture itself, or not in agriculture in the same geographical area, but is instead siphoned off for investment in industry, not to say industry in Great Britain, is another thing altogether. The fact that the British industrialised with the help of the drain – which was of course drained out of agriculture in India in large part – does not seem to me to be useable proof as UP seeks to do that Indian agriculture is feudal (or was).
> (Frank, 1973)

J. Banaji and H. Alavi belong to the group whose views were closer to those of the dependency school (Banaji, 1972 and Alavi, 1975). Banaji rejected the 'thesis of capitalism' as well as the 'thesis of feudalism', and tried to identify a mode of production that was peculiar to the colonial areas: a colonial mode of production. In this way he avoided the artificial superimposing of European models on areas in which they are not suited and where they confuse the issue.

Alavi was closer to the Marxist terminology than to the dependency school, but he also emphasized the need for some kind of 'world system' approach:

> We would like to emphasise that, both the concept of 'feudalism' in India (during the period of direct colonial domination) as well as the contemporary phenomenon of rural 'capitalism' cannot be grasped theoretically in all their implications except specifically, in the context of the world-wide structure of imperialism into which it is articulated. A consideration of that fact should lead us towards a conception of a colonial mode of production and the structural specificity that distinguishes it from both fuedalism and capitalism in the metropolis.
> (Alavi, 1975, p 1235)

Alavi's solution to the problem of using Marx's conceptual apparatus and its link to national economies without dropping world capitalism in the process, was at the time (he has since reconsidered) to work with a special mode of production – *the colonial mode of production.* He supported Laclau's argument that Frank's definition of capitalism was insufficient, but he nevertheless felt that the attacks on Frank – particularly those originating in India – paid scant attention to the theoretical problem raised by that author: Frank may not have solved the problem, but Laclau's idea of a feudal and a capitalist mode of production coexisting in the same economic system had not solved it either. The existence of two, widely different modes of production within the same economic system would, from a Marxist point of view, inevitably mean that they were in contradiction with each other. 'But, on the other hand, the Brazilian reality like that of the other countries of the Third World, is that the 'feudal mode of production' in agriculture is precisely at the service of imperialism rather than antagonistically in contradiction with it' (Alavi, 1975, p 1247).

As previously mentioned, Alavi found the solution in the construction of a special mode of production, 'that might be conceptualized not in terms of a diffuse generalized conception of world-wide capitalism, nor by a dichotomy of the "feudal" and the "capitalist" in a mechanistic unity, but their hierarchical structuration in a world-wide imperialist system'.

As will be seen, certain Marxists tend to bypass the Marxist tradition's obvious difficulties with an analysis of 'Third World formations' by identifying new modes of production. Later, we shall also deal with the theory that explains underdevelopment by the dominance of merchant capital (as opposed to industrial capital, which dominates the developed countries). Banaji – who also seems to have abandoned the concept of a 'colonial mode of production' in his later articles – has followed this line (Banaji, 1977).

Although, in this context, we are unable to dwell on all the nuances of the Indian mode of production debate, it clearly shows the breadth and vitality of Marxist research in India. Despite certain dogmatic streaks, this Marxian tradition is, we believe, one main reason why the Latin American version of the dependency theory was criticized at an early stage and subsequently met with so little success in India.

Self-reliance v. Modernization in China

Turning to other parts of Asia, the debate on dependency along Latin American lines is even more conspicuous by its absence than in India. Of course China has been important for the strategy of self-reliance, implied in Mao Zedong's ideas of development. Mao, like Gandhi, was deeply rooted in the soil of his country, but also in his case the Western impact seems to have had a catalysing effect on his ideas. Mao is often pictured as a Marxist-Leninist, but it is of importance to point out that the influence of Marxism came rather late in his life. Like Gandhi he was early influenced by the anarchist and populist thinking of Kropotkin, Bakunin and Tolstoy. In fact the first great Chinese Marxist, Li Dazhao, who had a great impact on the young Mao, seems to have been equally influenced by Russian Narodism and Marxism. Even if he never directly referred to the Narodnik writings he took a strikingly similar stand in emphasizing the village community and the need for the intellectuals to 'go to the people'. His Marxism, like that of Mao later, was therefore of a very unorthodox kind.

The Maoist Approach

The Cultural Revolution was a revitalization of Maoism. Assisted by the army, Mao cut the bureaucracy to pieces and all but crushed the Communist Party. In terms of the Chinese power structure it was a strengthening of the military element. In terms of the regional balance of power it was a strengthening of the Shanghai group. In terms of Marxist philosophy it pointed to the need for a continuous revolution in the superstructure of society, where there was a permanent danger of capitalist revivalism which could affect the socialist infrastructure as well. In terms of development strategy it was a re-emergence of populism and the indigenous Maoist model of development.

This model contains six important components. As its core was the elimination of 'three unequal relationships': between *city* and *countryside*, between *industry* and *agriculture*, and between *intellectuals* and *manual labourers*. Mao conceived these relationships as contradictions to be resolved in a dialectic process, resulting in completely new economic, social and political structures.

The model is furthermore based on the principles of *self-reliance, participation (mobilization)*, and *decentralization*. Self-reliance, the antithesis of 'dependence', was, as we noted, one of the key concepts in the discussion on development and underdevelopment in the 1970s. It is not wrong to say that Mao was one of the great popularizers of the concept.

Participation and mobilization were characteristic features of Chinese economic policies under Maoist inspiration. It is not correct to evaluate these features primarily as *means* to development. They should also be regarded as *ends* in themselves, reflecting the Maoist emphasis on equality and popular involvement. The principle of decentralization is an application of the same values to regions and levels of administration.

Towards Modernization

In 1972-3 the economic policies of Maoism were increasingly criticized. 1974-5 saw a counter-attack led by the infamous 'Gang of Four'. In January 1975, at the Fourth National People's Congress, Zhou had given a speech on the Four Modernizations which can be seen as the programme of the moderate group. In 1976 both Zhou and Mao died, and the power balance thereby changed significantly. Without the support of Mao the radicals were isolated and their defeat a question of time.

Soon after 'the decisive victory over the Gang of Four' new economic signals appeared. The *People's Daily* ridiculed the self-reliance of the 'Gang of Four' and emphasized that 'economic and technical exchanges between countries with different social systems are completely normal activities'.

The goal of modernization is no longer disputed but there may of course be many shifts in approach and emphasis as the imbalances and contradictions of the new strategy appear.

One way to summarize the recent changes in economic policy is to relate them to the six components of the Maoist model. To start with *self-reliance*, there is of course no explicit refutation of this goal. The difference is rather one of interpretation. Today self-reliance is stressed as a reason for importing foreign technology (rather than importing commodities), thus strengthening the productive base of the country. The cultural aspect of dependency is completely ignored. The training of thousands of young intellectuals abroad, thus exposing them to an alternative ideology and way of life, is a case in point. Mao's self-reliance and Deng's do not belong to the same world. Today *mobilization* is not supposed to be based on moral but on material incentives. Furthermore the trend is towards a hierarchical organization in the factories, putting an end to the chaos of popular participation in decision-making. The revolutionary committees are being abolished at lower levels of administration.

During a period of major policy changes it is not possible to retain a system of *decentralization*. In order to get China on the path of economic growth all sectors of the society must respond to the new signals and make their contribution to the Long March Towards Modernization. As an article in *Beijing Review* (15 June 1979) made clear: 'modernization requires a political environment of stability and unity, stable and good social order, strict regulations and rules and labour discipline and centralized, unified command'.

As far as the three contradictions (*urban-rural, agricultural-industrial* and *intellectual-manual*) are concerned, the dialectic process has obviously taken a turn in a non-Maoist direction. Deurbanization was a major component in the Maoist model and it is likely that during the 1960s China succeeded in at least keeping its cities from growing faster than the countryside. This policy has been terminated and many towndwellers, earlier dispersed in the countryside, are now returning to the urban world with aggressive demands for re-employment and rehabilitation. The policy of modernization is obviously not compatible with continued deurbanization. Rural industries are still emphasized but rather in terms of their overall functions in the industrial system that as an asset in themselves, or as a means of achieving self-sufficiency at the commune level.

The new relationship between industry and agriculture is still unclear. The initial emphasis on industry (particularly steel) in the modernization programme was modified during the 1979 'slowdown' and the importance of the agricultural sector was stressed. Within this sector a significant shift from grain production to the production of cash crops took place. Regional specialization according to the principle of comparative advantage and productivity – raising measures were also stressed. All this points to a more conventional pattern of economic development. Today Mao is history, and the Chinese development strategy does not put much emphasis on self-reliance. The key word is modernization, and modernization implies Western technology and modes of organisation.

The Capitalist Havens of Asia

The urge for modernization along rather conventional lines (a revival of the modernization paradigm) is even more intensely felt in the capitalist miracles of East and South-east Asia. First of all Japan, secondly the 'four little dragons', South Korea, Taiwan, Hong Kong and Singapore, and thirdly the more doubtful cases of Malaysia, the Philippines and Indonesia. We consider them as 'doubtful' since the contradictions of the capitalist path are more obvious and the bright future of that path less certain.

Japan is a case *sui generis*. Paul Baran stressed that Japan escaped colonial exploitation and therefore could build the foundations for indigenous capitalist development. According to Samir Amin, Japan is the *last* country to achieve this (Hettne and Wallensteen, 1978, p 20). Thus, to the dependency theorists Japan is a capitalist success story and orthodox neo-classicists are equally enthusiastic.

The Prototypes

The development policy of the South-east Asian group of countries seems quite unconcerned about the problem of blocked development supposedly associated with a dependent position. As is well known, they have been referred to as cases contradicting the basic thesis proposed by the dependency school, as will be discussed in our concluding chapter. A closer look at these cases, however, suggests that their experiences are not easily generalizable, and that, furthermore, they differ quite substantially among themselves. Hong Kong and Singapore are city states, and therefore completely atypical. Hong Kong derives much of its prosperity from being the key to the Chinese market, but the uncertainty of its political status after 1997 is already affecting the confidence of the business community. Regardless of the outcome of the British-Chinese negotiations, Hong Kong illustrates the problems of dependence rather than the opportunity of indigenous capitalist development. Much the same can be said about Singapore, although the *political* situation of this city state is more secure. In spite of this, Singapore leaders have recently become concerned about security problems, obviously thinking about what happened to another cosmopolitan centre for banking and tourism – Beirut (*Far Eastern Economic Review*, 13 Jan 1983). Thus, the military component in the Singapore miracle is becoming more and more conspicuous and the future progress of this city state is becoming dependent on arms exports.

South Korea and Taiwan must be taken more seriously as possible models of development, although some non-repeatable features emerge more clearly on closer scrutiny. Let us briefly examine the case of Taiwan, which has been considered by many as an 'economic miracle'. It has then been argued that the main reason for its success is the effort to get its prices right in relation to international opportunity costs and thereby to promote exports (see e.g. Bhagwati, 1978). Furthermore, it is said that this is the solution to the problems of many Third World countries and thus something to emulate (see e.g. Keesing, 1979).

Undeniably, Taiwan is a success story that has achieved 'growth with equity' under a relatively free market regime. The above-mentioned neo-classical explanation to why this country has succeeded is, however, more doubtful, since it ignores several important features of Taiwan's history. Wynn (1982) identifies five such features that, according to him, make Taiwan a special case. First, Taiwan's unusual colonial experience. Japan's policy differed remarkably from that of European colonizers, mainly in that primary production was not confined to a foreign enclave with limited spill-over on subsistence agriculture. The agriculture in Taiwan was, therefore, generally commercialized. Furthermore, a land reform similar to that undertaken in Meiji Japan was initiated by the Japanese. 'A parasitic class of great landlords was [thereby] destroyed, while a middle stratum of landlords was given incentives to produce more, thus minimizing their opposition to taxation, while their tenants were squeezed to the maximum.' Secondly, another land reform was engineered by the Quomindang in alliance with the Americans which destroyed landlordism and created a class of smallholders. According to Wynn, this explains to a great extent why income distribution is far less unequal in Taiwan than in most Third World countries. Thirdly, Wynn points to the fact that the Quomindang authority was provided with substantial aid from the USA. Fourthly, Taiwan's export boom and growth rates coincided with an extraordinarily favourable international situation, very different from the present one. Finally, Wynn stresses the cultural differences between Taiwan and most other underdeveloped countries. 'The philosophy of Confucianism in Taiwan (and in South Korea and Japan as well), with its *sui generis* attitudes about work and authority, undoubtedly influences Taiwan's development capability. Other factors aside, it may be quite impossible to copy the Taiwan model in dissimilar cultures.'

Wynn also discusses some myths that have surrounded Taiwan's development model. One is that Taiwan, unlike the Latin American countries, resisted the temptations of infant industry protection and efforts to initiate a process of import substitution industrialization. However, a regime of import substitution preceded the export of labour-intensive manufactures and this was 'hardly a trivial episode in Taiwan's economic history'. Another myth is that the seed of industrialization bore fruit in Taiwan because the environment which supported it was free from state interference. Even this could not be further from the truth. 'Government management of capital accumulation is as conspicuous in the export oriented era of economic development as in the import substitution phase.'

Going through different factors contributing to the South Korean economic boom of the late 1960s and early 1970s, Don Long (1983) shows that repression played an important role in keeping down the farmers' and workers' incomes. This radically accelerated the process of capital accumulation, according to Long. Such an aspect of a development strategy must, of course, also be taken into consideration by those who want to emulate the 'newly industrialized countries (NIC) model'.

The Emulators

When one turns to the 'emulators', as distinct from the 'prototypes' (Lamb,

1981) the question marks multiply. Countries like Malaysia, the Philippines and Indonesia are still far from repeating the 'NIC model', and one may ask if that sun will ever rise in these countries. Malaysia's recent 'Look East' policy may serve as an example. This policy, announced in the latter part of 1981, implies that the government explicitly refers to Japan as the model for emulation. The reason for not mentioning the 'four little dragons' as models must be their Chinese character.[5]

The new policy has apparently been pursued at two levels (Saravanamuttu, 1983). At the external economic policy level, Japanese governmental and private sector aid, technical assistance and training is being sought and contracted for in Malaysia. At the domestic level, the Malaysian government itself seeks to inculcate the 'Eastern' work ethic through various propaganda devices and through concrete promotion and implementation of policy in the private and public sectors.

What the new government means by 'Look East' has been explained by the President himself in the following:

> This means emulating the rapidly developing countries of the East in an effort to develop Malaysia. Matters deserving attention are diligence and discipline in work, loyalty to the nation and to the enterprise or business where the worker is employed, priority of group over individual interests, emphasis on productivity and high quality, upgrading efficiency, narrowing differentials and gaps between executives and workers, management systems which concentrate on long term achievement and not solely on increases in dividends or staff incomes in the short term, and other factors which can contribute to progress for our country.
> (Mahathir, 1983, p 276)

Furthermore, he wants to see his country as a company: 'Malaysia Incorporated': 'The Malaysia Incorporated concept means that Malaysia should be viewed as a company where the government and the private sector are both owners and workers, together in this company. In a company, all owners/workers are expected to co-operate to ensure the company's success' (Ibid.).

The Malaysian government is thus attributing Japan's success to three main factors: work ethics, management system (incorporating a belief in group achievement), and technology. Although these have been important features in Japan, there are also other important factors that are more difficult and sometimes even impossible to emulate. To mention only a few, one is the early reorganization of landownership and the taxation system to mobilize and redirect a surplus (see Halliday, 1975). In fact, land reforms have been an important prerequisite in all the prototypes. In Malaysia, however, the sultan system, among other things, prevents land reforms. Another characteristic of Japan is the cultural, ethical and religious homogeneity. In this respect Malaysia is very different. The same can be said concerning the attitude to foreign capital. While Japan has always been very restrictive to foreign firms the situation is the opposite in Malaysia.

Considering the fact that export promotion is of central importance in the NIC strategy another question mark arises in the case of Malaysia, since the country has already put all its eggs in the world markct basket. In 1980 export comprised 60 per cent of the gross domestic product. This economic policy, which had made the Malaysian economy extremely vulnerable to fluctuations in the world economy, has rarely been questioned by the academics, since the bulk of them belong to the modernization school.

There is not much of a development debate in Malaysia, and there are several reasons for that. One is the political situation, which excludes a free intellectual debate. Although the situation has improved during the new administration (installed in 1981), the recent withdrawal of the periodical *Nadi Insan*, because it contained an interview with a leader of an underground nationalist movement, clearly shows that there are still limitations. Another reason is that the academics are heavily involved in consulting activities. Most of the research done at the universities consists of rather bland, empirical studies commissioned by the government or some private company. As will be seen in the next chapter, a similar situation is found in Kenya. There, however, several foreign scholars are involved in development research, which is not the case in Malaysia. The state of art in the development discussion in Malaysia may, perhaps, be seen in the university bookshops, which sell mainly literature on management and corporate efficiency, but very little on development problems.

The political leadership also seems bent on continued modernization in accordance with the recommendations from the recurrent orthodoxy.

However, since 1980 the Malaysian economy has been hard hit by the international recession. This has provided an opportunity for a few critics of the free trade-modernization orthodoxy to come to the fore. Some of them take a modified version of the dependency theory as their point of departure, and try to point out the relevance of more self-reliance in the present Malaysian context (e.g. Khor, 1983). What effects this critique will have on the government's strategy is still an open question, but there seem to be at least some in the government who are inclined to introduce more self-reliance.[6]

The prospects for those countries trying to emulate the newly industrialized countries are, at least for the moment, not very promising. On the one hand this is due to the fact that several important internal conditions that have been crucial for the NIC success are absent in the emulators. One must also remember that the NIC phenomenon appeared in a favourable, international context. Although, as Warren has rightly pointed out (1980), it is a myth that industrial production in the NIC only takes place in free zones, one cannot ignore the fact that the success of the NIC coincided with a changing international division of labour and favourable export possibilities. This underlines the fact that the NIC phenomenon may not be analysed outside the context of the changing world economy. Was this not the problematic that the dependency school brought to the fore?

Notes

1. A.C. Minocha says: 'Prebisch, Singer and a host of others have built theses of exploitation of developing countries on the basis of their worsening terms of trade. These analyses are in line with Dadabhai, though the political conditions are vitally different today from what they were in the days of Dadabhai and the nature of drain has also undergone a change' (Minocha, 1970, p 42).
2. Various interviews with social scientists in Delhi, Calcutta and Bombay have revealed that the dependence debate, as we know it from Latin America, had little effect on the Indian debate (interviews conducted during March 1980).
3. The periodicals *The Economic and Political Weekly* (Bombay) and *The Social Scientist* (Trivandrum) were the main vehicles of this debate.
4. Summaries may be found in Alavi (1975), McEachern (1976) and Thorner (1982), which also contain more detailed references. We provide only a limited number of references to the individual contributions.
5. Malaysia is a multiracial society with some 55 per cent Malays, 35 per cent Chinese and 10 per cent Indians and others. Historically, the development of this plural society can be traced to the colonial era (see Li Dun Jen, 1982, and Bedlington, 1978). Different waves of migration were distinct not only in racial composition and in location (the Malays have been overwhelmingly rural dwellers while the Chinese generally were urban dwellers), but more important in economic functions. The historically based identification of race with economic function resulted in the 1969 racial riots in Kuala Lumpur. The polarization of poor and rich corresponded to a significant extent with the polarization of Malays v. Chinese. The proclamation of the New Economic Policy (NEP) helped defuse the political situation after 1969, and its main objectives were summarized in the second Malaysian Plan as follows: 'Comprising two prongs, the NEP seeks to eradicate poverty among all Malaysians and to restructure Malaysian society so that the identification of race with economic function and geographical location is reduced and eventually eliminated, both objectives being realized through rapid expansion of the economy over time' (Quoted in Fisk and Osman-Rani, 1982, p 8). NEP thus aims at creating a new *bamiputra* (Malay) middle class. Furthermore, the current Malay-dominated government strives for one culture, one language and one citizenry (see *Far Eastern Economic Review*, 5 May 1983). This means that they want the Chinese to assimilate more, and with such a policy it would be awkward explicitly to spell out the 'four little dragons' as models because of their Chinese character.
6. Khor said, for instance, talking of this: '. . . a couple of years ago, when I warned what effects a world recession may have on the Malaysian economy because of its external dependence, nobody listened to me. Today the situation is quite the opposite. Every week I am invited by different government institutions to discuss with them how to achieve more self-reliance' (conversation in Penang, September 1983).

7. The Scramble for African Capitalism

The Idea of Dependence in an African Context

The 'scramble for Africa' began during the latter part of the 19th Century. Africa was thus the last continent to be incorporated into the world capitalist system. The societies that took shape were distinctly colonial, although differences between them, of course, existed in accordance with physical (resources, population, location) as well as sociocultural characteristics. Furthermore the colonial powers themselves exerted their distinct influences on the colonized areas.

Extensive political movements against colonialism were relatively rare in Africa with the exception of Algeria, Kenya, and the more recent struggle against Portuguese domination. The effect of the colonial economy on the social structure was also relatively limited (as compared to Latin America, the Caribbean and Asia). The bourgeoisie and the working class were relatively undeveloped. The small elite which took over the position of the colonial power had been educated abroad in a Western way of thinking. Therefore, this 'modern elite' not only assumed the position of the former colonial masters, but also the latter's general views on development and modernization.

To some extent these views were modified to suit African conditions as they found ideological expression in the concept of *African socialism* (see e.g. Friedland and Rosberg, 1964). As an ideology it encompassed many diverse viewpoints (Klinghoffer, 1969). The *Afro-Marxists* emphasized Marxist-Leninist ideas of economic development and political structure. Ghana (Kwame Nkrumah), Guinea (Sekou Touré) and Mali (Modibo Keita) during the first half of the 1960s could be mentioned as major examples. The *moderate socialists*, including Kenyatta of Kenya and Kaunda of Zambia, favoured a state-controlled 'socialist' economy but were at the same time anxious to attract foreign investment capital. The *social democrats* were closely connected with European socialism and frequently pro-Western in outlook, for example Leopold Senghor of Senegal and Tom Mboya of Kenya. The *agrarian-socialists* (populists) were associated with Nyerere's Ujamaa philosophy (see below). Rather than looking for foreign models of socialism Nyerere found it in traditional African society:

> Both the 'rich' and the 'poor' individual were completely secure in African society. Natural catastrophe brought famine, but it brought famine to everybody – 'poor' or 'rich'. Nobody starved, either of food or of human dignity, because he lacked personal wealth; he could depend on the wealth possessed by the community of which he was a member. That was socialism. That *is* socialism.
> (Nyerere, 1968, p 3-4)

As the above examples show, African socialism covered a wide ideological spectrum from more or less pure Marxism-Leninism to populist ideas, in fact rather similar to the Russian Narodniks or Gandhi in India. The concept of African socialism, however, obviously contained an anti-capitalist element which, in turn, was due to the fact that the 'modern elite' associated capitalism with colonialism. It is also important to note that the elite, consisting of bureaucrats, professional politicians and intellectuals, did not share their power with the 'bourgeoisie'.

Compared to the other regions that we have discussed so far, Africa is the economically least developed one, with a comparatively limited foreign penetration. This is important, when we consider the idea of dependence in the African context. The economies of the African countries south of the Sahara (excluding the Republic of South Africa and Zimbabwe) are dominated by rural, small-scale production. This is particularly pronounced in the agricultural sector which normally forms the backbone of these economies. Most of the farms are small, while the larger and more scientifically operated ones (which, of course, are the ones the foreign corporations are mainly interested in) are rare. The manufacturing industry displays a similar pattern, and since this sector is quite small in these agrarian economies, the multinational industrial corporations' share of total production is also small. The mining industry is, on the other hand, totally dominated by foreign firms; it is also the most important component of the formal sector in certain countries, such as Zaire and Zambia.

The Social Science Infrastructure

Africa did not have a social science debate like the Latin American, the Caribbean or the Indian one during the 1950s and the 1960s. This is not surprising if we consider the infrastructure for social science in Africa. At the moment of political independence, which came later than elsewhere in the Third World, the nations of the continent were among the economically least developed in the world, with an almost non-existent system of higher education. After independence, the number of Africans with an academic degree was very small, as was also the number of universities in Africa. Those who did have an academic degree were educated mainly in Europe, or in the United States (or, to some extent, at European universities in South Africa).[1]

The system of university education expanded rapidly during the 1960s. Between 1960 and 1966 eleven new universities were founded in the former British colonies (Leys, 1971, p 31). This provided a basis for the development of alternatives to the hitherto dominant Western view on economic development. However, the alternatives never did materialize,[2] for reasons which may be sought at several levels: a lack of traditions and resources, as well as the general political situation with strong ties to the former colonial powers, etc.[3] Furthermore, the close connection between the universities and the government may also have been an important factor, since social science research was extremely policy oriented, aiming at solving the most acute problems of development (Court, 1975, p 15). The universities had little time left over for creating alternative development theories.

The dependence upon theories and models which had been developed in Europe and in the United States was thus greater in African universities than anywhere else in the Third World. Development was thought of as a straight path along which the industrialized nations had already travelled, and along which the underdeveloped countries were now to travel.

> This was the moment of optimism, when economists seemed capable of planning prosperity for the underdeveloped world, when sociologists and social psychologists felt certain they could convert Weberian Traditional Man into a Marshallian maximizer, and when systems analysis seemed to have reached the point where political scientists knew what inputs, through-puts and outputs were needed to maintain stability in a decolonized world.
> (Hopkins, 1976, p 31)

Nor did the African interregional institutes, which were established outside the universities during the 1950s and the 1960s, distinguish themselves as their Latin American counterparts had done. As we have already seen, the ECLA played an important role in the development of alternative views on the problems of the Third World. The *United Nations Economic Commission for Africa* (ECA) in Addis Ababa did not play that kind of role. The prevailing ideas about development were wholly accepted – which was also the case in the ECA's 'sister institute', the IDEP (the *United Nations African Institute for Economic Development and Planning*), established in 1963 in Dakar. Like its counterparts in Latin America (the ILPES) and in Asia (the UNADI), the IDEP was, in accordance with the UN objectives, supposed to train economists and planners, to carry out research in connection with this training programme, and, when requested to do so, to function as an advisory body to the various African governments. The purpose of the latter was to study local and national development problems, and to use the results from these studies both in the training programme and in the development of theories.

During the 1960s, the IDEP functioned merely as a training centre for African top civil servants. Both the research and the advisory functions were neglected, which is why this institute, unlike the ILPES, in no way differed from any other African institute of higher education.[4]

As in the rest of the Third World, the optimism of the 1960s subsided in Africa as well. This decade did not turn out to be the 'Decade of Development' proclaimed by the United Nations. Instead Africa fell into the usual development pattern of 'growth without development'. It was therefore quite natural that many intellectuals, in their search for new, explanatory models felt attracted to the new currents from Latin America. Here was an alternative to the Western development theory with a simple message that seemed to explain everything: the dependence on the centre was the cause of the 'development of underdevelopment'.

The dependency school became more important in Africa than in Asia, but never as important as in Latin America and the Caribbean. It was in this context that the IDEP eventually came to play a significant role. Its profile changed radically in 1970, when one of the professors, Samir Amin, who had been quite critical of its previous orientation, became head of the Institute. Along the lines of the ILPES in Latin America, he planned to tone down the IDEP's role as an 'uncritical intermediary of methods', and to build up an independent, Pan-African training and research centre. The following excerpt is from an official report on the period between 1964 and 1975:

> As modest institutions whose costs are insignificant compared with the vast resources, called international aid, allocated for development, the regional institutes are nevertheless capable of fulfilling important functions. I.L.P.E.S. has already made a decisive contribution in this respect; it is a known fact that the whole new current of thought from Latin America in the last decade originated from that Institute. For ever associated with the name of that Institute will be the analyses of dependency and the historical formation of Latin American underdevelopment which are undoubtedly the most important contemporary contribution to the study of development and underdevelopment. (IDEP, DIR/2605, pp 4-5)

Under Amin's direction the IDEP changed the research orientation towards uniquely African development problems. Questions concerning development strategy were given top priority, and the basic research objective was now to enable the scholars to challenge the 'know-how' of the existing development strategies by increasing their understanding of the 'know-why' of underdevelopment (ibid., p 10). To answer the question 'why', Amin used a dependency approach. The views held by some of the Institute's researchers and teachers meant that the dependency school's ideas, to some extent, were disseminated to other African nations through courses, seminars and conferences, as well as through the fact that members of the IDEP staff often worked as advisers to various African governments.

However, the effect of the dependency theory varied considerably from country to country. It was diligently applied in some countries and completely ignored in others. Before we attempt to explain this, we shall examine Amin's extensive production, which we believe to be justified, not only because he was an important participant in the African debate, but also because of his significant contributions to the further development of the dependency school.[5]

Blocked Development: Samir Amin

Samir Amin began to study the problems of underdevelopment from a global perspective. In his doctoral thesis, which was published in 1957 (Amin, 1957), he described the structural effects of international integration on the underdeveloped economies. Amin was at that time greatly influenced by French growth theorists such as Perroux, but even more so by Raúl Prebisch and the ECLA. In this respect he differed little from his Latin American colleagues. However, Amin himself also emphasized discussions with the Egyptian Communist Party as influential.[6]

Amin's doctoral thesis formed the basis for his more empirically oriented research during the 1960s, in which he attempted to deepen his analysis by concrete studies of a number of West African countries (Amin, 1965, 1967a, 1969a, 1971a). Common to all of these studies is an eclectic view in which orthodox economic theory forms a dominating part.

What is commonly known as Amin's theory of global accumulation of capital emerged towards the end of the 1960s. In this section we shall deal exclusively with this theory, the main ideas of which appeared in 1967 in a book on the Ivory Coast (Amin, 1967b). They were elaborated upon and later published in his *L'échelle mondiale* in 1970 (Amin, 1970).

Amin defined underdevelopment by means of three structural criteria: (1) unevenness of productivity as between sectors; (2) disarticulation of the economic system; and (3) domination from outside. In order to show how this underdevelopment came about Amin constructed a model of capitalist accumulation on a world scale. Like other dependency theorists, he believed that underdevelopment was merely the result of the fact that the accumulation in the periphery was patterned to the advantage of the centre. The starting point of his analysis was therefore the global system, or the global capital accumulation, because of the intimate relation between the development of the centre and the underdevelopment of the periphery.

The crucial premiss in Amin's model, and thus the very foundation of his theory, was that the global capitalist system contained two types of capitalism: on the one hand, an autocentric, dynamic capitalism in the centre, and on the other, a blocked capitalism in the periphery. Both types were structurally linked, and the system was therefore reproducing itself at the global level. In order to understand and analyse the problems in the Third World which, according to Amin, included social, ideological and political issues, it was necessary to identify the differences between a self-centred and blocked capitalism. This difference is illustrated in Figure 7.1.

According to Amin there must be a link between the production of consumption goods and capital goods (intended for the production of Sector 2) in order to create a self-reproducing, growing capitalism. The laws of capitalism in Marx's analysis were based on this 'pure' capitalism in which wages may be looked upon in two different ways – either as income, or as costs. The higher the wages, the higher the capitalist's costs of producing a commodity. On the other hand, higher wages enable the workers to buy more

Figure 7.1
Samir Amin's Model of Central and Peripheral Capitalism

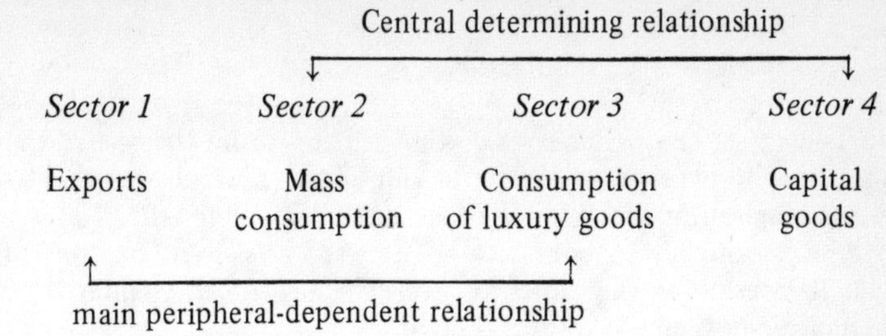

commodities; and in order to realize his profits, the capitalist must sell his commodities. A 'normal' or 'balanced' growth of 'pure' capitalism will therefore impose a lower limit to wages. The size of the capital goods sector as well as that of the consumption goods sector are also given in this pattern of growth, since there is an 'objective' or 'necessary' relation between these and the distribution of wages and profits in the system.

The intimate relationship between demand and the wage level in the centre made the economic systems there self-perpetuation at the national level. This implied that as soon as feudalism had been replaced by capitalism, which, according to Amin, was a result of internal factors, capitalism continued to develop on its own. In the periphery the situation was, however, different since the origins of the peripheral model of accumulation were to be sought in external rather than internal factors. The politically dominating centre created an export sector in the periphery according to its own needs.

> The underlying reason which rendered possible the creation of this export sector must be sought in the conditions which make the establishment 'profitable'. There is no pressure for central national capital to emigrate as a result of insufficient possible outlets at the centre; it will however emigrate to the periphery if it can obtain a better return. The *equalisation* of the rate of profit will redistribute the surplus arising from the higher return and use the export of capital as a means to fight the trend of a falling profit rate. The reason for creating an export sector therefore lies in obtaining from the periphery products which are the basic elements of constant capital (raw material) or of variable capital (food products) at production costs lower than those at the centre for similar products such as coffee or tea.
> (Amin, 1972, p 13)

In this context it is also necessary to consider the question of modes of production in the periphery. Unlike André Gunder Frank, Amin claimed that 'the world capitalist system did not represent a world capitalist mode of production. Rather it should be seen as a conglomerate of systems' (Amin,

1971b, p 36). The mere integration into the world capitalist system did not necessarily imply the imposition of a capitalist mode of production. The pre-capitalist modes of production might instead survive, at least partially, which made it possible to lower the wages in the export sector, since the workers in that sector received part of their subsistence minimum from the traditional (pre-capitalist) sector.

The export sector in the periphery was thus isolated from the rest of the economy. The link between the wage level and demand, which was characteristic of 'pure' capitalism, was missing because the demand for the products of the periphery lay outside its boundaries. The wage level could be lowered even more in the periphery than in the centre which, in turn, facilitated an 'unequal exchange' between the countries involved.

In other words, the centre forced the periphery into a system which destroyed the basis for a 'pure', capitalist development – and as soon as that had happened this system reproduced itself. The growth of the demand for mass consumption goods was effectively throttled, since the wages in the export sector were kept low by means of repression. Instead, the incomes of various domestic 'parasitic' social groups formed the most important part of the demand, which meant that it was concentrated on 'luxury goods'.[7] This also meant that the periphery's investment resources were channelled to the luxury goods sector, rather than to the consumption goods sector. The local production of 'luxury goods' tended to be capital intensive with minimal effects on the employment level. The result was a 'development of underdevelopment' in which the great majority of the population was marginalized.

The situation in the periphery may be summarized in Figure 7.1. As can be seen, the link between the consumption goods sector and the capital goods sector is missing; instead, there is a link between the export sector and the sector producing luxury goods. Thus, capitalist development is blocked, since the dynamics lie outside the countries' control, resulting in dependence upon the centre.

From this, Amin reached the conclusion that a break with imperialism was necessary if development in the periphery was to come about. In this context, he emphasized that development was meaningless if it did not include the 'masses' and their standard of living. To achieve this kind of development it was necessary to change the linkages between sectors, so that the production of consumption goods and capital goods was more emphasized; this, in turn, required an expansion of the internal market and an increase in mass consumption. An internal dynamic was thus to be created in the periphery, which at the same time led to independence from the centre.

We shall now examine the dependency theory's role in the African debate. We are specifically interested in the conditions that have caused the dependency theory to be accepted in one country, and not in another. This goal can be achieved by focusing on Tanzania and Kenya. The case of Tanzania is discussed in more detail, since its government has tried to apply the dependency approach in its development policies. Furthermore, we examine the ensuing African criticism of the dependency theory.

The Rise and Fall of the Dependency Theory in Tanzania

Dar es Salaam – A Secondary Centre

During the 1970s Tanzania was an important centre of the theoretical debate on dependence and underdevelopment in the English-speaking parts of Africa.[8] After political independence in 1961, the rulers of the country were strongly influenced by the contemporary ideas of modernization (Ståhl, 1980).[9] In an economy which was (and still is) primarily agrarian (90 per cent of the labour force was employed in agriculture in 1976), one important task was to modernize the primitive agricultural sector. In accordance with the development strategy of the modernization paradigm, modern, capital-intensive farms were favoured. The same kind of development thinking was also reflected in the industrialization strategy. The industrial sector was almost non-existent at the time of independence; only 220 industrial firms employed more than 10 workers (ibid., p 93).

Tanzania's first five-year plan established several ambitious development goals. How they were to be achieved was, however, not too carefully specified. In his analysis of the plan, Brian van Arkadie made the following observations:

> it emphasized dependence on external financial support and failed to reflect all the implications of the rural nature of Tanzanian society. Moreover, although the Plan was in principle comprehensive, much of the economy was dominated by external influences which were only in small part susceptible to influence by available policy instruments. Not only was the economy heavily dependent on external trade, and therefore primary commodity markets, but each sector of the 'modern' economy (e.g. banking, insurance, industry) was foreign owned, while a significant segment of exports was produced on foreign-owned estates. The available policy tools largely consisted of fiscal policy (at the outset of the Plan even monetary policy was largely passive under the Currency Board system) and development programmes in the traditional areas of central government concern (e.g. education, agricultural extension, roads).
> (van Arkadie, 1973, p 25)

Subsequently, it became obvious to the Tanzanian leaders that the path they followed would not in fact lead them to the established goals. A more radical restructuring of the economy was needed. The new strategy, greatly influenced by Nyerere's social philosophy, was proclaimed in the so-called Arusha Declaration of 1967 (see e.g. Nyerere, 1968).

From this moment on, capitalism was seen as the main enemy. The alternative was to revitalize the 'traditional' African socialism, an original approach which attracted much international attention at the time. The new development strategy gave priority to the development of the rural areas, since the previous strategy was thought to have too much favoured the urban population. It was primarily a question of increasing the agricultural production. How was this possible in a country in which the population was widely dispersed with only small lots at their disposal? The so-called *Ujamaa* villages were thought of as the solution: more efficient production should be achieved by the peasants' moving together in villages, which also facilitated the provision of improved social services.

The policy of industrialization carried out until then was criticized: the small Tanzanian industrial sector was characterized by its extensive use of capital-intensive methods of production and was heavily dependent upon imported goods. This did not create the desired development effects. It had also emphasized the existing pattern of localization, in which industry was concentrated in a few urban areas. Since that was contrary to the new strategy, industries which stimulated the development of the rural areas were now to be favoured in order to create a balanced and integrated national economy. An increased emphasis on small-scale industrial production in the towns and villages was therefore part of the rural development programme.

Another important objective of the new strategy was to increase the degree of 'self-reliance'. The dependence on foreign countries was to be thwarted. Strategically important firms were nationalized and foreign investment was no longer to be allowed as long as it 'favoured only the urban aristocracy'. Foreign aid was to be channelled to projects which increased domestic activity, and imports were to be controlled so that no commodities that could be produced domestically were imported. Increased trade with other underdeveloped nations was to lessen Tanzania's commercial dependence on the centre. That is what later came to be called South-South cooperation.

Of course, these changes stimulated the intellectual atmosphere at the University of Dar es Salaam, popularly known as 'the Hill'. It attracted a number of foreign teachers and researchers, of whom most were neo-Marxists with clearly defined views on dependence.[10] As already mentioned, Samir Amin was an important link in the process of transferring the dependency theory from Latin America to Africa, but the expatriate teachers at 'the Hill' also played a significant role in this context.

On the one hand, there was a group of Western intellectuals who had come to the university during the late 1960s. Lionel Cliffe and John Saul were the most important among these. On the other hand, the ideas of the dependency school came to Tanzania via the Caribbean. Both Walter Rodney and Clive Thomas from Guyana and more or less associated with the University of the West Indies, played a central part in the African dependency debate. Thomas was perhaps primarily known for his attempt to construct an economic model for the transition to socialism in African countries like Tanzania, i.e. raw material producing countries with relatively small populations, whereas Rodney, in addition to his radical writings on African history, became well-known as a prolific political debater. We have already pointed out that Rodney's views on dependence differed somewhat from those of the other Caribbean dependency theorists in that he emphasized the racial aspects of the dependency complex. He was a black-power theorist, apart from being a dependency theorist, although his East African production suggests a more clearly defined dependency theoretical view compared to his later work in Jamaica. This shift appears natural in view of the fact that Tanzania had neither the racial problems, nor the lack of a relevant cultural identity, peculiar to Jamaica.[11]

Most foreign social scientists who came to Tanzania during this period were greatly influenced by the Latin American dependency school. When trying to explain underdevelopment in Africa, the standard approach was a rather uncritical application of problems and methods borrowed from the *dependentistas*, primarily A.G. Frank. Walter Rodney's book *How Europe Underdeveloped Africa* (Rodney, 1972), which was also diligently read and discussed outside Africa, was a typical example.[12]

According to our classification system described in Chapter 4, Rodney ends up far to the left on all axes. He emphasized the external factors[13] and claimed that underdevelopment was a result of the fact that the satellites had been deprived of their economic surplus.[14] The result of his analysis was, inevitably, 'development of underdevelopment'. His political solutions, furthermore, clearly contained voluntaristic elements.

In addition to the expatriates, a group of Tanzanian scholars now began to study the African development problem in a dependency perspective. This group also accepted the Latin American method of analysis rather uncritically in their efforts to show the 'development of underdevelopment' in Tanzania. In this context, the two most important Tanzanians were Justinian Rweyemamu and Issa Shivji. As early as 1969 Rweyemamu wrote an article in which he claimed that foreign domination was the cause of underdevelopment in the periphery (Rweyemamu, 1969). On several subsequent occasions, he elaborated on this issue (see Rweyemamu, 1971 and 1973). However, his role was not limited to the discussions at the university, where he held a chair in economics; his political influence grew, since he later became President Nyerere's personal adviser.

The publication of Issa Shivji's, 'Tanzania – The Silent Class Struggle' (Shivji, 1970) was perhaps the most interesting event in the Tanzanian dependency debate, as well as a true milestone in the development of African development theory. It contains unmistakable attempts to provide a Marxian analysis:

> without a real class analysis, it is impossible to chart out a correct strategy and formulate appropriate tactics. More important still: it is impossible to make correct alliances. How can we talk about a 'Tanzanian Revolution' without even knowing the friends and the enemies of such a revolution? An analysis of the socioeconomic formation of Tanzania is, therefore, urgently needed.
> (Ibid., p 2)

This was in fact the first time that the development in Tanzania was criticized from a radical point of view. Shivji wanted to show that the chosen approach did not lead to socialism: Tanzania was, despite nationalizations, for instance, trapped in the neo-colonial system, mainly because the rapidly growing government bureaucracy now formed the basis for a new class stratification. In Shivji's opinion, Tanzania was still a neo-colonial society, i.e. a class society.

In this article, however, he never really abandoned the dependency approach, and Marxists outside the dependency school regarded his 'class analysis' as not too different to that of André Gunder Frank (Nabudere, 1975, pp 502-3). The debate started by Shivji was, however, more important than his actual theoretical contribution, since it eventually led to a Marxian alternative to the dependency school. Initially, a group of 'senior Marxists on the Hill' (Hyden, 1977, p 55) were invited to comment upon the article. Although they were all sympathetic to Shivji's ideas, opinions differed. Tamás Szentes (see Note 11) did not find the government bureaucracy as autonomous as Shivji would have it, whereas John Saul found it even more independent.[15] In Shivji's analysis there were several points which, if stated more clearly, might have resulted in an interesting alternative to the dependency theory already in the beginning of the 1970s. As it was, several years passed before such an alternative did appear.[16]

The case of Tanzania is important for a study of the practical, political role played by the dependency school, as well as its consequences. During the 1970s the country became a development strategic 'laboratory'. There were clearly-defined objectives of 'self-reliance' and 'socialism', and the dependency theorists saw it as their mission to provide theoretical models in support of these objectives. Since there was a strong link between the university and the administration (as in Jamaica, a number of the dependency theorists were taken from the university and put into various positions in the administration), they were also able to influence the country's development strategy.

The most important question was that of the role of industry. The Arusha Declaration shifted the interest entirely to the development of the rural areas. A number of dependency theorists soon reacted to the fact that industry was left behind. They claimed that if Tanzania were to lessen its dependence upon foreign countries, and if it were ever to stand on its own feet, it was necessary to build a domestic industry. A rapid industrialization was the only means of achieving true 'self-reliance'.

Clive Thomas was, without doubt, a driving force in the discussions on this question. During his time in the Caribbean, where he worked on problems of development planning, Thomas had sketched strategies of development, the purpose of which was to eliminate foreign dependence (see e.g. Brewster and Thomas, 1971). These 'sketches' were completed and fully drawn up in Tanzania where they were published in the book *Dependence and Transformation: The Economics of the Transition to Socialism* (Thomas, 1974). A draft from 1972 attracted a great deal of attention in Dar es Salaam; in it, Thomas outlined a strategy for a transition to socialism for small, dependent countries like Tanzania.

Thomas claimed that underdevelopment was mainly a result of foreign penetration, which, in turn, had started a cumulative process in which domestic production had gradually swung away from not only domestic demand, but also the basic needs of large parts of the population. The counteracting of this process, thus achieving a convergence of domestic resource use and domestic demand was of great importance. To Thomas the first step in his plan was to abandon capitalism and sever the ties with imperialism (ibid., p 123).

The convergence of resource use and demand was thus the first iron law of transformation. The second was the convergence of needs with demand. In underdeveloped economies there is (due both to inequities of income distribution and to low levels of absolute income per capita) an acute divergence between the basic needs of the population and consumption expenditure. *Consumption planning* should therefore aim at the 'progressive expansion of the range of socially and collectively consumed commodities' in order to reduce the distributive role of the market (ibid., p 260).

Granted that this basic strategy was implemented, there was much scope for regional integration and international trade, but, claimed Thomas, it was likely that many of the small underdeveloped countries would have to advance towards socialism in relative isolation from their neighbours. The efforts at agricultural transformation and industrialization must therefore take this constraint into account.

The strategy of convergence should not only lead to a shift towards production for basic needs, but also rationalize agriculture through the spread of industrialization techniques and shift the balance in favour of industry. Under capitalism this process would lead to capitalist farms and the rise of the modern agro-businessmen. Under socialism there would instead be state and co-operative farms. There was no conflict between industry and agriculture according to Thomas since 'industrialization is a social process necessary to enable society to master the material environment in the service of its own needs' (ibid., p 181).

The limited applicability of the 'Soviet industrialization model' to small underdeveloped economies had led even radicals to doubt the feasibility of industrialization programmes. This pessimism was, however, according to Thomas, unwarranted. A strategy of comprehensive planning required the domestic production of those *basic materials* which were required as primary inputs for the manufacture of the *basic goods* of the community. It was necessary to ensure that these basic materials were substantially derived from domestic resources. This constituted the necessary condition for the growth of an *indigenously oriented technology*. The scope for structural transformation would be heavily dependent on the resource configuration in each and every society. Economies of scale should be judged from the point of view of a *critical minimum* rather than idealized optimum levels.

Justinian Rweyemamu's book *Underdevelopment and Industrialization in Tanzania* (Rweyemamu, 1973) was another important component in the discussions about the Tanzanian industrial policy. His contribution was primarily an analysis of the effects on the country's industrial structure of colonialism and continued foreign dependence. However, the book also contained a section on how to get rid of the 'perverse' industrial structure which was the result of the dependence – including some ideas that were closely related to those of Thomas. Rweyemamu and Thomas were both advocates of rapid industrialization and a high level of self-reliance. Possibly they underestimated the contradictions involved.

The debate about the Tanzanian industrialization strategy, initiated by the dependency theorists, eventually led to a renewed and intensified concentration on industry. In fact, the third five-year plan (1976-81) emphasized the important role of large industries in the process of development, a view that constrats sharply to the Arusha Declaration. We shall return to this new strategy and its conseuqences after having examined the critique of the dependency school in Tanzania.

Imperialism or Uncaptured Peasantry?

The position of the dependency school in Tanzania was unchallenged during the first half of the 1970s, although the mood at the university started to change as early as 1972-3,[17] mainly as a result of Issa Shivji's critique of the Tanzanian development strategy, which paved the way for a critique of the dependency school.[18] The ensuing debate turned into a showdown between different scholars influenced by Marxism.

The early Marxist critique was theoretically abstract, and differed little from what has already been discussed in Chapter 4. Those who contributed were familiar with the international debate, which thus again was imported to Africa.[19] We shall, therefore, confine ourselves to Marc Wuyts's comments on Samir Amin's work (Wuyts, 1976). Wuyts did not object to the fact that Amin's analysis was based on the accumulation of capital and its various forms:

> Indeed the analysis of the accumulation of capital is essentially a study of how the reproduction of the social relations of production condition the development of productive forces, and of how this development of productive forces may give rise to the development of contradictions within the social formation. It follows if we postulate that there is a fundamental difference between capital accumulation in the 'centre' and in the 'periphery', our attention should be drawn to analysing whether the configuration of social relations of production and the way in which they condition the development of productive forces and contradictions which arise from this, develop differently in the 'centre' as against the 'periphery'. Furthermore, we should be equipped with a theoretical analysis of how the 'periphery' links up with the 'centre' at the level of social relations of production.
> (Ibid., pp 2-3)

Wuyts did, however, object to the way in which Amin carried out this analysis. In his model of global capital accumulation Amin distinguished between two types of capitalism: one was 'autocentric' and another was 'blocked'. Defined by the links between various sectors in the economy, these two types of capitalism formed the backbone of Amin's analysis, and that, in Wuyts's opinion, was a fundamental mistake: Amin saw the capital accumulation as a process of structural interaction between economic sectors, rather than seeking its determining factors at the level of social relations of production.

Amin did in fact, analyse the formation of new social relations of production in the Third World. According to Wuyts, he then came very close to an understanding of the 'process of partial dissolution and the partial conservation of pre-capitalist modes of production', but he never got down to an analysis of how these new social relations of production conditioned the development of productive forces. Rather he related it back to the structural level (ibid., p 5). Amin's analysis of underdevelopment was therefore structuralist, not Marxist, since it was based on a 'structuralist definition of capitalism'. In other words, the links between different economic sectors explained why some countries were developed and others underdeveloped.

The ensuing Marxist debate was kept at an abstract level and contained no attempts to provide concrete explanations of 'African underdevelopment'. Hypotheses which had been empirically tested elsewhere in an attempt to disprove some of the dependency theory's fundamental postulates, were instead 'imported' and thoroughly studied. Gradually, however, a more 'African' critique of the dependency school emerged. By African critique, we mean a critique that was based on uniquely African experiences. In view of the fact that the African economies are mostly agrarian, it was also quite natural that such a critique should pay special attention to the peasant's role in the process of development. Thus, based on concrete studies of these agrarian economies, several authors attempted to elaborate on new Marxist approaches (see e.g. Bernstein, 1976 and 1977a). These types of studies might be thought of as contributions to the new more or less Marxist trend in development theory, built on African experiences. One example of such studies is a book written by Goran Hyden (Hyden, 1980), which is interesting since it deals with uniquely African development problems, in an original way. Presumably, some Marxists will react to the fact that we place Hyden in the Marxist camp, but we consider his contribution as an independent attempt to provide an analysis within the Marxist framework.

During his time as a professor at the University of Dar es Salaam (1972-7) Hyden remained aloof as far as the ongoing development debate was concerned.[20] In his opinion, the intellectual discussion was somewhat 'unreal':

> The parameters of our discussions were set almost exclusively by expatriates to whom modern capitalism and modern socialism were the only known social systems. We were at best able to open the doors to the social realities of Tanzania, but the discussions never led us closer to them. Instead, these discussions often became ends in themselves.

> It was a struggle to set the rules for our intellectual exercises. It was a matter of who could convince whom, regardless of any test of validity of that viewpoint in the context of the Tanzanian situation. We saw social structures where none exists. We detected enemies where there were none. There was a danger that our expertise, instead of being used to help Tanzania overcome its problems of underdevelopment, was reduced to that of producing social-science fiction. Like Don Quixote we were engaged in an imaginary struggle that kept us going intellectually but turned us into caricatures in the eyes of non-academic observers. We were about to lose our credibility as people concerned with the problem of overcoming underdevelopment. We were indeed part of that problem ourselves.
> (Ibid., pp. 5-6)

As we have already seen, the Marxists were of the opinion that underdevelopment in the Third World was not only a result of foreign penetration. Instead they pointed out the existence of pre-capitalist modes of production which were so strong that they blocked the progress of the capitalist mode of production. Thus, at an abstract and theoretical level there was, in fact, a Marxist explanation of the causes of underdevelopment, but what is this social formation like which, so effectively, has stood in the way of development in Africa? It is uniquely African, and how does it affect development?
ment in Africa? Is it uniquely African, and how does it affect development?

Hyden's analysis starts with the process of material production, based upon which he defines different modes of production. What is unique about the countries south of the Sahara is a specific mode of production which Hyden calls 'the peasant mode of production' (he excludes the Republic of South Africa and Zimbabwe). This mode of production has three characteristics. First, a rudimentary division of labour. Each unit of production is small, and without any real product specialization there is a little exchange between the production units. But although the peasant households are not usually self-sufficient, management decisions are taken in the light of domestic needs and capabilities, and this is important. This mode of production thus contains no structural links that lead to interdependent relations between the households – which, in turn, would lead to the development of the productive forces. In fact, the production units are independent of each other, and the extent to which producers co-operate is not governed by structural factors, but rather by a common concern for survival. Co-operation between peasants is therefore incidental, e.g. in emergency situations only, irregular and informal.

Secondly, agriculture is resource based, i.e. the African peasant's production is limited to that which nature provides in his immediate surroundings, and not easily improved by modern agricultural machinery.

Thirdly, the peasant mode of production is characterized by the fact that the state forces itself upon the peasants. They do not need the state for their own reproduction, and prefer to do without its interference.

Each mode of production gives rise to its own type of economy. A capitalist society is dominated by the market economy, in which the fundamental contradiction is the contradiction between labour and capital. This is not the case in 'the peasant mode of production'. As Hyden describes it:

> The peasant mode gives rise to an economy in which the effective ties based on common descent, common residence, etc. prevail. We refer to it here as an 'economy of affection'. In the absence of contradictions that characterize social action in capitalist and socialist modes of production, familial and other communal ties provide the basis for organized activity. Communal action prevails and conflicts naturally tend to arise between communities rather than between other forms of social organization. Peasants are not likely to engage in class action unless their chances of reproducing their own mode of production are in danger. As long as the peasant mode is kept alive, other forms of social action will prevail. This is the case even in situations where the peasantry may be effectively incorporated into the capitalist or socialist economy. The main reason for this is that the economy of affection is primarily concerned with the problems of reproduction rather than production.
> (Ibid., p 18)

Hyden claims that the cause of African underdevelopment should not be sought in the international system, but in the rural areas of that continent, where a unique pre-capitalist (or pre-socialist) mode of production, following specific rules, has not only managed to survive, but to dominate the social formations in these countries. A 'modern' mode of production, like the capitalist one, has not managed to eliminate 'the peasant mode' and clear a path for development. This is because the pre-capitalist mode has blocked all roads to cheaper production of the means of subsistence, i.e. it represents an obstacle to capitalism, the expansion of which is based on a continuously rationalized and cheapened production of these commodities. The capitalist mode of production has therefore become weakened and incapable of eliminating 'the peasant mode' (ibid., p 22).

The power structure, and particularly the role of the state, in the Third World constitute central issues in the dependency school's analyses. A brief discussion of Hyden's views on the role of the state in Tanzania, and a comment on the differences between Hyden and the approaches taken by the dependency theorists in this respect is therefore called for.

A modern society (capitalist or socialist) is characterized by the fact that the state is an integral part of the existing production system, implying that those who control the state also control society. Thus, when the dependency theorists claimed that the African economies were dominated by the capitalist mode of production, while they at the same time claimed that the dominant class was still the foreign bourgeoisie, the inevitable conclusion was that these economies were dominated by foreign capital. This picture of the Tanzanian power structure is, in Hyden's opinion, completely misleading, because it is based on the notion that those who control the state also control society. Tanzania is not dominated by capitalism, but by 'the peasant mode of production', and the peasants have remained relatively independent because of the lack of effective instruments of power to influence their actions. 'Small is powerful.' Those in control of the state have therefore not been in control of society. The state has simply not had at its disposal the means to increase agricultural production (ibid., p 23).

Dependency Theory in Action: The Tanzanian Experience

At the risk of oversimplifying, we might say that while the dependency theorists blamed the country's ailments on imperialism, the Marxist critics to a larger extent included internal causes. This led to a politically coloured power struggle at the university. The first round went to the dependency theorists, supported by the rulers of the country who, of course, were not interested in admitting their own mistakes.

A large number of the foreign visitors were forced to leave the university as a result of the power struggle. It is interesting to note that some of the members of this group were among those who introduced the dependency theory in Tanzania, e.g. John Saul and Lionel Cliffe, who both subsequently changed their views about the dependency school. One might say that Tanzania suffered a 'brain drain' during the period 1972-5. Some of the scholars returned home (e.g. Saul, who went back to Canada), while others continued their work in other African countries. One group went to Mozambique (including Wuyts) and another to Zambia (Bhagavan and Cliffe among others). This latter group soon ran into the same kind of problems it had faced in Tanzania, and was later forced to leave Zambia as well. The pointing out of internal problems had once again proved to be dangerous.[21]

Meanwhile, the dependency theorists in Tanzania consolidated their position at the university by outmanoeuvring most of their critics. However, attitudes began to change when the country experienced an economic crisis during the mid-1970s. Many abandoned the dependency school, not so much because of their theoretical convictions, but rather because of their practical experiences. It had been difficult to translate the dependency theory into practical, usable policies.[22] One of the most important objectives of the Tanzanian development strategy was to achieve 'self-reliance'. The dependence created by imperialism was to be broken by the mobilization of domestic resources, but the expected surplus from agricultural production had not materialized. Agricultural production was almost at a complete standstill – a situation which could not be ascribed to imperialism alone. New ideas were needed, including a look at the country's internal problems.

Above we described how the third Tanzanian five-year plan (1976-81) shifted to industrial development, with a special emphasis on heavy industry. This new line of thought was inspired by dependency theorists like Clive Thomas, whose writings led to a heated debate on the relevance for a small economy like Tanzania of a large-scale 'Soviet-type model' of industrialization. Experience had now shown that the practical application of this type of model required a number of revisions (e.g. the early realization of the fact that the time frame was totally unrealistic). Tanzania is a poor country lacking the resources required to carry out the strategy in its entirety; thus, the practical application of the model necessitated a number of compromises. The results were not exactly what the dependency theorists had expected, particularly in the area of international relations. Large international industrial corporations are, for example, no longer viewed with the same amount of scepticism – after all, they do possess both capital and technology, which are sorely needed in Tanzania. Thus, in conclusion, we might say that the Tanzanian experiences during the 1970s once again proved that the real world is far more complex than the dependency school figured it to be.

Capitalism or Simple Dependency: The Kenyan Debate

Leaving Tanzania, and looking at the other English-speaking countries in Africa, we find the effects of the dependency school wearing off noticeably. We also find that research from a dependency perspective was primarily done by non-Africans. In this respect, however, it is no different from other social science research on Africa. For instance, of all the social science research published in East Africa during the period 1963-75, only 12 per cent was done by Africans (Killick, 1975b, p 4).

The low level of interest in the dependency school was partly due to the low priority afforded development issues in both research and education in those countries. As late as 1973, some 70 per cent of the students enrolled in African universities studied literature and administrative subjects (N'Diaye, 1973, p 51). Many therefore saw the educational system as both obsolete and irrelevant to the needs of African societies. Ki-zerbo described it as a 'malignant tumor', and Perceira conceived of the universities as a place 'where you fiddle while Rome burns' (Perceira, 1971, p 40).

As far as research done by Africans is concerned, we have already pointed out that the opportunities for development research were almost non-existent before the advent of the dependency school. This is still the case in many countries. We have found that development problems at one university belong to the subject of sociology, at another to political science, and at a third to economics. The choice of problems has, furthermore, been rather *ad hoc*, which explains the lack of continuity in the research on African development problems. Paul Streeten has, for example, characterized it as irrelevant to the needs of the countries, and claimed that its basic purpose has been to intensify foreign exploitation (Streeten, 1974).

Why have development issues played such a minor part in these countries compared to Tanzania? The most important reason is, of course, that the general political conditions have been so totally different. Whereas Tanzania provided opportunities for development research and education, particularly in a dependency perspective, the other English-speaking countries did not. Here we could compare the Tanzanian case to that of Jamaica in the 1970s. The institutional conditions were similarly poor: most African social science research is done at the universities, but since education has first priority, research is afforded a relatively minor role (Ghai, 1974b, p 1). Several governments created research institutes at various universities during the 1970s, but these institutes have not only suffered from a serious shortage of personnel, but have also been employed mainly in the construction of development plans, in the formulation of policies, and in the evaluation of various projects (ibid., p 2). The preconditions required for *theoretical* research on development have thus been missing.

In trying to explain why the dependency theory was so important in Tanzania, President Nyerere's role as the country's intellectual leader must not be forgotten.[23] Although he criticized the dependency theorists occasionally (as they criticized him) they nevertheless always worked under his protection. Again a comparison could be made with Michael Manley in Jamaica.

In order to provide a contrast to the Tanzanian development debate, we may examine the debate in Kenya. The preconditions for a successful application of the dependency theory in Kenya may have seemed particularly good, not least because of the greater influence of foreign capital. Colin Leys was the foremost advocate of the dependency perspective in Kenya. As a professor at the University of Nairobi, and as author of a number of articles (see e.g. Leys, 1970), he was able to disseminate the ideas of the dependency school during the 1970s. A number of foreign dependency theorists at the Institute for Development Studies[24] (e.g. Raphael Kaplinsky and Steven Langdon) concentrated their research efforts on the Kenyan development problem during that same period.

These dependency theorists started a debate among the teachers and students at the university, but it never went beyond the discussion stage and the university campus.[25] A thorough analysis of Kenyan society from the dependency perspective was not made until 1975; behind that was, of course, Leys (Leys, 1975). Although his book was diligently read and discussed at the university, the dependency school never really gained much influence in Kenya. The few Kenyans who were involved in development research were rather critical of the dependency school,[26] not least because of the fact that Leys, only a year after the publication of his dependency analysis, rejected the approach (Leys, 1977 and 1979).

On the surface, the political conditions in Kenya for more radical development research seemed favourable during the 1970s. The media, for instance, carried a relatively open debate and offered some criticism of the government. 'All' that was required was that the debate be confined to the intellectuals and never used for practical or political purposes.[27] This type of research was, nevertheless, almost totally absent in Kenya among indigenous researchers. One of the reasons might be the country's system of remuneration: it is neither economically nor academically rewarding to work with these issues, which explains why the work that has been done has been done almost exclusively by visiting, foreign scholars. Moreover, the dialogue between the expatriates and the Kenyan authorities, as well as the formers' influence on practical policies, have, for all intents and purposes, been almost non-existent.

A lack of resources combined with the fact that the 'market mechanism' has been used to allocate the educated Kenyans since independence are additional factors affecting social science research in Kenya.[28] A great deal of research has, as a consequence, been done in the form of official reports. A multitude of consulting firms have sprung up, all specializing in official reports, and all sorely lacking in the area of data collection and in thoroughness.[29] This has also affected the country's academic education. University teachers often neglect their teaching responsibilities, since it is more profitable to work on consulting jobs, either for private firms, or for some government authority.[30]

Although domestic research on development in Kenya was negligible, there were other students of Kenya who made important contributions. We have already mentioned Colin Leys. His reversed attitude to the dependency approach gave rise to a considerable debate on whether or not a dependency model was applicable to Kenya. The particular point of concern in this debate was the proper characterization of the indigenous industrial bourgeoisie. Since this debate is important, not least because it is presumably the most comprehensive debate between Marxists and dependency theorists concerning the relevance of the dependency approach to one particular country, it is worth going into in more detail.

In his 1975 book, Leys was pessimistic about the prospects for Kenyan capitalism, the reason being that the indigenous bourgeoisie was largely defined by its relationship to foreign capital. Furthermore, this, as he called it, 'auxiliary' bourgeoisie ran its alliance with foreign capital. The view that Kenya could not 'adopt the bourgeois mode of production' and develop their productive forces within it, was also supported by several of the scholars at the Institute of Development Studies (IDS) in Nairobi, for instance Steven Langdon (Langdon, 1974, 1975a, 1975b and 1977).

Other students of Kenya, particularly Michael Cowen and Nicola Swainson, were, however, of a different opinion. They had concentrated their research on the historical roots of the indigenous bourgeoisie. Using comprehensive empirical material, Cowen, for instance, argued that the indigenous capital accumulation not only was substantial and growing, but that it had its roots in pre-colonial Kenya (see Cowen, 1972, 1976, 1979a, 1979b, 1980a, 1980b; and Cowen and Kinyanjui, 1977). By tracing the roots of the indigenous bourgeoisie back to pre-colonial times he rejected the characterization of this bourgeoisie solely in relation to foreign capital. Furthermore, the political base of the post-colonial state was, according to Cowen, founded on the interests of the Kenyan bourgeoisie.

Swainson also objected to the thesis about the indigenous bourgeoisie's inability to act in accordance with national interests (Swainson, 1977 and 1980). She tried to show the existence of a relatively independent and productive investing group of Kenyan capitalists by pointing at such evidence as the expansion of the number of joint ventures between Kenyans and foreigners, the Africanization of management in the foreign firms, the recent state of regulatory mechanisms *vis-à-vis* foreign firms, etc., and her conclusion was that

> in comparison with large multinational firms in Kenya, indigenous capital is small and insignificant. Nevertheless, at the *present stage* of accumulation in Kenya it is still the case that value formation is *nationally* based and the state is able to support the interests of the internal bourgeoisie. During the independence period, within the limits set by Kenya's position in the global economy, the indigenous bourgeoisie have extended their control over the means of production.
> (Swainson, 1980, p 289)

Influenced by these studies, Colin Leys returned to the debate (Leys, 1978). His pessimism about the prospects for Kenyan capitalism was now gone, and he criticized his own previous work:

> Instead of seeing the strength of the historical tendency lying behind the emergence of the African bourgeoisie I tended to see only the relatively small size and technical weakness of African capital in the face of international capital, and to envisage the state as little more than a register of this general imbalance; rather than seeing the barriers of capital, scale and technology as relative, and the state as the register of the leading edge of indigenous capital in its assault on those barriers.
> (Ibid., p 251)

Leys now emphasized the extension of capitalist relations of production: the principal force in this process was the emergent indigenous bourgeoisie and the state apparatus under its control. Influenced by Cowen and Swainson he argued that the settlers' capital had radically undermined the pre-capitalist relations of production, and prepared the way for the take-over by an indigenous bourgeoisie. Its control of the state had recently been used to make considerable encroachments on manufacturing industry and the prospects for the indigenous bourgeoisie to play a leading role in the transition to industrial capitalism were favourable.

Several scholars, of course, reacted strongly to this sudden change of view, trying to show that Leys's earlier dependency position was in fact more correct. Raphael Kaplinsky and Steven Langdon both presented impressive empirical evidence to support the thesis that Kenya was still a dependent country (Kaplinsky, 1980 and Langdon, 1980). In his review of the post-independence industrialization in Kenya, Langdon reached the conclusion that 'growing industrialization is having only limited effects on social transformation, because of restricted employment and linkage effects', and Kaplinsky continued:

> I believe that the evidence shows that, although an indigenous capitalist class has managed to carve out a slice of the benefits arising from accumulating in large scale industry, this has arisen from the alliance between this class and foreign capital. Not only does little prospect emerge for indigenous capital to squeeze out foreign capital, but the inbuilt contradictions of economies of this type make it difficult to foresee that such a pattern of accumulation – with or without foreign capital – can proceed in a viable form.
> (Kaplinsky, 1980, p 31)

Leys answered his critics by accusing them of empiricism and of being a-historical. The question was, however, who was 'correct'? Both sides obviously had empirical evidence to support their conclusions. In a most valuable comment on the debate, Björn Beckman had the following answer:

> On the whole, I believe that the overall picture of a dependent, neo-colonial economy and its ruling class, as summarized above, can be sustained by contemporary Kenyan evidence more or less point by point, just as it could in the case of Nigeria. I also believe that the evidence summoned by Leys and Swainson to indicate new elements in the situation can be largely incorporated into the dependency perspective as changes which do not significantly alter the overall pattern of dependency and underdevelopment. It may even be shown, as ventured by Kaplinsky and Langdon, that some of these changes, such as indigenous private and state participation industry, may in fact reinforce the underdevelopment syndrome as defined by the dependency line. However, the opposite also seems true. It seems quite possible to integrate the empirical evidence quoted by Kaplinsky and Langdon into the anti-dependency pursued by Leys. The continued (or growing) presence of foreign capital, the close links between foreign and domestic capital (private and state), the low employment and linkage generating capacity of the present pattern of industrial growth, are all compatible with an emphasis on the growing influence (power) of the domestic bourgeoisie, on its own and via the state apparatus.
> (Beckman, 1980, p 53)

Beckman thus reached the conclusion that the differences of emphasis in the interpretation of the overall growth potential of the Kenyan economy were inconclusive.

> The evidence on its own is neither here nor there. Its significance depends on the interpretation given to it, which (again) is determined by the theoretical position taken. The inconclusive nature of the

> argument is caused not by contradictory or inconclusive evidence but by the weaknesses of the theoretical positions from which such evidence has been selected, ordered, and interpreted.
> (Ibid., p 54)

The Kenyan debate, whether or not a dependency model is applicable to the country, clearly shows that the early dependency conclusion, i.e. that capitalist development in the periphery is impossible, was not defensible. However, it also shows the imperfections of the alternatives to the dependency approach. The revised and current dependency position has obviously overcome the simplistic ideas of the earlier *dependentistas*. The dependency theorists have thus accepted and incorporated much of the Marxist critique, without totally rejecting the dependency position. In the Kenyan debate, for example, they accept the fact that the domestic bourgeoisie has roots in the pre-colonial past and has developed a momentum of its own (Godfrey, 1982, p 272). One may therefore conclude that, as long as the Marxists refer to development only as 'the development of the productive forces', it is difficult to see their alternative to the dependency school as their last word.

Notes

1. Exemplified by the situation in East Africa (Kenya, Tanzania and Uganda). In 1961 there was only one university in the entire region; Makerere in Kampala, which was not an autonomous university, but merely a branch of the University of London. The number of students who obtained their degree during this particular year was 99. This figure should be seen in relation to the population of 23 millions for the entire region (see Court, 1975 and Anyang' Nyong'o, 1978).
2. See Anyang' Nyong'o (1978) and James (1979). An excellent bibliography of research done on East Africa between 1963 and 1975 is found in Killick (1975).
3. An extensive analysis of this is found in Ashby (1966).
4. A UN sponsored evaluation of the IDEP's first years of activities criticized this narrow-minded orientation, referring to the IDEP charter and the needs of the African nations. It was also pointed out that the teaching was much too conventional, and that similar skills could be acquired elsewhere at lower costs.
5. It is interesting to note that Amin is considered to be of Nobel Prize class in *Economic Development and Cultural Exchange*, a periodical which mainly sticks to the modernization paradigm (October 1978, p 195). However, the author of this somewhat surprising article, Martin Bronfenbrenner, is not quite sure that his readers have heard of Samir Amin. As a safety precaution, he adds that this Amin should not be mistaken for another well-known African with the same surname!
6. 'I have probably not reminded the readers sufficiently of the debt which

I, as well as the entire non-apologetic economic theory of underdevelopment, owe to Latin America. The initiator is Raúl Prebisch, and it is to him and the ECLA that we must be thankful for the main part of the critical theory to which I belong; the ECLA has initiated the reflections out of which the current Latin American thoughts have grown; i.e. the critique of the policy of import substitution and the theory of dependence' (Amin, 1970). The reference to the Egyptian Communist Party is from a conversation in Gothenburg, March 1981.

7. Amin defines 'luxury goods' as goods the demand for which arises from the consumed part of the profit (Amin, 1971b, p 25).
8. Tanzania is usually considered to be part of the English-speaking region, although its official language is Kiswahili.
9. Tanganyika became independent in 1961. In 1964 it entered into an association with Zanzibar under the common name of Tanzania.
10. Nabudere describes this period as follows: 'Most of the first 'left' academics who came to the Hill particularly after 1967 were the neo-Marxist type, neo-Marxism being a by-product of Trotskyism in Western Europe, USA and Latin America. This phenomenon was strengthened by the literature that was characteristic of the Dar es Salaam University Bookshop in the period 1968-1972. These were mainly Trotskyist books by people like Isaac Deutscher and Trotsky himself. Then we had the Monthly Review group of Paul A. Baran and Paul Sweezy, and lastly in the later period the Gunder Frank Latin American 'underdevelopment' school. This latter group of literature was later popularised on this continent by the prolific neo-Marxist Samir Amin. The late-comer to this neo-Trotskyist piling literature was the British New Left Review. Marxist-Leninist classics were kept in the background and were not encouraged for these neo-Trotskyists regarded the classical works as 'too difficult' and as not helpful in the present epoch' (Nabudere, 1977a, pp 61-2).
11. Tamás Szentes was another interesting name in Tanzania during the early 1970s. He held a chair in Economics in Dar es Salaam between 1969 and 1971. Greatly influenced by the dependency school, he published *The Political Economy of Underdevelopment* (Szentes, 1971) after his return to Hungary, and was thus able to disseminate the thoughts of the dependency school in Eastern Europe.
12. The works published by dependency theorists visiting Tanzania were, of course, not all written in the spirit of André Gunder Frank. As in Latin America, there were several different views in Tanzania; however, it is outside the scope of this book to discuss them, since they, in our opinion, have added very little original thought to the dependency school. We have therefore chosen Walter Rodney as an example. The interested reader may turn to Arrigi and Saul (1973); Cliffe and Saul (1972 and 1973); Seidman (1972 and 1976) and Tachanneerl (1976).
13. Rodney (1972), p 34. Like Frank, he also uses the concept of metropolis and satellite.
14. In his extreme emphasis on the economic factor he also uses the following: 'the fact that over $500 million flowed outward from the underdeveloped countries in 1965 . . . gives some idea of the extent to which the wealth of Africa is being drained off . . .' (ibid., p 32).
15. Together with Shivji's original article these comments have been pub-

lished under the title *The Silent Class Struggle* (Tanzania Publishing House, 1973a).

16. A summary of the entire discussion that followed Shivji's thesis is found in Omwony-Ojwok (1977). See also UTAFITI, Vol. 111, no. 2, 1978, which is a special issue on the African class struggle.
17. M.R. Bhagavan; conversation in Stockholm, August 1980.
18. See particularly Nabudere (1975) and Wuyts (1976).
19. Wuyts (1976) indicates that this criticism was theoretically inspired by authors with whom we have already dealt. He himself refers to e.g., Geoffrey Kay's book *Development and Underdevelopment* as an important source of inspiration. Goran Hyden has, in this context, emphasized the important role played by Henry Bernstein, during his tenure as a professor in Tanzania (conversation in Nairobi, March 1980).
20. Goran Hyden; conversation in Nairobi, March 1980.
21. M.R. Bhagavan; conversation in Stockholm, August 1980.
22. E.g. Justinian Rweyemamu, who left his position as Nyerere's economic adviser and began to work for the Brandt Commission.
23. Goran Hyden; conversation in Nairobi, March 1980.
24. The Institute for Development Studies (the IDS) was founded in 1965, and has, since 1970, enjoyed the status of a faculty at the University of Nairobi. The Institute is primarily a multidisciplinary research centre which, to a great extent, has been financed by foreign means. Up until the mid-1970s, visiting scholars dominated at the IDS, but the number of Kenyan researchers is now on the rise.
25. Kabiru Kinyanjui; conversation in Nairobi, March 1980.
26. For instance Kabiru Kinyanjui. See Cowen and Kinyanjui (1977) and Kinyanjui (1979).
27. The writer Ngugi wa Thiongo is a good example. As long as his plays were written in English he was allowed to carry on, despite his often biting critique of the authorities (see e.g. *Petals of Blood*, Nairobi, 1976). His audience, largely intellectuals, was considered to be relatively 'harmless'. But he was interned when he staged a play based on class consciousness, in the rural district and in a language spoken by the locals (Kikuyu).
28. A thorough discussion on this is found in Court (1975).
29. David Court, conversation in Nairobi, March 1980.
30. A number of students in Nairobi felt that this was the real reason for the student riots at the university in the beginning of the 1980s, and not the 'infiltration of world communism', as the authorities claimed (see *Nation*, 6 March 1980).

8. Beyond Dependency: New Trends in Development Theory

Judging from the current debate in development theory, the demise of the dependency school has left an awkward theoretical vacuum. The critics are generally less successful in pointing out *new* theoretical directions. In this chapter we attempt to identify the major current alternatives to the dependency school from the different reactions to the challenge from the *dependentistas*. There have been four such reactions. First, the fundamentalists, who have totally rejected the dependency approach. Secondly, the theoretical traditions that try to incorporate the dependency perspective within their own frameworks. This has been done both by Marxists and non-Marxists. Thirdly, the current Marxist mode of production approach, which seems to be a more genuinely *new* Marxist direction, and, fourthly, different attempts to elaborate on the dependency approach. This fourth category contains approaches showing a strong continuity back to the dependency school. In what follows we examine these alternatives and we also try to assess their relevance.

Fundamentalist Reactions

The weakening of the dependency school has resulted in a revival of both *classical Marxism* and the *modernization paradigm*. This is quite natural, since both these theoretical traditions were the main targets of the critique from the *dependentistas*. Although it is wrong to call these *new* theoretical developments, they must be included among current trends in development theory since they have both experienced a renaissance.

The Return to Classical Marxism

It appears from Chapter 1 that Marxism may be thought of as a theory of development, a theory of the development of capitalism containing some indications of an eventual transition from capitalism to socialism. In connection with our discussion of Marx's views on the 'backward' countries (Chapter 2), we also mentioned some of the difficulties involved in applying his theory to the problem of 'underdevelopment'. These difficulties include, for instance, Marx's view on 'progress' which he shared, of course, with the prevailing 19th Century evolutionism (including the ethnocentric presumption), the tying of the conceptual apparatus to a 'national economy', the notion of different national economies going through a basically similar process of capitalist development, etc. Considering the Marxist claim to universality, its contributions to the solution of the problems of underdevelopment are rather meagre – in fact, this entire area must be considered one of the great gaps in classical Marxist theory. This is the light in which we should see not only the rise of so-called neo-Marxism, but also the latter's need to be tangibly free in its relations with its Marxist heritage.

In connection with our survey of the critique of the dependency school we also commented on the fact that neo-Marxism is more and more being regarded as divergent from Marxist theory. This criticism has prepared the ground for the return of a classical, Marxist view on underdevelopment. The best example of this is Bill Warren's brave effort to revive the original Marxian idea of capitalism (including imperialism) as historically progressive (Warren, 1973 and 1980). Although Warren correctly revealed many of the mistakes made by the *dependentistas*, he uncritically repeated a rather sterile and mechanical Marxism. According to Warren, 'imperialism was the means through which techniques, culture, and institutions that had evolved in Western Europe over several centuries . . . sowed their revolutionary seeds in the rest of the world' (Warren, 1980, p 136). He also claimed that capitalism and democracy were 'linked virtually as Siamese twins' (ibid., p 28).

The kind of Marxism Warren represents has aptly been called 'neo-classical Marxism' by Dudley Seers (Seers, 1978). This term refers not only to the return to the Master, but also to the logical conclusions of the analysis. Although Warren explicitly starts from a Marxist position he nevertheless comes to much the same conclusions as do the neo-classical economists. This, according to Seers, is because both schools have their roots in the classics – Smith and Ricardo – and because both of them were developed in Europe during the 19th Century, thus having numerous common elements. 'Both doctrines assume competitive markets and the over-riding importance of material incentives. They are both basically internationalist and also optimistic, technocratic and economistic. In particular, they both treat economic growth as "development" and as due primarily to capital accumulation.' (Ibid.)

The political implications of Warren's analysis are even more clearly shown by Ronaldo Munck, referring to Warren's political activities in Ireland:

> In the early 1970s he [Warren] was a prime mover of the British and Irish communist organization which became notorious for its support of the most reactionary social groups in Ireland. It supported the pro-imperialist settlers of the Northeast whose historic mission was to build capitalism (in association with British imperialism) against the reactionary pretensions and outdated myths emerging from the 'green fog' of Irish nationalism.
> (Munck, 1981, p 169)

Most Marxists find Warren's evolutionistic views on development untenable (see e.g. Leys, 1978 and Taylor, 1979), but that does not mean that they approve of the kind of 'Marxism' expressed by the dependency school. As an example of the growing awareness of the fact that Marx's original views on development were in need of a revision, we quote the following:

> The appearance of systematic barriers to economic advance in the course of capitalist expansion – the 'development of underdevelopment' – has posed difficult problems for Marxist theory. There has arisen, in response, a strong tendency sharply to revise Marx's conceptions regarding economic development. In part, this has been a healthy reaction to the Marx of the *Manifesto*, who envisioned a more or less direct and inevitable process of capitalist expansion: undermining old modes of production, replacing them with capitalist social productive relations and, on this basis, setting off a process of capital accumulation and economic development more or less following the pattern of the original homelands of capitalism.
> (Brenner, 1977, p 25)

The Rise of Neo-Liberalism

The development perspective associated with the modernization paradigm has also revived after the demotion of the dependency school. Significantly enough, *monetarism*, which in the context of development strategies implies an extreme *laissez-faire* policy, has experienced a renaissance in Latin America. This has been the case particularly in Chile, the former stronghold not only of the dependency school but also of the ECLA tradition. The current modernization theory is, however, hardly different from that discussed in Chapter 1, so its theoretical value today is therefore negligible. Its actual importance should rather be explained by political factors.

The current free trade-modernization orthodoxy (as well as the neoclassical Marxists) generally refers to the 'phenomenal' growth of the 'four little dragons' in Asia as examples of what positive impact the integration into the 'modern' world may have. The experiences of these countries are referred to as cases contradicting the dependency perspective and as triumphs for the free play of the market forces. In Chapter 6 we argued, however, that this simple explanation to the NICs' success does not contain the whole truth. First of all, the 'phenomenal' growth of the NICs has not been unrelated to their political systems – repressive military regimes, whose popularity among the proponents of the free market forces is hard to understand. Moreover, it is problematic to regard the NICs as a group with one single strategy, since they differ quite substantially among themselves. We also pointed to some myths surrounding the NIC model by showing not only that a regime of import substitution preceded the export-oriented policy, but also that extensive state intervention had been present.

If one is interested in studying the effects of the strategy recommended by the free trade-modernization orthodoxy, one would do better to look at the Chilean experience. Chile is one country that really has tried to follow the recommendations from this orthodoxy without restrictions. During the 1970s this country became almost a laboratory for the 'Chicago boys', and their purpose was to 'transform Chile not into a nation of proletarians but into a nation of proprietors'. The catastrophic experiences of the monetarists' experiments in Chile, as well as in other Latin American countries, particularly Argentina and Uruguay, are familiar enough.

At the CANCUN meeting in October 1981 the modernization philosophy was translated into *global Reaganomics* and the 'Keynesian' strategy of the Brandt Commission report *North-South: A Programme for Survival*, which was meant to provide the framework for the discussion, was tacitly buried. In terms of development strategy the Brandt report articulated a 'Keynesian' solution to world poverty by proposing a massive resource transfer. The poor people of the world were to function as the unemployed in Keynes's system. As they made use of the financial resources (petrodollars in particular) to buy goods produced by the industrial countries, the economic problems of the latter would be solved as well. The rich and poor countries were to move forward together rather than the poor countries being given benefits at the expense of the rich world, which was the strategy of the earlier UNCTAD reform proposals. But instead of this *global Keynesianism*, the 'developing countries' were now advised to liberalize their economies, encourage their entrepreneurs and find out their comparative advantages, all in accordance with the neo-classical theory.

Incorporation and Reabsorption of the Dependency Problematic

Another approach to the challenge posed by dependency theory has been to incorporate the problematic into existing theoretical frameworks, Marxist or non-Marxist. In what follows we shall give some examples from both traditions.

The Marxification of Dependency

One way of eliminating classical Marxism's inherent theoretical difficulties with the phemenon of underdevelopment has been to elaborate on Marx's own distinction between *industrial* and *merchant capital*, blaming the latter for the persistence of underdevelopment. This may be seen as an effort at 'Marxification' of dependency.

The basic difference between merchant capital and industrial capital is that only the latter is capable of generating surplus value, despite the fact that all the commodities in the process are exchanged at prices that are equivalent to their values. Merchant capital must therefore be created by means of non-equivalent or 'unequal exchanges'. This type of capital is, according to Marx, historically prerequisite to the growth of the capitalist mode of production. It promotes the production of commodities in the pre-capitalist societies, thus increasing the division of labour and the productivity in these societies. However, merchant capital can never by itself bring about the transition from one mode of production to another, since it is dependent upon some kind of non-capitalist class exploiting the labour force; consequently, it is forced to support this class while in the long run undermining its existence. Thus, merchant capital stimulates development while at the same time it constitutes a barrier.

> The history of underdevelopment is the fullest expression we have of these contradictionary tendencies of merchant capital to both stimulate and repress the development of the forces of production and to both open and block the way for the full development of capitalism.
> (Kay, 1975, p 95)

In a capitalist society, merchant capital is only part of the circulation of capital; moreover, it is subject to the productive capital which, as opposed to merchant capital, is basically a social relation. In pre-capitalist societies, however, merchant capital lives a life of its own. The merchant capitalist obtains his profits by arranging trade between different societies and economic systems. This type of trade is something entirely different from trade in a fully developed capitalist society, where it is a question of 'trade between regions that have been integrated into the same system of production and reproduction' (Weeks and Dore, 1979, p 82). Only under these circumstances will capital be accumulated in the Marxist sense. Merchant capital may, of course, grow by a skilful use of the production costs in different economic systems ('unequal exchange'), or as a result of a deterioration of the producers' situation caused by various kinds of political oppression (colonialism), but it will never revolutionize the relations of production and create capitalism. Nor is it possible to say that the 'unequal exchange' generates underdevelopment:

> To argue that the loss of surplus product itself is the cause of backwardness is to see accumulation (or more generally, economic development) as purely a quantitative process. It is also to assume that all the necessary conditions for accumulation were present in precapitalist societies prior to the spread of merchant's capital and the world market. The basis for accumulation is a particular set of social relations, not the availability of a surplus product.
> (Ibid., p 84)

In other words, underdevelopment was not created by 'unequal exchange', but that does not imply that the effects of the latter on the 'backward' nations were positive. The pre-capitalist mode of production was instead strengthened by political alliances between the comprador bourgeoisie and pre-capitalist ruling elites. In fact, this view is not very far from the dependency theoretical standpoint, but the terminology is different, as are the theoretical conclusions. It is further corroborated by the following provocative comment by Kay: 'Capital created underdevelopment not because it exploited the underdeveloped world but because it did not exploit it enough' (Kay, 1975, p X). This often-quoted phrase by Kay has a long history in Marxist thought. In the debate with the Narodniks, Plekhanov and other Marxists repeatedly stated 'We suffer not only from the development of capitalism, but also from the scarcity of that development' (Schwarz, 1955, p 55). Even Joan Robinson used this argument when she said: 'As we see nowadays in South East Asia, or the Caribbean, the misery of being exploited by capitalists is nothing compared to the misery of not being exploited at all' (Robinson, 1962, p 45).

The analysis of merchant capital is the key to Kay's writings about underdevelopment. For reasons which obviously had not been foreseen by classical Marxism, merchant capital remained relatively independent, although subject to industrial capital. However, to accuse merchant capital of being the cause of 'underdevelopment' would be to take the easy way out. First, the definiition of the concept of merchant capital appears to have become somewhat wider than originally intended. The trade between centre and periphery has, after all, been quite different from the classic, long-distance trade between pre-capitalist societies. Nor should it be forgotten that the former type of trade has, occasionally, required extensive changes in the relations of production in the periphery. Kay's claim that industrial capital left the carrying out of these changes to merchant capital, is therefore not just another doubtful widening of Marx's definition of merchant capital (which was limited to the sphere of circulation), but a shattering of it (Bernstein, 1977b, p 57). One might well ask if this is not the distinction between *central and peripheral capitalism* (which the dependency theorists never managed logically to clarify), now appearing in the guise of a distinction between industrial and merchant capital with much the same inherent theoretical difficulties.

What, then, is the role played by merchant capital in the 'underdeveloped' world today? Is it still dominating, and is it still causing the problems facing these countries? The answer according to Kay is no. He uses merchant capital merely as an historical explanation of the origins of 'underdevelopment'. The pressure on merchant capital in the Third World culminated during the 1930s as a result of the declining raw material prices; this, in turn, led to increasing nationalism and demands for economic and political changes. The resulting industrialization has led Kay to believe that it is wrong to think of these countries as producers of raw materials only. After all, industrial production is one of their most important characteristics (Kay, 1975, p 125).

Kay's view of this industrialization is, however, different from that of 'neo-classical' Marxists like Warren: his description of it is, in many ways, similar to what the dependency school called 'dependent', or 'peripheral' capitalism, but it is only a partial development, since only certain sectors are developed and only a small part of the population is employed in these sectors. However, Kay firmly rejects the term 'dependent capitalism'. The high level of unemployment, he says, 'is a *normal* feature of capitalist development, and as such, independent of particular forms of ownership or dependence' (ibid., p 153).

The fact that the manifestation of industrialization in the underdeveloped countries is different from that in the now developed countries is explained by the inability of capital to erase its own history and start all over, as if nothing had happened. Kay says:

> It was forced to operate in the conditions of underdevelopment which it had itself created: conditions that were quite different from those that prevailed in the developed countries in the eighteenth and nineteenth centuries. Thus when industrialization finally started in the underdeveloped world in the 1930s and picked up steam in the post-war period, it was a process altogether different from that which had taken place earlier in the developed countries. It took place in conditions of deeply established underdevelopment which it could not overcome but only reinforce.
> (Ibid., p 124)

Kay speaks, however, of 'conditions of deeply established underdevelopment', without identifying them. His analysis of the ongoing industrialization in the Third World is therefore inadequate. We have returned to the simple notion of merchant capital being the root of all evil.

The Modern Structuralist Approach

Another example of the process of absorption is the *structural* tradition which started with Myrdal, Prebisch, Seers and Singer. It is true that structuralism means different things to different disciplines and therefore covers other theoretical currents. There are, for instance, several structuralist oriented Marxists. We shall, however, limit our discussion to *non-Marxist* authors who view the problems of underdevelopment in a structuralist perspective, authors who believe that the problems of the underdeveloped countries are more or less unique, implying that universally applicable development models are of limited value. Since the difference between the developed and the underdeveloped countries are many and considerable, and since the latter do not constitute a homogeneous group, it is necessary to tailor models for their development to their structural characteristics.

In Chapter 1 we mentioned that some scholars had proposed a structural approach as early as the 1950s. They criticized the neo-classical economists for their almost superstitious belief in the price mechanism's ability to lead the economy into a situation of equilibrium, and pointed out that specific structural factors in the underdeveloped economies, such as the permanently high level of unemployment, required alternative development models. This idea did not become generally accepted until the 1970s. By that time it had become obvious for empirical reasons that the old paradigm was no longer able to provide the answers to the researchers' questions, or to serve as a basis for development strategies – facts which the United Nations 'Development Decade' (the 1960s) had proved to be sadly true. A number of studies indicated *growth without development* instead. One of the leading development economists summed up the experiences gained during that decade:

> It is now clear that more than a decade of rapid growth in underdeveloped countries has been of little or no benefit to perhaps a third of their population. Although the average per capita income of the Third World has increased by 50 per cent since 1960, this growth has been very unequally distributed among countries, regions within countries, and socio-economic groups. Paradoxically, while growth policies have succeeded beyond their expectations of the first development decade, the very idea of aggregate growth as a social objective has increasingly been called into question.
> (Chenery, 1974, p XIII)

The optimism with regard to the underdeveloped countries' development positions was now toned down, and analyses of the problems of development by means of the existing economic models were no longer thought possible. A number of the structural and institutional 'rigidities', which originally had been expected to disappear as a result of economic growth, were still present.

For the economists working on development issues the time had come to let bygones be bygones. Underdevelopment could no longer be explained by the lack of capital. It was rather a question of an entire spectrum of restrictions. A number of 'dogmas' from the early theory of development therefore had to be rejected. We quote Pan Yotopoulos and Jeffrey Nugent:

> The field of development economics, which has thus far been based largely on neoclassical analysis, has considerably underplayed the costs, as opposed to the benefits of development. As a result, it needs both revision and refinement to fit the realities of developing countries . . . there has been too much emphasis on development as a uniform, smooth, and equilibrating process of continuous marginal adjustments. Conversely, too little attention has been devoted to the study of structure and of discontinuous processes and disequilibria, such as those that appear as 'costs' of development. Efforts to deal with disequilibrium and structural changes have been limited either to describing institutions or to discovering correlations among variables. Seldom, if ever, have discussions of disequilibria and structural change delved into the cause and effect relationships in an analytic way . . .far too much attention has [also] been given to a variety of fundamentalist dogmas, such as capital fundamentalism, sectorial fundamentalism, import substitution fundamentalism, and planning fundamentalism.
> (Yotopoulos and Nugent, 1976, p 10)

The alternative to the existing paradigm was what we call the structuralist approach – hardly a new paradigm, but certainly a new way to look at things. The theoretical basis of this was discussed in Chapter 1, where we pointed out that underdevelopment was seen as a problem of structural relations. The structural variables thus entered the analysis explicitly. The early attempts at formulating a 'General Theory of Underdevelopment' were, however, less successful. It turned out to be difficult to find factors and relations that were sufficiently stable over time and space (Bigsten, 1983). Instead, there is now a growing interest in partial analyses, in which separate problems in a development process are put under the magnifying glass. These analyses also use a broader, interdisciplinary approach. The modern structuralists have thus abandoned narrow economic thinking, and the former 'poor cousins' are no longer considered equally uninteresting – *au contraire*: the social, political and cultural factors play an important role in the modern structuralist approach.

The early structuralists furthermore tended to overemphasize either external or internal obstacles to development. Prebisch provides an example of the former, while an example of the latter may be found in Myrdal's *Asian Drama* (Myrdal, 1968). The modern versions on the other hand emphasize the importance of *both* domestic and international structures, as well as the importance of considering the history of the underdeveloped countries. Development is thus no longer thought of as a 'race' in which some of the participants have fallen behind. Since it is more a matter of methodology than theory, the structuralist approach is the least homogeneous of the current trends in modern development thinking. The explicit inclusion of structural relations in the analysis may be considered a common denominator at the abstract level, but at the concrete level, we find different authors emphasizing different relations. This is partly a result of the open attitude which structuralists have displayed *vis-à-vis* other theoretical currents, such as Marxism and/or neo-classical economics. Those who have been influenced by Marxism tend to place greater emphasis on social and political factors than those who take as their point of departure neo-classical economics. What structural relations are emphasized is, of course, also a result of the type of society under study. It seems quite natural for students of Latin America to emphasize international structures, since the role played by foreign capital there is more important than anywhere else in the Third World. It is therefore difficult to offer a concise definition of the modern structuralist approach. However, we believe that more modern structuralists agree with the following:

> This approach (i.e. 'the structural-internationalist' models) views underdevelopment in terms of international and domestic power relationships, institutional and structural economic rigidities, and the resulting proliferation of dual economies and dual societies both within and among the nations of the world. Structuralist theories tend to emphasize external and internal 'institutional' constraints on economic

> development. Emphasis is placed on policies needed to eradicate poverty, to provide more diversified employment opportunities and to reduce income inequalities. These and other egalitarian objectives are to be achieved within the context of growing economy, but economic growth per se is not given the exalted status accorded to it by the linear stages model.
> (Todaro, 1977, p 51)

The Pioneers: Prebisch and Seers: To illustrate the fact that the 'early' structuralists have been influenced by the dependency school, we shall examine some later writings of Raúl Prebisch and Dudley Seers. In the former's recent works it is argued that peripheral capitalism is 'unique' in many respects (Prebisch, 1976, 1978, 1979 and 1980b). The difference between central and peripheral capitalism is that the former is *innovative*, while the latter is *imitative*. This is clarified in the following five points:

1) Technique and consumption.
Owing to the great heterogeneity of the social structure, the fruits of the penetration of technique are appropriated mainly by the privileged strata. Of course, this was also the case in the centres as they began to develop, but there is an important difference:

> The difference lies in that, owing to this form of distribution, consumption patterns are adopted in the Periphery which developed gradually in the centres, as capital accumulation allowed technique to penetrate more and more deeply into the social structure. In the Periphery, in contrast, we are imitating these consumption patterns when accumulation is not sufficient to fulfil its labour-absorbing function; and this situation is aggravated in as much as the centres siphon off income by virtue of their technical and economic supremacy and the weight of their hegemony.
> (Prebisch, 1980b, p 183)

2) Degree of development and democratization.
The democratization process made its breakthrough in the centres when considerable capital accumulation had already been achieved. Peripheral democratization, on the other hand, has evolved before capital accumulation could meet the dynamic requirements of development.

3) Land tenure.
The prevailing system of land tenure in the periphery has been an obstacle to development. In the centres this obstacle was removed at an early stage, with favourable social and technical consequences.

4) The formation of surplus.
In the periphery, the appropriation and distribution of surplus and its effect on capital accumulation has resulted in dualism. This was never the case in

the centre.

5) Population growth.
The development in the centre brought down the rate of mortality, while the changes in the social structure and the social consequences of these changes led to a fall in the birth rate.

A population explosion in the centre was thus prevented. Although the rate of mortality in the periphery has also come down, the birth rate has remained high. This has resulted in a population growth which has only aggravated the problem of insufficient capital accumulation.

Since peripheral capitalism is unique, it also requires a theory of its own.[1] In Prebisch's analysis of peripheral capitalism the appropriation and distribution of the economic surplus is of central importance. The lion's share goes to the 'upper strata' of the social structure, since they own the means of production. This surplus might have been invested to increase the economy's rate of growth, but that is not done. In a way reminiscent of Paul Baran, Prebisch claims that the unequal distribution will lead to luxury consumption (to a 'premature imitation of the consumption patterns of the centres'), and thus waste the potential accumulation of capital. This, and the explosive growth of the population, explains in essence why the 'lower strata' have not been absorbed into the modern, dynamic sector.

However, Prebisch is forced to go one step further in order to find an explanation for the fact that these economies do, in fact, grow, despite the negative effect on capital accumulation of luxury consumption. This growth provides a basis for demands for increased welfare from new social groups, which, in turn, represent new demands for a share of the economic surplus. On the one hand, pressure builds up in the market sphere. As a result of the process of democratization workers form trade unions which provide them with the political power needed to secure a part of the surplus produced. The government, on the other hand, must appropriate part of the surplus in order to be able to absorb a steadily growing part of the labour force. Government employees also form trade unions in order to raise their salaries.

This capitalism, however, lacks a set of norms regulating the actions of the 'middle strata', which implies that a demand from this group for a larger share of the surplus will affect the accumulation of capital negatively; and, as a result of that, the upper strata's profits will decline followed by a series of crises.

> Enterprises react by raising prices in order to reestablish the dynamic of the surplus, and this is followed by a counter-reaction on the part of the labour force, provided it has sufficient power, with the consequent wage increases. Thus an inflationary spiral is triggered off: a new type of social inflation which is superimposed upon and aggravates the effects of other factors. This is how the crisis of the system begins in the later stages of development, when the play of power relations gains great momentum with the unrestricted advance of the democratization

> process.
> (Prebisch, 1980b, p 156)

Peripheral capitalism is thus dual in nature. A large portion of the population finds itself outside the modern, dynamic sector (or in the terminology of the dependency school, it is 'marginalized'), because it lacks the power to increase wages at the same rate as it increases its productivity. This dualism, in which a modern sector, with a dynamic of its own, has been placed 'on top of' a traditional sector, will continue to exist as long as there is peripheral capitalism, which precludes any development that will benefit the entire population. The system must be transformed so that the surplus can be used in a better way if any development is to be achieved.

In view of the importance Prebisch attaches to the distribution of income in his analysis of peripheral capitalism, it is interesting to note that he is rather critical of the advocates of the 'basic-needs' strategy:[2]

> I sometimes think – if I may be excused a touch of misgiving – that some of those who offer such formulas to the Periphery from the Centres do so in order to evade the problems of the new international economic order. Why listen to all this disturbing rhetoric, instead of mounting a direct attack on poverty? Would it not be assumed for a moment that by virtue of some such benevolent magic poverty could be eradicated without the need to accumulate more capital in order to absorb the lower strata at rising levels of productivity. At best, the exclusive tendencies of the system would have been precariously corrected, but not its conflictive tendencies. Rather might these latter be aggravated.
> (Ibid., p 187)

As pointed out in Chapter 1, Dudley Seers felt that the Latin American *estructuralistas* during the 1950s had a better theory (at least as far as the understanding of underdevelopment was concerned), and later he accepted the more ECLA-oriented part of the dependency school. In his last works, Seers was prepared to accept the dependency theory as an alternative way of studying the world economy and as the basis for a classification which was better than the established, unviable division into 'three worlds' (Seers, 1979b). Note, however, that Seers viewed dependence as a *dimension* of the international division of labour, and not as a state that was characteristic of a certain group of countries. The dependency theory appears to be most useful in studies of the 'world economy'.

Seers's classification implies that there are no 'independent' countries, since he distinguishes between 'least dependent countries' (e.g. Japan, Nigeria and Argentina), and 'dependent countries', such as Brazil, Cuba and Portugal. The classification is based upon the import structure, in which the key inputs are oil, cereals and technology. This is, of course, only a suggestion, but it is an interesting example of how 'modern' structuralism has managed to assimilate not only the perspective of the dependency school, but also the critique of this perspective. Seers's dependency approach is flexible and facilitates an analysis of the centre as well. We shall return to this latter point in the concluding chapter.

The Transnationalization Thesis: Sunkel: If modern structuralists like Prebisch and Seers may be said to have stimulated the growth of the dependency school with their early critique of the theory of development, then Osvaldo Sunkiel may be referred to as a structuralist with his roots in the dependency school. After the military take-over in Chile, Sunkel moved to the *Institute of Development Studies* (Sussex) for some years before returning to the ECLA in Santiago. This is probably what Marxist critics are hinting at when they speak of 'conservative re-absorption' (Kay, 1975, p 8). At the IDS Sunkel continued his work, based on the ideas of the dependency school (Sunkel and Fuenzalida, 1976 and 1979). He was primarily concerned with an analysis of the process of transnationalization, of which we find traces in his earlier works. His theses may be summed up in the following points:

1) The capitalist system has in recent years been changing from an international system to a transnational system. It has been eliminating elements that do not fit into it, remnants of earlier sociocultural systems, and has been integrating the remaining elements into a whole of remarkable consistency. This process is associated with and symbolized by the increase in the number, size and diversification of the transnational corporations.
2) Because of transnationalization, national societies in the capitalist sphere, both 'underdeveloped' and 'developed', are suffering deep changes in their social structure. In the first place, a process of disintegration has set in. This is most obvious in its effect on the economy, but disintegration is also discernible in other organized social activities, such as scientific research, architecture, and urban/regional planning, medicine, education, the arts, and on a cultural/personal level.
3) Meanwhile, national societies are generating a variety of counter-processes of reintegration, with a reassertion of national and/or subnational values and meanings that sometimes finds political expression in an attempt to assert the separate identity of the nation. These processes are sometimes reactionary, sometimes progressive, and appear in different degrees and terms in all organized social activity.
4) As a consequence of all these processes, distinct communities are emerging within national societies. One of these is a transnational community integrated at a worldwide level, in spite of the fact that its members live in geographically and politically separate territories. The other communities, incarnating different national and local sociocultural configurations, usually lack any structural basis for becoming globally integrated in this way.

Sunkel believes that the theory of transnationalization provides a useful conceptual framework in several ways (Hettne and Wallensteen, 1978, p 39).

First, because it indicates why growth and poverty are so closely connected in the periphery. Secondly, because, by *combining* transnational integration and national disintegration, it offers a more diversified concept of dependence. Thirdly, because it is particularly important that the analysis is capable of showing how this effect cuts right through the conventional categorization of classes. Certain parts of the bourgeoisie and the working class are integrated into the transnational system, while others are left out. This requires a refined class analysis.

Structural Imperialism: Galtung: The growing interest of radical peace research in structural power and the relations between rich and poor countries represents a structuralist tradition which is far removed from that of the economists we have discussed so far. This change of interest is obviously linked to the paradigm shift, around which this work is circling, as well as to the growth of the 'new left' in Europe and the USA during the latter part of the 1960s. The theory of conflicts had, until then, concentrated its efforts on the contrasts between principally equal parties in terms of military and economic power, with empirical links to the so called East-West conflict. One of the key assumptions was that international tension could be reduced by a more adequate basis for decision making. The question was whether there was a need for a special theory and fundamentally different conflict solutions in the case of structural conflicts, in which the relation between the two parties systematically favoured one at the other's expense. A typical example of this type of conflict was that between the developed and the underdeveloped countries, in which the tension could hardly be reduced, unless the very nature of the relation was fundamentally changed. The concept of *structural violence* (coined by Johan Galtung) played an important role in this discussion. It was believed that, in addition to *direct military violence*, there existed a kind of violence which, through exploitation, undernourishment and oppression, affected individuals, and whose origins could be traced back to the social structure. During the 1970s a number of peace researchers, with this as a common starting point, devoted their time to studies of structural conflicts at the local, national or international level. The conflict solutions that were discussed in this context might almost be characterized as processes of liberation from historically given positions in a social structure which *itself* generated conflicts. This social structure might be a village in Latin America, or the world system as a whole.

This shift of perspective is, to a great extent, associated with Johan Galtung, who in 1971 published the now classic article 'A Structural Theory of Imperialism' in the *Journal of Peace Research*. Like most of the authors discussed in this chapter, Galtung describes a global structure, which he calls 'imperialism', although his analysis in many respects departs from the Marxist approach. The most striking difference is the fact that Galtung's imperialism is not *necessarily* associated with capitalism, but rather viewed as a more general phenomenon which, in reality, is a special kind of *dominance*. This dominance is characterized by the fact that the centre has established a bridgehead in the periphery. This bridgehead is made up of an elite, whose position is heavily dependent on external support. The relation of dominance is maintained by what Galtung calls a *feudal pattern of interaction*. This is best described by the fact that the centres maintain direct communication with each other and their respective peripheries. However, the latter hardly communicate with each other, or with metropoles other than those upon which they are dependent. The fact that telephone communications between two African capitals may go via London is a concrete example of the feudal pattern of interaction. While the process of establishing the bridgehead and the ideological influencing of the peripheral elite together are called *penetration*, the process of reducing communications between countries of the periphery is called *fragmentation*.

The most important cause of 'underdevelopment' in the dependent countries (which thus may be thought of as lack of power) is what Galtung calls the *vertical division of labour*.

According to Galtung, the vertical division of labour leads to a widening material gap between the centre and the countries of the periphery (exploitation). A study of the economic interaction with respect to the economic exchange *between* the countries will not, however, provide an adequate explanation of this type of development. This is one of the limitations of the so-called Prebisch-Singer thesis, claims Galtung. It is much more important to focus on the development effects of the international division of labour *within* the countries. In the case of the division of labour we find that different forms of production affect social organization, technological development, education and research differently. An advanced form of production has positive secondary ('spin-off') effects on a number of other sectors in the community, while a more primitive form of production does not. Static theories, like the theory of comparative advantages, lack the ability to reveal this kind of relationship, which, from a development theoretical point of view, is fundamental. By examining the effects of the vertical division of labour both from an historical and a structural perspective, it is possible to see that the 'spin-off' effects often go to only one of the parties, and that the advantage of the division of labour may be rather limited, as far as the other party is concerned. The mechanisms of structural imperialism are illustrated in Figure 8.1.

However, the international structure, which Galtung calls imperialist, consists of more than just relations of economic dependence. As opposed to Marxist authors, Galtung emphasizes not only the economic dimension of imperialism, but also the *political, military, communications* and *cultural* dimensions as well. These dimensions are all parts of a *generalized imperialiism*, which in Galtung's opinion are convertible, i.e. they may merge into each other. Political imperialism may, for instance, change into economic imperialism via 'dictated' terms of trade; the imperialism of communication may change into cultural imperialism via control of the flow of information, and cultural imperialism may change into economic imperialism via the export of development models.

Figure 8.1
The Mechanisms of Structural Imperialism

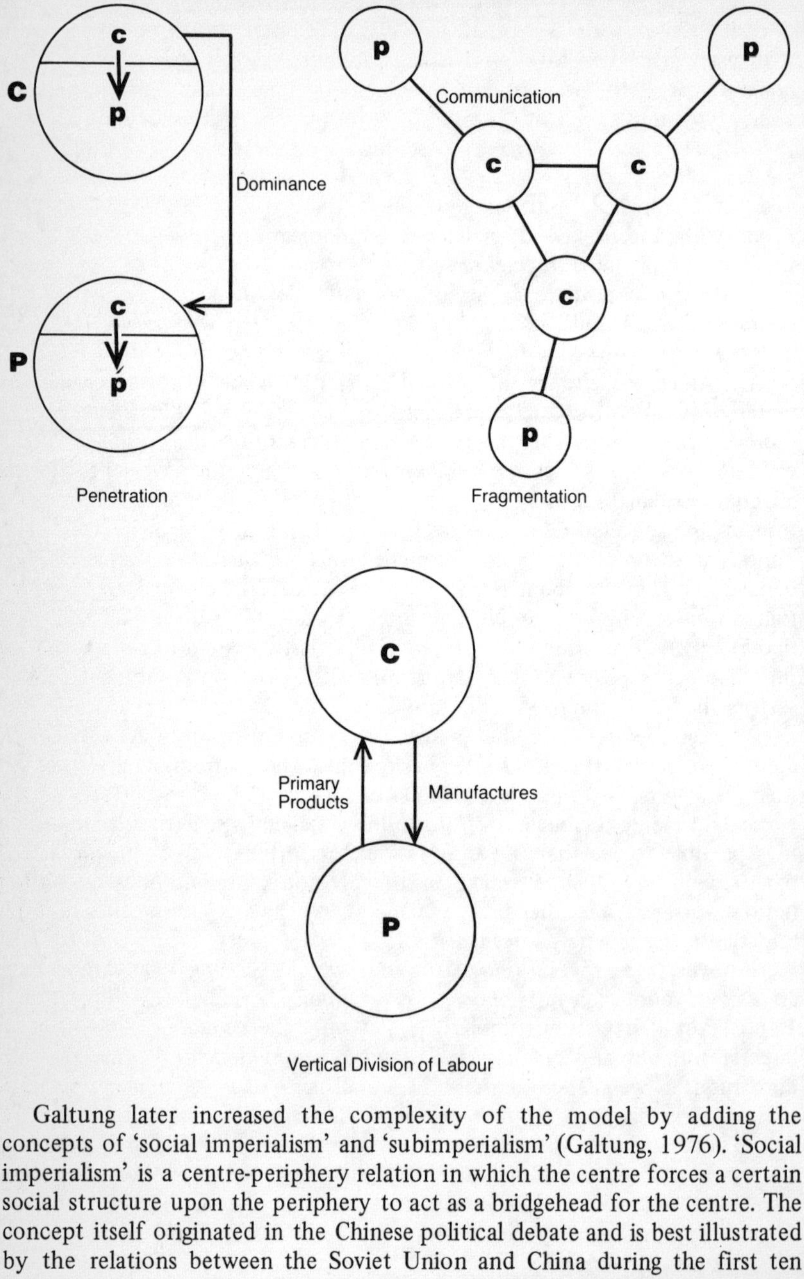

Galtung later increased the complexity of the model by adding the concepts of 'social imperialism' and 'subimperialism' (Galtung, 1976). 'Social imperialism' is a centre-periphery relation in which the centre forces a certain social structure upon the periphery to act as a bridgehead for the centre. The concept itself originated in the Chinese political debate and is best illustrated by the relations between the Soviet Union and China during the first ten years after the Chinese Revolution, when China relied heavily on the Soviet Union. Subimperialism is imperialism by proxy, which is illustrated by the relations between the United States and Brazil, and a Latin America dominated by Brazil. We have already met the concept of subimperialism when we discussed Marini, who also used the concept when dealing with Brazil. His interpretation of the phenomenon was, however, more in line with the Marxist theory of imperialism. The control mechanisms in Galtung's model are only partly economic and contain no indications of the fact that the nature of the ultimate driving force behind an imperialist structure must be economic. Instead, the most important factor behind subimperialism appears to be the political weakening of the United States. Galtung's theory of imperialism is therefore more of a theory about power and the use of power, than a theory about underdevelopment.[3] However, the difference is in fact minimal.

New Directions in Marxism: The Mode of Production Approach

We shall now pay some attention to the scholars who, while trying to answer the dependency school's challenge, also defended the core of the Marxist theory and the relevance of its conceptual apparatus. The critique of the dependency approach reveals the indispensable elements of the Marxist heritage, i.e. the fact that analysis is based on the 'sphere of production' rather than on the 'sphere of circulation', and that explanations of social change require a greater emphasis on class analysis. Robert Brenner has claimed that the class relations and the structure of government determine the way in which, as well as the extent to which, specific demographic and commercial changes affect long-term income trends and economic growth – not the other way around (Brenner, 1979). This position is based on an analysis of the transition from feudalism to capitalism, but is probably representative of the current Marxist understanding of how to analyse the development of capitalism wherever or whenever it occurs.

The *mode of production* appears to be one of the cornerstones in Marxist development research. This abstraction acquires its empirical form through the *articulation* of different modes of production in a concrete social formation. Laclau proposed such an approach in his critique of Frank and defined the concept of an 'economic system' as:

> the mutual relations between the different sectors of the economy, or between different productive units, whether on a regional, national or world scale . . . An economic system can include as constitutive elements, different modes of production – provided always that we define it as a whole, that is, by proceeding from the element or law of motion that establishes the unity of the different manifestations.
> (Laclau, 1971, p 33)

A similar view is found in the much discussed 'theory of articulation', the intellectual background of which is at least as complicated as that of dependency theory. To the extent that it deals with current Third World problems, the theory of articulation must, in our opinion, be seen as *a*, but not necessarily as *the,* Marxist answer to the challenge of the theory of dependence – an answer which, rightfully so, appears to be formulated primarily by Marxist anthropology. More than the other social sciences social anthropology has resisted the Marxist influence, since what Marx and Engels had to say about the societies, the study of which was the very purpose of anthropology, was embarrassing to a science trying to gain respectability by breaking with its colonial heritage. Yet, anthropology must also repudiate the neo-Marxist view, despite its attractive 'Third Worldism', since it, in turn, had rejected the anthropological level of analysis, the 'local community'. What happened at the local level was, according to one popular interpretation of dependency theory, merely a reflection of processes in a remote centre. Thus, Marxist oriented anthropologists were strongly motivated in their search for a solution to both of these problems: the theoretical poverty of Marxism *vis-à-vis* the study of non-European cultures, and the neo-Marxist tendency to deny the local level its own dynamics. There are, obviously, no easy solutions to these theoretical problems, and it is certainly too early to say that any solutions are close at hand.

The approach which we have called the 'theory of articulation' has its roots in French anthropologists like Claude Meillassoux and Pierre Philippe Rey. Briefly, the concept of 'articulation' means the concrete manifestation of the hierarchical coexistence of different modes of production. Although Marx used the concept mode of production (in referring, for example, to feudalism and capitalism), it was the French Marxist, Althusser, who pointed out its theoretical importance, when making the distinction between the abstract concept of *mode of production* and the real *social formation*. The latter will always contain several different modes of production, since the transition from one mode of production to another can be neither sudden nor complete. Thus, the concept of *articulation* refers to this 'coexistence' of different modes of production which, rather than being parallel, constitutes a structured, hierarchical whole, characterized by the domination of one mode of production over the others. In Rey's opinion the articulation between feudalism and capitalism was 'protective', i.e. the reference to coexistence, in the true sense of the word, was justified. All other pre-capitalist modes of production respond negatively to capitalist penetration, but that does not mean that they cannot be strengthened by it, at least for short periods of time. Capitalist penetration is, in all cases but one (i.e. its articulation with feudalism), associated with violence. In other words, capitalism may come about spontaneously (the 'normal' case), or be introduced by force. Aidan Foster-Carter has pointed out that this distinction should have led Rey to develop a wider theoretical framework – which he did not.[4]

English anthropologists have finally assimilated the French debate in an attempt to move beyond the strong structuralist-functionalist tradition, and have managed to establish a theoretical link between the new French anthropology and the dependency school.[5] Is it then correct to speak of an intellectual breakthrough – a paradigm shift? At this point we should clarify the distinction between the Marxist anthropology, which deals with pre-capitalist modes of production, and that which deals with the current problems of underdevelopment. The former more or less ignores world capitalism, which undoubtedly constitutes a fundamental, theoretical challenge as far as the study of what was formerly known as 'primitive societies' is concerned. The study of the problems of underdevelopment, which is what concerns us here, therefore still appears to be in a 'pre-paradigmatic' phase. This problem has, as already mentioned, been discussed primarily in England. The dependency school and French anthropology are explicitly linked together in *Beyond the Sociology of Development* (Oxaal *et al.*, 1975), a collection of papers which came about as a result of a conference at the University of Hull in 1973. The title is somewhat inadequate since the scope of the conference was not only to go beyond the 'sociology of development' (the old, evolutionist social science), but to transcend the 'sociology of underdevelopment' (the dependency school). Both the dependency school and Frank were subjected to critical analyses (see contributions of O'Brien and Booth), and the collection of papers also contained empirical studies which attempted to bypass the weaknesses of the dependency school by resorting to French anthropology (introduced by Clammer in the same volume). The approach may be described in the following ways:

The starting point is the dependency school's vision of capitalist expansion and penetration into the periphery, the development of which is subject to that of the centre and thus distorted and blocked (underdevelopment). The vision is, however, expressed in a different (Marxist) terminology, the intent of which is to improve the basis for deeper theoretical analyses.

The articulation of different modes of production must, essentially, be studied empirically, but in such a way that *a priori* assumptions are excluded. New questions are instead generated, questions which the dependency theory never considered: which relation between the modes of production is expressed in the articulation? Which are the real production relations? How is the exploitation manifested within the class structure of a particular social formation? What is required for a capitalist mode of production not only to dominate, but also to eliminate other modes of production?

The elimination of pre-capitalist modes of production is the true meaning of capitalist development. The problems of underdevelopment 'discovered' by the dependency school would, in this theoretical context, be described as a 'stalemate' in the process of articulation. The pre-capitalist modes of production successfully resisted the attacks of the capitalist mode of production for reasons which (once again) can only be explained by a concrete analysis; this, in turn, implies a long, but not necessarily everlasting, period of stagnation or, in the terminology of the dependency school, 'underdevelopment'.

Does this represent the solution to the theoretical problem of analysing underdevelopment? The editors of the Oxaal volume are very cautious on this issue: 'This is a partial and not a final synthesis' (ibid., p 5). Caution is indeed a virtue. Many appear to be of the opinion that the solution is to be found in the concept of a mode of production, but this kind of solution, typically, generates new problems. We do not see the modes of production concretely manifested until we use the concept of articulation, but on that level of analysis these modes are no longer recognizable because of their intermixing. When an author claims to be studying a formation which consists of modes of production A, B and C, is there any way for the reader to verify that it really is a question of modes A, B and C, and not B, C and D? Or if one anthropologist, after having studied some valley in the Andes, finds that this social formation (A + B + C) is dominated by mode of production A, and if another anthropologist, after a later 'restudy' finds B to be the dominant mode of production, are we then to assume that this social formation has changed, or could it be that one of the two anthropologists has a preconceived idea about which mode of production *ought* to be dominant?

A practical problem is now added to these theoretical ones. The number of different modes of production has lately shown an alarming tendency to increase. A number of 'newly discovered' modes of production has been added to Marx's classical list ('in broad outlines we can designate the Asiatic, the ancient, the feudal and the modern bourgeois modes of production as so many epochs in the progress of the economic formation of society'). We have already discussed Hamsa Alavi's 'colonial mode of production'. In the French analyses of West Africa we find the 'lineage mode of production', Joel Kahn has discovered the 'petty commodity mode of production' in Western Sumatra (Clammer, 1978, p 112); Marshall Sahlins speaks of a 'domestic mode of production', Samir Amin and Goran Hyden of a 'peasant mode of production (although defining it in different ways), etc. The number of social formations determined by various combinations of modes of production will be infinite if the number of different modes of production continues to grow at this rate. Of course the number of 'articulations' should not exceed the number of historical and contemporary societies, if this method of analysis is to form a stable basis for continued research in the area of development and underdevelopment problems.

Continuity and Elaborations

Under this last heading we shall examine various attempts to elaborate on the dependency approach. These current theoretical trends thus show a strong continuity back to the dependency school.

The Internationalization of Capital

The fact that some Third World countries, which according to the dependency school were doomed to underdevelopment, suddenly showed impressive growth figures during the 1970s, inspired the development of different theories of the internationalization of capital. There are several such theories (see Marcussen and Torp, 1982), but what keeps them together is the view that the industrialization in the periphery is the result of the export of capital from the centre. It is argued that changing historical conditions for capital accumulation in the centre have led to new ways in which the periphery is integrated in the reproduction of the centre's capital, which in turn has led to the argument that some Third World countries very well may break with the 'blocked development' situation. The static form of statements asserting a permanent division of the global economy into a centre and a periphery, and treating capitalist development in the latter as an impossibility, is thus no longer accepted here.

Just as in the classical theories of imperialism, the point of departure for the theories of internationalization of capital is to analyse how capital accumulation results in a tendency for capital to broaden its sphere of operation internationally. Perhaps the most well-known attempt at such an analysis is Fröbel, Heinrichs and Kreye (1980). According to them, the decreasing strength and protective power of the national states implies an intensive competition among various fractions of capital. The transnational capital benefits from the structural changes and further reinforces them by combining the new technology, the emerging market in industrial sites and the worldwide industrial reserve army. The pattern of international investment is changing, in a first phase, from the traditional industrial centres in Europe to the European periphery (in America the corresponding shift is from the East to the South – and 'south of the border'), and, in a second phase, to any country in the Third World where there is a good supply of labour, political stability and other incentives, usually described as 'an appropriate investment climate'. This reallocation of industrial investment depends on a number of technological developments. There are improvements in communication and information, facilitating quick decision-making on how to take advantage of the changing global structure of comparative advantages in different branches. There are improvements in transport technology reducing the importance of geographical distances. There are, finally, changes in technology and labour organization, making it possible to decompose complex production processes. Thus, skilled labour in the traditional centres is replaced by unskilled labour, for example in free trade zones. All this is shown in the new process of Third World industrialization.

As far as analyses of the periphery are concerned, the only real difference between the dependency approach and the internationalization of capital approach seems to be that dependency is no longer synonymous with underdevelopment. It rather means development. The export of capital no longer blocks development in the periphery. Instead the centre 'permits' some (but not all) Third World countries to develop. But just as in the dependency literature, the centre determines the accumulation process in the periphery, and even if some Third World countries today are 'permitted' to develop, their future is still dependent on the same factors that characterized the 'blocked development'. The fundamental critique of the dependency approach, namely its exaggeration of the importance of the 'external' factors, thus remains valid also for the internationalization of capital approach. Consequently this approach is not much more illuminating.

The World System Approach

The *world system approach* is usually associated with Immanuel Wallerstein, and with more recent works by André Gunder Frank and Samir Amin.

Amin and Frank: Samir Amin takes the broadest approach from a theoretical point of view and seems to be moving between Marxist theory and the world system approach. In one of his latest books Amin tries to rethink basic concepts in the tradition of historical materialism and asserts that the classic line of development (slavery – feudalism – capitalism) is largely mythical. The much discussed contrast between a European and a so-called Asian development path merely expresses eurocentrism. What Amin calls 'the unity of universal history' is, however, recreated by the necessary succession of three families of mode of production: the family of communal modes, that of tributary modes and the capitalist mode (Amin, 1980).

In a paper originally written in Chile in 1972 Frank looks back at the dependency school and its critics. Although he defends the dependency school on the basis of what happened during the 1960s, he also shows that it became *passé* during the 1970s:

> The evidence is accumulating that 'dependence' has ended or is completing the cycle of its natural life, at least in the Latin America that gave it birth. The reason is the newly changing world economic and political reality that in a word may be summarized as the crisis of the 1970s.
> (Frank, 1977, p 357)

Frank is obviously of the opinion that the dependency school became obsolete mainly because of the changes in the world economy, and not because of its critics.

Frank has lately been concentrating his efforts on the complex problems of *capital accumulation on a global scale*. He claims that the world economy (= world capitalism) is currently in a state of crisis, which is reminiscent of the crises during the 1870s and the 1930s, in so far as it leads to a structural change towards new areas of investment, such as energy technologies. The crisis can be traced back to the mid-1960s, and manifested itself in the currency crisis of 1970-1, in the oil crisis of 1973-4, and in the depression tendencies that started to appear during 1974 and 1975 and have become successively worse. Since it is not only a question of an unusually deep recession, but also of more fundamental disturbance, the process of adjustment will be painful and conflict ridden.

The nature of the problem in the Third World is somewhat different, depending on the role each country plays in the international division of labour. On this basis Frank identifies four possible reactions:

1) In industrial economies based on cheap labour (Korea, Taiwan, Hong Kong, Singapore) the shortage of capital in a worldwide economic crisis will lead to a lowering of wages and to repression, which, in all probability, will be maintained by a militaristic, corporativistic state apparatus.

2) The 'Chile model' will be used extensively in raw material producing economies based on cheap labour, like Sri Lanka, Bangladesh and several other Latin American countries. In this case the 'solution' will consist of generous invitations to international capital to co-operate in the exploitation of dormant resources.

3) The more developed, industrial economies who have already tried the strategy of import substitution (Brazil, Mexico, India) may participate in the international division of labour in other ways, e.g. by concentrating on capital accumulation and industrial export, supported by the state.

4) The fourth category consists of old and new subimperialistic nations with Brazil as their model. In this group Iran, at least for a while, seemed to have excellent prospects of development based on economic, political and military control of a large region (summary of a seminar presentation in Gothenburg, (1978).

Frank's current writings (Frank, 1978) have turned into a political chronicle of global events in which everything that happens in this world is explained by referring to the global accumulation of capital. His historical works on this theme have, however, been thrown into the shade by Immanuel Wallerstein's magnum opus *The Modern World-System.*

Wallerstein: The crucial point in Wallerstein's theory – the point at which he progresses beyond the dependency theory – is the question of internal versus external factors; nor does he work with two kinds of capitalism, i.e. a 'central' and a 'peripheral' capitalism. Both of these pitfalls are avoided by the use of the central concept of a 'world system'.

The world system is a 'social system' which, according to Wallerstein, is characterized by the fact that life within it is largely self-contained and that the dynamics of its development are largely internal (Wallerstein, 1974, p 347). The expression 'largely self-contained' is, of course, somewhat vague. According to Wallerstein, the definition is based on a contrafactual hypothesis: if it were possible to screen off the system from external factors, the system would continue to function in basically the same way.

We know that various parts of the world are, above all, economically dependent upon each other, a situation which is nowadays described by the term 'interdependence'. However, if we go back about 1,000 years, this kind of of 'interdependence' was almost non-existent. The world was then made up of a number of relatively independent 'mini systems'; there was no world system, i.e. no *world economy* per se.

On the other hand, history has yielded a type of world system which Wallerstein calls the *world empire*. The unifying factor in that system does not consist of various economic relations, but is made up of a central, political power, which, in the process of expansion, has forced peripheral areas under its control. This kind of expansion is naturally limited by the size of the territory that can be effectively controlled by a central power. Contact between the central power and the provincial *governors* must be maintained, and it must be possible to put down rebellions in the more remote regions of the empire. Transport technology is therefore of great importance: it took forty to sixty days to move from one end of the Roman Empire to the other; after the transport revolution the same amount of time was needed to move goods from one end of the world to the other.

The main difference between a 'world empire' and a 'world economy' (the two historically given versions of a world system) lies in the fact that the latter is able to exist without a system of supreme political control, which also proves the world economy to be more viable than the world empire. A number of world empires have been created and destroyed while the world economy, which has expanded steadily since the 16th Century, today covers most of the world. In other words, it is the one and only world system. The problem of the external versus the internal factors, which caused the dependency theorists a great deal of trouble, has ostensibly been solved when Wallerstein internalizes the external factor. Like Frank, Wallerstein describes the world system (i.e. the world economy) as being capitalist. However, he does not make the basic distinction between development and underdevelopment made by most dependency theorists. Thus, there is only *one kind* of capitalism, namely that of the world system, although its various branches may manifest themselves differently. By avoiding the prerequisite polarization between centre and periphery (development-underdevelopment, central capitalism-peripheral capitalism), Wallerstein circumvents another one of the pitfalls of the dependency school.

Wallerstein's 'world system' is composed of the *core-states* (corresponding to the dependency school's 'centre', or 'metropolis') the *semi-periphery*, the *periphery* and the *external arena*. The semi-periphery consists of an intermediate but functionally important category of countries which are either turning into core-states, or losing their status as such, disappearing out into the periphery. The external arena is the set of areas which have not as yet been affected by capitalist penetration from the core-states. Thus, 'the global accumulation of capital' (in Amin's and Frank's terminology) is a long historical process in the course of which parts of the external arena are incorporated in the world system (*peripheralization*). The fact that this process is now more or less completed, is confirmed by the protests raised by the few remaining 'aboriginal peoples' of the world.

Wallerstein's work provides an impressive vision of world-historic development but his conceptual apparatus is, as can be seen, quite simplistic and at times appears rather haphazard. The great impact of his work was due more to the way in which these concepts were used in a concrete, historical analysis, than to their inherent theoretical attractiveness.

The above applies to the first two volumes of a planned series of four, covering the period between 1450 AD and the present. The fact that a number of years lie between the publication of the first volume (1974) and that of the second (1980) seems to indicate that the author may have had difficulties in applying his fundamental principles to a later, and far more complex phase in the growth of the world system.

In Volume 1, Wallerstein describes the growth of the modern world system from circa 1450 to 1640, when the world system appears in its embryonic form. England, the Netherlands and France were then competing core-states. True core-states are, apart from a more diversified economy and the beginnings of industrial production, characterized by strong and centralized governments. This is why the Netherlands rapidly fell behind, while England and France were involved in several wars during the 18th Century – wars which essentially were concerned with the achievement of world hegemony. Portugal and Spain, the former leaders of the 16th Century European expansion, had lapsed into semi-peripheral positions. The tradition of empire building is, in Wallerstein's books, represented by Charles V, whose empire was centred around Spain, but included large parts of the rest of Europe; for a while it competed with the other world system alternative: the capitalist world economy.

During the mid-17th Century, the periphery consisted of Eastern Europe, providing the core-states with cereals, and Latin America, which served as the silver and gold mine of Europe. The external arena, which, in other words, had not as yet been 'peripheralized', was made up of the rest of the world, i.e. Africa, Asia and Russia. Africa was at that time still an unexplored continent. In contrast Asia had a number of early established trade routes (dominated by Arab traders) connecting a number of relatively powerful nations, which the Europeans took a long time in subjugating. Russia was still an independent empire with a strong central government, much like the political structures that were developing in Western Europe.

A history of such grandiose dimensions is bound to contain some contradictions and flaws, and Wallerstein's work has been the subject both of admiration and of criticism. The latter has grown in intensity during the past few years. A Swedish historian might wonder where Sweden fits into Wallerstein's scheme of things. Is it not true that Sweden was a particularly centralized power and a militarily aggressive nation during the 17th Century? Yes, indeed. Is it therefore true to say that Sweden was one of the core-states? Hardly. At this point we might question the validity of the hypotheses about the core-states having strong governments. However, in this context, it is not this type of empirical critique that is the most interesting, but the critique directed at Wallerstein's theoretical approach to the study of the problems of development and underdevelopment.

Compared with the dependency theory, the world system approach constitutes a theoretical improvement. It effectively does away with the classical Marxian preoccupation with Europe without turning into the same cul-de-sac. However, this does not mean that Wallerstein's world system puts an end to the Marxist critique of the dependency school. Many feel that Wallerstein's way of handling basic Marxian categories is much too free, and also that he is too eclectic to be truly acceptable from a Marxist point of view. It is beyond the scope of this book to deal with these objections in any detail but we would like to provide a brief summary, in which we shall touch upon three distinct problems: the transition from one social formation to another, the question of what constitutes capitalism, and the class analysis.

As far as the transition problem is concerned, Wallerstein's first period (1450-1640) coincides with what in Marxist terms is usually described as the transition from a feudal to a capitalist mode of production. The reason why Marxists attack Wallerstein is that he stirs up a classical Marxist debate which is generally considered to be over and done with (Hilton, 1976). The debate, which dates back to 1950, was concerned with the dissolution of feudalism, i.e. whether it was caused by 'internal' factors, such as the stagnating feudal mode of production and the rise of a class of capitalist peasants (Dobb), or by 'external' factors, such as the growth of the cities and markets (Sweezy). Marx's work suggests that both explanations might be valid, but the consensus is now that the main cause is to be found in the mode of production, i.e. among the internal factors.[6]

From the Marxist critique of the dependency school the reader might recall that Laclau's most severe criticism of Frank was the latter's definition of capitalism. Frank had managed to get himself into a situation in which he identified capitalism with production for the market. Rather obviously, Laclau pointed out that the Marxian definition of capitalism was associated with a specific mode of production, characterized by the free sale of labour power. This difference of opinion might be thought of as a variation on the above-mentioned debate between Dobb and Sweezy; Wallerstein explicitly supports Frank (and Sweezy):

> I believe both Sweezy and Frank better follow the spirit of Marx if not his letter and that, leaving Marx quite out of the picture, they bring us nearer to an understanding of what actually happened and is happening than do their opponents.
> (Wallerstein, 1979, p 9)

Wallerstein continues by saying:

> If proletariat, then capitalism. Of course. To be sure. But is England, or Mexico, or the West Indies a unit of analysis? Does each have a separate mode of production? Or is the unit (for the sixteenth-eighteenth centuries) the European world-economy, including England *and* Mexico, in which case what was the mode of 'production' of this world economy?
> (Ibid., p 10)

Here, the antagonists are obviously talking about different things. The Marxists appear to base their critique on the idea that the world system is composed of national economies (or modes of production) and that the relations among these must take the form of some kind of trade. In the world system perspective the 'international' economy is in fact a worldwide system made up of specific zones of production characterized by various types of labour control (from wage labour to slavery). The question of trade thus does not arise. Therefore the ironical comparison to Adam Smith ('neo-smithianism') appears less appropriate (Brenner, 1977).

Thus, Wallerstein equates 'world system' and 'capitalism', and, like the dependency theorists, he shifts the analytical focus to the world system, while the concept of the mode of production – although used occasionally – is relegated to a lesser position. The fact that he acknowledges only two modes of production (the world system and not yet incorporated so-called 'mini-systems') makes the concept rather trivial from an analytical point of view.

As far as class analysis is concerned, it is quite obvious that Wallerstein's (and the majority of the *dependentistas*) view of the importance of the concept of class differs somewhat from that of classical Marxism, to whom the class struggle *was* History. The following excerpt is liable to cause some concern: 'To say that there cannot be three or more classes is not, however, to say that there are always two. There may be none though this is rare and transitional. There may be one, and this is most common. There may be two and this is most explosive' (Wallerstein, 1974, p 351). Wallerstein associates the class concept with situations of conflict only, implying the existence of two opposing parties, and that there therefore can never be more than two classes. The situation with only *one* class is explained by the fact that, historically, capitalists have subjectively seen themselves as a class (*für sich*) in relation to other groups (*an sich*), who never had a similar, permanent feeling of class consciousness.

The concept of class is afforded only a peripheral role in Wallerstein's conceptual apparatus, and is therefore, like the mode of production, of little importance as an analytical tool. Thus from a Marxist point of view it is correct to claim that Wallerstein does not use the concept of class as such in his analysis, but chooses to work with a mass of undefined status and interest groups.

We shall finally give a concrete example of how students of the world system tradition deal with the problems of underdevelopment. The fact that Wallerstein is an Africanist makes it all the more interesting to find out what his views on the African process of underdevelopment are (Wallerstein, 1976). The world system theory views both the 'eurocentric' and the 'afrocentric' interpretations of African history as being deceptive. Wallerstein claims that both Europe and Africa, at a given point, were made parts of a larger system, and that the latter therefore determined their subsequent development. In other words, he fully agrees with those critics who accuse him of not allowing the individual actors to be autonomous:

> All systemic analysis denies the real autonomy of parts of a whole. It is not that there are not particularities of each acting group. Quite the contrary. It is that the alternatives available for each unit are constrained by the framework of the whole, even while each actor opting for a given alternative in fact alters the framework of the whole.
>
> An analysis then must start from how the whole operates and of course one must determine what is the whole in a given instance. Only then may we be able to draw an interpretative sketch of the historical outlines of the political economy of contemporary Africa, which is in my view an outline of the various stages (and modes) of its involvement in this capitalist world-economy.
>
> (Wallerstein, 1976, p 30)

Which are the stages to which Wallerstein refers? The first phase of the African *peripheralization* (i.e. incorporation into the world system) was the period between 1750 and 1900. Africa and Europe therefore represented external arenas to each other before 1750. Trade was in 'luxury goods', the function of which was unimportant in both economies. It was governed by effective supply rather than by demand, implying that the effect of interruptions was relatively small. There was a qualitative change in the relations between Europe and Africa around 1750 (it is difficult to determine the exact year), which is suggested by the fact that the slave trade expanded rapidly during the first half of the 18th Century, culminated around 1750, and then remained constant for the remainder of the century until 1810. The African states (Ashanti and Dahomey) who organized the slave trade (and whose structures were therefore determined by this) were now peripheralized, while the regions in which the actual slave hunt took place belonged to the external arena. The world system as such was therefore not affected by the destructive consequences of the slave trade. It is significant that the peripheralization put an end to the slave trade; there are, after all, other and much more profitable ways of using a periphery than to use it as a hunting ground for slaves. West Africa gradually changed into a colonial, raw material producing economy, while the slave trade moved to East Africa, whence it eventually disappeared as the region was peripheralized.

The past 80 years constitute the second phase of the African peripheralization. It should be seen in the light of the so-called 'scramble for Africa', which eventually led to the partition and use of Africa as a production area for the core-states. For various reasons (on which there is no need to dwell) unique forms of production were created in different parts of the continent: African 'rural capitalism', white farmer settlements, and plantations. These forms of production, brought about by the peripheralization of Africa, have greatly influenced African social development. The dependency perspective has, obviously, been accepted as the basis for an explanation of the process of underdevelopment.

In Wallerstein's vision of the future of Africa, i.e. the third phase, the reader will recognize the dependency school's rather dreary outlook: the inexorable process of 'underdevelopment' which must continue to the bitter end. As already mentioned, Wallerstein avoids the concept of 'underdevelopment', and seems more inclined to use Cardoso's and Faletto's concept of 'dependent development'. The classic core-states will eventually be weakened, while the *semi-peripheral* regions will assume an increasingly important role. The Republic of South Africa, Zaire, Nigeria, Algeria and Egypt are some of the countries that are strong enough (in terms of size, raw materials and industrial capacity) to play a semi-peripheral role. The peripheral nations' position will deteriorate, which implies that their only hope is a revolutionary transformation of the world system into a *socialist* world system. Once again, we return to the dependency ideas. 'Semi-peripheral countries' roughly correspond to Marini's 'subimperialism'; we also recognize the fundamental dilemma: underdevelopment or revolution.

Wallerstein forecasts that Africa, during the next 50 years, will be completely incorporated in the world system, and that the capitalist process of expansion, which started during the 16th Century, will be successfully completed. Marx's model of the capitalist system would, in that case, finally correspond to the reality. The inherent tendencies which Marx identified and analysed within the framework of a national capitalist economy have constantly been checked by the existence of a periphery and an external arena. Since the frontiers of the world system will soon be reached, we might expect a different kind of dynamics – perhaps the kind about which Marx prophesied over 100 years ago?

Similarities and Differences: To what extent do former dependency theorists such as Amin and Frank and the world system theorists share a common outlook? This is conveniently made explicit in a recent book co-authored by Samir Amin, Giovanni Arrighi, André Gunder Frank and Immanuel Wallerstein (Amin *et al.*, 1982, pp 9-10):

(1) There is a social whole that may be called a capitalist world economy, which came into existence in the 16th Century and has since expanded historically from its European origins to cover the globe. The appropriation by the world bourgeoisie of the surplus value created by the world's direct producers has evolved direct appropriation at the market place as well as unequal exchange.
(2) No analysis of individual states can be made without placing them in the context of the capitalist world economy.
(3) Throughout the history of the capitalist world economy there has been increasing organization of oppressed groups and increasing opposition to its continuance.
(4) After the Second World War, the United States was the hegemonic power and able to impose relative order on the world system. This hegemony is now in a decline.
(5) The struggle between capitalist and socialist forces cannot be reduced to a struggle between the US and the USSR. The 'crisis' is worldwide and in-

tegral, and must be analysed as such.

In a concluding discussion the four authors also spell out their differences. Without going into much detail it can be noted that Frank and Wallerstein are more positive about the existence of a single world system dynamics. They believe, for example, that the so-called long waves represent parts of the recurrent pattern of the functioning of the system, whereas Amin and Arrighi rather emphasize the specificity of each wave. The latter are also more 'voluntaristic' than are Frank and Wallerstein, who perceive the behaviour of the world system in a somewhat mechanistic and deterministic way. This rather important difference leads to different views on a number of issues, for example whether the decline of the US is similar to earlier declines of Dutch and British hegemony, and whether the Soviet economic system is an integral part of the world division of labour governed by the rules of the capitalist world economy, or if it is more or less outside the world system. Thus a world-system position, typically expressed by Frank and Wallerstein, would put heavy stress on the capitalist world economy as one integral system covering the whole globe and being moved by a single dynamics completely overpowering the individual states that make up the system. As can be seen, this position has a clear paradigmatic resemblance to the dependency tradition, although the level of analysis has been shifted from the periphery to the centre-periphery structure of the world system.

Notes

1. He offers the following comment on the possible uses of neo-classical theory: 'Their arguments are hopelessly divorced from the realities of the Periphery . . . Where is that "invisible hand" which was to assign those productive resources wisely, and equitably disseminate the fruits of development?' (Prebisch, 1980b).
2. A thorough discussion of the implications of this strategy is found in Streeten (1979).
3. Today, Galtung sees 'social imperialism' as a social dimension of a structurally defined imperialism. Thus, the implication of this dimension is the transfer of a social system or structure from the centre to the periphery. The five dimensions have, in other words, turned into six. As far as 'subimperialism' is concerned, Galtung now sees it as being more of a defensive than offensive strategy, i.e. the phenomenon of subimperialism is an expression of a weakening and internal division in the centre. So-called regional great powers in the Third World, like Brazil, India, Nigeria, etc. may, of course, during longer or shorter periods of time have interests in common with the centre; they may even be dependent upon the military technology of the centre, but their long-term ambition is probably to increase the level of autonomy. (Conversation with Johan Galtung in Gothenburg, September 1980.)
4. See Foster-Carter (1978). A critique of the theory which stays within th

framework of an analysis of Rey's theoretical contribution is found in Bradby (1975).

5. French Marxist anthropology was introduced in England through a collection of essays (Seddon, 1978; Bloch, 1975; Clammer, 1978) and via the periodical *Critique of Anthropology* (see particularly its French issue, 1979). The connection appears from the following autobiographical notes taken from Seddon's foreword to his introduction of the new anthropology (Seddon, 1978, pp VII and VIII): 'During the last year of my own anthropological fieldwork in north-east Morocco (carried out between 1968 and 1970) I was introduced by a Danish sociologist friend to a book that had an immediate and profound effect on my thinking about the study of society and in particular of social and economic changes: *Capitalism and Underdevelopment in Latin America*, by A.G. Frank. Firstly, it seemed to suggest an approach to the study of 'underdeveloped' countries that was sharp and powerful and which, in contrast to the majority of studies by 'bourgeois' economists, sociologists and anthropologists, denied the conventional dichotomy between "modern" and "traditional" sectors and developed an essentially holistic and dynamic approach to the phenomenon of underdevelopment; secondly, it appeared to apply quite remarkably directly to what I knew of Morocco, the history of its progressive involvement in the international capitalist economy over the last few centuries, and the transformations undergone by the pre-capitalist social and economic formations of the Maghreb.' Unfortunately, these great expectations never came true. 'In French, however, I discovered a body of fascinating and directly relevant literature revealing the development of a lively and critical discussion which directed its attention primarily at the investigation and analysis of pre-capitalist formations – the general "field" of economic anthropology. Beginning with the work of Jean Suret-Canale and developed in various somewhat different directions by Maurice Godelier and Claude Meillassoux this discussion had produced, by the end of the 1960s, a considerable body of extremely important work which asked, among other things, the "key questions" . . . which British and American anthropology had rarely and unsatisfactorily asked.'
6. It is interesting to note how this feud runs through the entire Marxist debate. The following examples should suffice: Dobb-Sweezy; Bettelheim-Emmanuel; Laclau-Frank; Brenner-Wallerstein. An unbiased, methodological analysis of this intellectual conflict should be well worth the effort.

Conclusions

We have in this book tried to describe the origins and growth of a new theoretical tradition: development theory. Initially, the orientation of this theory was determined by two different biases. First of all, the experiences of Western industrial society heavily influenced the attempts to understand the global dimensions of development. Only recently was it realized that development in different parts of the world does not consist of a series of isolated development processes. This has now led to a fairly widespread understanding of the fact that each country, to a great extent, has its own, unique development problems, dictated by both external and internal conditions. Furthermore, the discipline of economics initially assumed a dominant position *vis-à-vis* the other social sciences. Today, most development theorists find it quite natural to think of development as not only an economic problem, but also a political, social and cultural problem. The theory of development is therefore now thought of as an interdisciplinary field of research.

The Significance of the Dependency School

The bias in development theory was first pointed out by economists like Dudley Seers, who described the early theory of development as a 'special case'. Also Gunnar Myrdal suggested a broader, 'institutionalist' analysis, taking into account the 'poor cousins' of economics. The present book is, however, written from a Third World perspective, which means that we have emphasized Third World social scientists' contributions to the 'paradigm change'. As we have shown, most of the early contributions came from Latin America, particularly from the dependency school. We hope that our analysis of how that approach was received and elaborated in other underdeveloped regions illuminates the Caribbean, Asian and African debates as well.

It is true that the contents of this book can be summarized as 'the rise and fall of the dependency school'. This was actually the title of an earlier draft. However, that title may be interpreted as an outright dismissal of dependency theory. Our intent has, in fact, been quite the contrary. In our opinion, it has played a decisive role in many respects.

First, it had a lasting effect on the theoretical development. The mechanical evolutionism, which was characteristic of not only the conventional, but also the Marxist theory of development, was practically demolished by criticisms from the *dependentistas*. The dependency theorists claimed that there existed a set of unique preconditions based on a country's *position* in the international economic structure, and the development stage of this structure at the time when the country was incorporated. Although the dependency school has rightly been accused of exaggerating the importance of the 'external' factors, the questions it raised were relevant and will remain so, even if the answers and remedies were sometimes less than adequate. It is therefore quite easy to trace the influence of the dependency school in several contemporary theoretical currents.

Obviously the *Marxists* today struggle with the problematic that the dependency school brought to the surface. This problematic was a challenge for a eurocentric and basically evolutionist Marxism. However, the theoretical emphases of the new Marxism differ. Some are for instance tied to the French structuralist tradition, while others base their analyses on Marx's own distinction between merchant and industrial capital. What ties them together is their use of the conceptual apparatus and basic method of classical Marxism, as well as their rejection of 'neo-Marxism'. The new approaches are, nevertheless, far from unproblematic, and a long critical debate should be expected.

Another current can be traced back to the structuralist-institutionalist critique of the early development theory. Pioneers like Gunnar Myrdal, Raúl Prebisch, Dudley Seers and Hans Singer, no doubt, inspired the critique of the theory of international trade. Their structural approach is still very much alive, and has now assimilated the dependency school's broader approach. It should be noted that *modern structuralists* consider their method applicable not only to 'underdeveloped' countries. 'Underdevelopment' should thus be seen as a general phenomenon.[1]

The most obvious heir to the dependency school is the different *world system* approaches. Attempts have been made to circumvent the traps into which some dependency theorists were lured, such as the difficulty of providing a theoretically satisfactory way of operating with two kinds of capitalism (one 'central' and one 'peripheral'), as well as the similarly awkward attempt analytically to explain the 'external' and the 'internal' factors affecting the process of development.

The dependency school was the Third World's first real contribution to the social sciences. This generally increased the self-confidence of Third World social scientists who, until then, had been imitating the social science of the Western world. The changes have been felt in the institutional development as well, for instance in the growth of new research institutes and organizations of co-operation with a more or less militant Third World perspective (Hettne, 1981). Western dominance in the field of development research has thus declined noticeably. Of course, we are not saying that this is a direct *result* of the rise of the dependency school, but the latter did play an important role in the change in the intellectual climate that we have outlined.

Secondly, the impact on development strategies of the dependency school in Latin America and other countries, as well as on UN policies of international development, has been considerable. While the ECLA economists justified the import-substitution strategy in Latin America, far-reaching programmes of self-reliance, both on national and regional bases, must be seen as strategic consequences of a more radical dependency perspective. The so-called Cocoyoc Declaration was perhaps the most well-known example of a new development strategy stressing self-reliance:

> We believe that one basic strategy of development will have to be increased national self-reliance. It does not mean autarchy. It implies mutual benefits from trade and co-operation and a fairer redistribution of resources satisfying the basic needs. It does mean self-confidence, reliance primarily on one's own resources, human and natural, and the capacity for autonomous goal-setting and decision-making. It excludes dependence on outside influences and powers that can be converted into political pressure.[2]

An analysis of the implementation of this policy, which unfortunately has been far from flawless, is beyond the scope of this book. We have mainly dwelt upon two cases, Jamaica and Tanzania, which, of course, cannot be considered as success stories. Whether the dependency approach should be blamed for this is, however, still an open question. 'Responsible' dependency theorists in Jamaica point to the fact that although they held quite a few important positions in the different ministries, the most important positions were still held by conventional economists. In the case of Chile, Pedro Vuskovic, the Minister for Industries in the Allende government, denies that the *dependentistas* had anything to do with the strategy of the *Unidad Popular*. He claims that the inspiration came from the ECLA, which, in contrast to the dependency school did formulate concrete economic programmes.[3] Anyway, a great deal of the rhetoric around the demands for a new economic order has obviously been inspired by the dependency perspective. This has, in turn, added ideological fuel to the international struggle for domestic control over resources and better terms of trade.

Thirdly, the dependency school played an important ideological and political role in Latin America during the 1960s. The indirect effects were felt throughout the world (at least at the universities) in 1968 and for some years thereafter. The breakthrough of the dependency perspective was intimately associated with a political militancy which had little to do with the Latin American communist parties, whose orthodox policies have so far been relatively unsuccessful compared to broad popular movements inspired by the nationalist ideology of *dependencia*. Nicaragua might perhaps be seen in this perspective, but apart from that, the new radicalism of the 1960s had a limited positive impact. In a few cases it provoked a terrible reaction, but one decade is too short a time in which to assess political changes. Those changes we can see today in Latin America may not be unrelated to the new ideas of the 1960s. This book is not the right vehicle for an analysis of the generation of 1968 – the 'new left'. However, this new left might, without exaggeration, be said to have influenced the political climate also in the industrialized countries during the latter part of the 1960s – an influence that is still prevalent in various, often abstruse, political forms. In our opinion, the dependency school should be seen as an important part of our modern intellectual history, whose significance has been particularly strongly felt in the social sciences.

The dependency school is dissolved and dispersed, but far from dead. Although modified, its ideas live on in new theoretical currents, and its role as a milestone and a watershed in the growth of the theory of development is undisputed. We hope that this book has proved that.

Determinants of Paradigm Change

A secondary purpose of our study has been to shed some light on the question of how scientific views are born, changed and disseminated. The material we have gathered from interviews and by studies of the internal debate in certain intellectual centres of the Third World is, naturally, far from complete. It should nevertheless be possible to reach certain conclusions about the sociological prerequisites for theoretical change – conclusions which may be used as a basis for more systematic studies.

Sociological analyses of paradigm change may be done at several levels, the fundamental analysis being that which examines the relationship between theory and empirical facts. Kuhn's theory predicts that a theoretical crisis will be the result of reality and our notion of reality drifting too far apart. This proposition constitutes a necessary, but not sufficient condition, particularly if the theory in question concerns the social sciences.

Since society is in a continuous state of flux, the social sciences are particularly prone to paradigm crises; however, the process of adjustment is hampered by the fact that theories may serve both ideological and legitimizing purposes. The paradigm change must therefore be politically sanctioned. The political factor behind the rise of the dependency school is easily identifiable. Santiago de Chile became the Latin American centre of the dependency debate during the 1960s and the early 1970s. A number of scholars from oppressive Latin American countries, such as Brazil, found refuge there. After the fall of Allende in 1973 this role was taken over by Mexico, which, at that time, was more or less the only Latin American country allowing a radical debate. However, Mexico turned out to be a less suitable environment for the dependency debate than Chile was during the years of the *Unidad Popular*. The notion of dependence never gained the kind of acceptance in Mexico that it did in other Latin American countries. While the oil boom in Mexico has brought about a development debate of a more conventional nature (the modernization paradigm), the intellectuals of the left – firmly rooted in the

Marxist tradition – adopted a generally negative attitude towards the ideas of the dependency school.[4]

The political factor is also noticeable when we look at the spread of the dependency theory. It served as a development ideology both in Tanzania and Jamaica after the Arusha Declaration (1967), and after the election of the Manley government in 1972. On the other hand, the political climate in Senegal was such that the IDEP could function only because of its status as a UN organization.

Focusing on the university milieu, we find that the dependency approach served as an effective weapon in the hands of younger, more radical scholars demanding jobs and more influence, cheered on by a growing number of students with an increasingly uncertain future. Paradigm changes seem to imply both power struggles and power shifts – even at the university level.

Thus, the underlying current of academic conflicts, intrigues and power struggle must also be seen in relation to the general political climate. In Jamaica, for example, a group of 'conventional' and 'established' academics of British origin dominated the University of the West Indies during the first decade after independence. The dependency theorists were, on the other hand, younger, black, non-established intellectuals. Some critics are therefore inclined to view the dependency school as an *ideology* that legitimized the non-established intellectuals' struggle for power and influence at, first of all, the academic level, and subsequently at the political level. One way of undermining established academics' positions is to question the scientific universality, for instance by pointing to the need for methods and theories that are tailored to a specific region, such as the Caribbean. This argument is strengthened if it can be shown that the established methods and theories are nothing but a rationalization of foreign interests, and a cover for exploitation. On this basis – and with the support of radical student opinion – it is easy to favour a certain group of intellectuals, as far as employment, advancement and research grants are concerned.

> It should be obvious that this critique is written from the standpoint of someone who must admit to a personal investment in internationalism and believes this to be the best long-run for intellectual analysis and hence indirectly for public policy. It is open to anyone who wishes to argue that this belief is itself ideological, reflecting the fear or fact that the writer stands to lose by any closing of the intellectual frontiers on nationalist or racial lines. This would not in itself discredit the analysis . . . to demonstrate that an argument serves an ideological purpose is not to demonstrate its falsity in any objective sense. It does, however, sharpen one's sense of the need for some pragmatic test which will indicate whether an analysis goes beyond ideological validity to some kind of objective truth.
> (Cumper, 1974, p 478).

The 'pragmatic test' which this critic felt was necessary for a proper evaluation of the dependency theory's operational validity came during the 1970s, when a number of dependency theorists were placed in political or administrative positions in the Manley government. The dependency-inspired economic policy, as mentioned in Chapter 5, did not solve Jamaica's economic problems. The situation grew worse as a result of a deliberate policy of destabilization reminiscent of that applied to Allende's Chile. Thus, to the extent that it was of any practical use, the success of the dependency school depended upon certain political fluctuations which tended to be fairly short-lived. Once the opportunity was missed, the doors were again opened to more conventional development strategies, like monetarism in Chile and 'Industrialization by Invitation' in Seaga's Jamaica.

In the current development debate there seems to be an overreaction to the weaknesses of the dependency school and a pessimistic determinism as far as the strategy of self-reliance is concerned. Export-oriented industrialization strategies, successfully carried out by some of the so-called 'newly industrialized countries' (NICs) are recommended instead. This change in the theoretical debate on development should, like the new Cold War, be related to the changes in the world economy during the 1970s. The decline of the US and the ensuing rivalry between industrialized countries, in which Japan was particularly successful, created unique possibilities for certain countries with a reasonably advanced industrial base, cheap labour and stable (repressive) regimes. On the other hand, the scope for self-reliance and other more or less radical strategies was reduced due both to economic and to political reasons. The economic reasons were changes in the terms of trade: rising import prices for energy, food and capital goods; falling prices for many of those raw materials that still dominate many underdeveloped economies. Of the political reasons the most important was a felt need for streamlining the allies and better control over the spheres of interest of the two superpowers. Here the USA possesses a much more varied repertoire of instruments for economic destabilization, whereas the Soviet Union to a larger degree must rely on diplomatic and military means.

In conclusion, we would like to stress that the 'failure' of self-reliance must be understood in relation to structural and political changes in the world and should not only be explained by inbuilt weaknesses of *national* development strategies. These underlying changes, as expressed in the 'new' Cold War, have made it even more difficult to implement strategies of self-reliance. For social, political and cultural reasons only a limited number of countries can follow the NIC strategy today. The lesson of Iran illuminates the social and political reactions provoked by excessive modernization and a number of countries, such as the Philippines, Malaysia, Sri Lanka, Chile (after Allende), Jamaica (after Manley) and Puerto Rico, are now learning the difficulties of interpreting the NIC strategy. Thus, the relevance of self-reliance (thought of as a strategy rather than as a nationalist ideology), implied in the dependency approach should not be judged only by the setbacks of this strategy in the 1970s.

Notes

1. The late Dudley Seers's classic article 'The Limitations of the Special Case' was one of the first assaults on the Western development theory's claim to universality. Seers was in fact prepared to go one step further in his critique: the neo-classical theory is of limited use not only in the Third World, but in the developed world as well (see Seers, 1979b). 'I believe that was the correct thing to say at that time because not only were growth models and other theoretical devices derived from Western experience, but they were also imported into the universities, especially in Asia and Africa. Today one would say they were part of "cultural dependence". Afterwards I became increasingly sceptical about the relevance of these concepts for European countries as well. When I went to work in Portugal I felt I was in a Latin American situation: rural poverty, dependence on the transnationals, the type of bureaucracy, the educational systems etc. I felt that some of the theories developed in Third World countries, for example *dependencia* might be relevant there as well. And if Portugal, why not Greece, Spain, Turkey etc. In these cases I found that there were some elements in common with what I have observed in Third World countries. In a sense this is contrary to what I said in the 1963 article. The connecting link is that in that article I was saying that neo-classical, and I would add, crude Marxist theories should not be imported into Third World countries where they did not fit but had to be replaced by different approaches. Now I would say, perhaps those theories did not fit the First World either?' (Interview with Dudley Seers in Brighton, June 1980.)
2. The Cocoyoc Declaration was adopted by the participants in a UNEP/UNCTAD Symposium on the *Pattern of Resource Use, Environment and Development* in Cocoyoc, Mexico, in October 1974.
3. From discussions at seminars at the UWI, Kingston and CIDE, Mexico City, October 1981.
4. The following Thesis 15 of the Nineteenth Congress of the Mexican Communist Party (in 1981) concludes, for instance: 'Dependency theory has not died. It still permeates the analysis and theory of the left . . . That is why the ideological struggle against this theory is not something of the past; it is an urgent task for today' (quoted in Munck, 1981, p 162).

Bibliography

Ablin, E, 1979, *Technology Exports from Developing Countries: Thoughts in the Light of the Argentine Case.* Paper submitted to the Nordic Symposium on Development Strategies in Latin America and the New International Economic Order, Lund, Sept

Adelman, I, 1961, *Theories of Economic Growth and Development*, Stanford: Stanford University Press

Aguilar, L E (ed), 1968, *Marxism in Latin America*, New York: Alfred A Knopf

Alavi, H, 1975, 'India and the Colonial Mode of Production', *Economic and Political Weekly*, Vol X, nr 33-35 (Special issue)

Alba, V, 1968, *Politics and the Labour Movement in Latin America*, Stanford: Stanford University Press

Alexander, R J, 1973, *Trotskyism in Latin America*, Stanford: Hoover Institution Press

Almond, G A, 1970, *Political Development: Essays in Heuristic Theory*, Boston: Little Brown

Almond, G A and Coleman, J S, 1960, *The Politics of the Developing Areas*, Princeton: Princeton University Press

Almond, G A and Powell, C B, 1965, *Comparative Politics: A Developmental Approach*, Boston: Little Brown

Amin, S, 1957, *Les effects structurels de l'intégration internationale économies pré-capitalistes. Une étude théorique du méchanisme qui a engendré les économies dites sous-développées*, Paris

——— 1965, *Trois expériences africaines de développement: le Mali, la Guinée, et le Ghana*, Paris: PUF

——— 1967a, *L'économie de Maghreb*, 2 Vol, Paris: Ed de Minuit

——— 1967b, *Le développement du capitalisme en Côte d'Ivoire*, Paris: Ed de Minuit

——— 1969a, *Le monde des affaires sénégalais*, Paris: Ed de Minuit

——— 1969b, *Du Congo francais à l'UDEAC – Histoire économique de l'Afrique équatoriale 1880–1969*, Paris: Anthropos IFAN

——— 1970, *L'accumulation à L'échelle mondiale*, Paris-Dakar: Anthropos (English translation, 1974, New York: Monthly Review Press)

——— 1971a, *L'Afrique de l'Ouest bloquée, l'économie politique de la colonisation 1880–1970*, Paris: Ed de Minuit

——— 1971b, 'The Political Economy of Underdevelopment', interview in *Zenit*, No 24 (in Swedish)

——— 1972, 'Accumulation and Development: A Theoretical Model', *Review of African Political Economy*, No 1
——— *et al.*, 1982, *Dynamics of Global Crisis*, New York: Monthly Review Press
Anyang'Nyong'o, P, 1978, 'The Teaching of Social Science in East Africa', *Africa Development*, Vol 3, No 4
Apter, D, 1965, *The Politics of Modernization*, Chicago: University of Chicago Press
van Arkadie, B, 1973, 'Planning in Tanzania', in Cliffe and Saul (ed), 1973
Arrighi, G and Saul, J, 1973, *Essays on the Political Economy of Africa*, New York: Monthly Review Press
Ashby, E, 1966, *Universities: British, Indian, African: A Study in the Ecology of Higher Education*, London
Axline, W A, 1979, *Caribbean Integration. The Politics of Regionalism*, London: Francis Pinter
Baer, W, 1967, 'The Inflation Controversy in Latin America: A Survey', *Latin American Research Review* (Winter)
Baines, J M, 1972, *Revolution in Peru: Mariátegui and the Myth*, University of Alabama Press
Bambirra, V, 1972, *El capitalismo dependiente en América Latina*, México: Siglo XXI
——— 1978, *Teoría de la dependencia: una antierítica*, Mexico: Serie ERA Popular
Banaji, J, 1972, 'For a Theory of Colonial Modes of Production', *Economic and Political Weekly*, 1972: 52
——— 1977, 'Capitalist Domination and the Small Peasantry', *Economic and Political Weekly*, 1977: 33-4
Baran, P, 1957, *The Political Economy of Growth*, New York and London: Monthly Review Press
Barratt-Brown, M, 1972, 'A Critique of Marxist Theories of Imperialism', in Owen and Sutcliffe, 1972
Bath, C R and James, D J, 1976, 'Dependency Analysis of Latin America: Some Criticisms, Some Suggestions', *Latin American Research Review*, Vol XI, No 3
Bauer, O, 1907, *Die Nationalitaten Frage und die Sozialdemokratie*, Wien
Bauer, P T and Yamey, B S, 1957, *The Economics of Underdeveloped Countries*, Cambridge: Cambridge University Press
Beckford, L G, 1972, 'Persistent Poverty. Underdevelopment in Plantation Economies of the Third World', Oxford: Oxford University Press
Beckman, B, 1980, 'Imperialism and Capitalist Transformation: Critique of a Kenyan Debate', *Review of African Political Economy*, No 91
Bedlington, S S, 1978, *Malaysia and Singapore. The Building of New States*, Ithaca, N.Y.: Cornell University Press
van Benthem van den Bergh, G, 1972, *Science and the Development of Society*, Discussion paper to 20th Anniversary Conference 'Science and the World Tomorrow', NUFFIC
Bernstein, H (ed), 1973, *Underdevelopment and Development*, Harmondsworth: Penguin Books
——— 1976, 'Capital and Peasantry: The Epoch of Imperialism', mimeo, University of Dar es Salaam

——— 1977a, 'Notes on Capital and Peasantry', *Review of African Political Economy*, No 10

——— 1977b, 'Underdevelopment and the Law of Value: A Critique of Kay', *Radical African Political Economy*, No 8

——— 1979, 'Sociology of Underdevelopment vs Sociology of Development', in Lehman, 1979

Best, L, 1967, 'Wither New World', *New World Quarterly*, Vol 4, No 1

——— 1968, 'A Model of a Pure Plantation Economy', *Social and Economic Studies*, Vol 17, No 3

Bhagwati, J, 1978, *Foreign Trade Regimes and Economic Development. Anatomy and Consequences of Exchange Control Regimes*, Cambridge, Mass: Ballinger

Bigsten, A, 1983, *Income Distribution and Development, Theory, Evidence and Policy*, London: Heinemann

Bloch, M, 1975, *Marxist Analyses in Social Anthropology*, London: Malaby Press

Blomstrôm, M, 1983, 'Foreign Investment, Technical Efficiency and Structural Change. Evidence from the Mexican Manufacturing Industry', PhD thesis, University of Gothenburg

Blomstrôm, M and Hettne, B, 1981, *Dependency and Underdevelopment. A Latin American Contribution to Development Theory*, Stockholm: Prisma (in Swedish)

Blomstrôm, M and Persson, H, 1983, 'Foreign Investment and "Spillover" Efficiency in an Underdeveloped Economy', *World Development*, Vol 11, No. 6

Bodenheimer, S, 1971, *The Ideology of Developmentalism: The American Paradigm – Surrogate for Latin American Studies*, Beverly Hills: Sage Publications

Bradby, B, 1975, 'The Destruction of Natural Economy', *Economy and Society*, Vol IV, No 2, May

Braun, O, 1973, *Comercio Internacional e Imperialismo*, México: Siglo XXI

Brenner, R, 1977, 'The Origins of Capitalist Development: a Critique of Neo-Smithian Marxism', *New Left Review*, No 104

——— 1979, *Klasstrider och ekonomisk utveckling under feodalismen*, Arkiv studiehäften 5

Brewster, H, 1973, 'Economic Dependence. A Quantitative Interpretation', *Social and Economic Studies*, Vol 22, No 1

Brewster, H and Thomas, C, 1971, 'An Organic Theory of Economic Integration', mimeo, University of Guyana

Bronfenbrenner, M, 1978, 'A World Class Economist from Underdeveloped Africa', *Economic Development and Cultural Change*, Vol 27, No 1, Oct

Brookfield, H, 1975, *Interdependent Development*, London: Methuen

Caputo, O and Pizarro, R, 1970, *Imperialismo, dependencia y relaciones internacionales*, Universidad de Chile, CESO

——— 1974, *Dependencia y relaciones Internacionales*, Costa Rica: EDUCA

Cardoso, F H, 1965, *El proceso de desarrollo en América Latina: hipótesis para una interpretación sociológica*, Santiago de Chile, ILPES, Nov

——— 1967, 'The Industrial Elite', in Lipset and Solari, 1967

——— 1970, 'Teoría de la dependencia?', *Revista Latinoamericana de Ciencia Política*, FLACSO, Dec

——— 1972, 'Dependency and Underdevelopment in Latin America', *New Left Review*, No 74

——— 1976, *The Consumption of Dependency Theory in the US*, Paper submitted to the Third Scandinavian Research Conference on Latin America, Bergen, June 1976

——— 1977, *The Originality of a Copy: ECLA and the Idea of Development*, Working paper No 27, Centre of Latin American Studies, University of Cambridge

Cardoso, F H and Faletto, E, 1969, *Dependencia y desarrollo en América Latina*, México: Siglo XXI (English translation, 1979, University of California Press

Castillo, D, 1980, *Apuntes para una crítica a la 'Teoría de la dependencia'*, Memorandum, UNAM - Facultad de Economía, México

Chandra, S, 1975, *Dependence and Disillusionment. Emergence of National Consciousness in Later 19th Century India*, New Delhi: Manas Publications

Chenery, H *et al.*, 1974, *Redistribution with Growth*, Oxford: Oxford University Press

Choy, E *et al.*, 1970, *Lenin y Mariátegui*, Lima

Clammer, J (ed), 1978), *The New Economic Anthropology*, London: Macmillan

Cliffe, L and Saul, J (eds), 1972 and 1973, *Socialism in Tanzania*, Vol 1 and 2, Dar es Salaam: East African Publishing House

Clissold, S (ed), 1970, *Soviet Relations with Latin America 1918–1968. A Documentary Survey*, Oxford: Oxford University Press

Court, D, 1975, *The Experience of Higher Education in East Africa: Prospect for a Developmental Role*, Discussion Paper No 216, IDS - Nairobi

Cowen, M P, 1972, 'Differentiation in a Kenyan Locaton', East African Universities Social Sciences Council Conference, Nairobi

——— 1976, 'Capital and Peasant Households', mimeo, CDS Swansea

——— 1979a, 'Capital and Household Production: the Case of Wattle in Kenya's Central Province, 1903–1964', PhD thesis, University of Cambridge

——— 1979b, 'Notes on the Nairobi Discussion of the Agrarian Problem', mimeo, CDS Swansea

——— 1980a, 'The British State and Agrarian Accumulation in Kenya after 1945', mimeo, CDS Swansea

——— 1980b, 'Commodity Production in Kenya's Central Province', in J Heyer and G Williams (eds), *Rural Development in Tropical Africa*, London: Macmillan

——— 1981, 'The British State. State Enterprise and an Indigenous Bourgeoisie in Kenya after 1945', mimeo, CDS Swansea

Cowen, M and Kinyanjui, K, 1977, *Some Problems of Capital and Class in Kenya*, Occasional Paper No 26, IDS - Nairobi

Cruise O'Brien, D, 1979, 'Modernization, Order and the Erosion of a Democratic Ideal', in Lehman (ed), 1979

Cueva, A, 1974, 'Problemas y perspectivas de la teoría de la dependencia', *Historia y Sociedad*, No 3, Mexico (English translation in *Latin American Perspectives*, Fall 1976)

——— 1977, *El desarrollo del capitalismo en América Latina*, México: Siglo XXI

Cumper, G E, 1974, 'Dependence, Development and the Sociology of Economic Thought', *Social and Economic Studies*, Vol 23, No 3

Davies, H E, 1972, *Latin American Thought: A Historical Introduction*, New York: The Free Press
Debray, R, 1971, *Conversations with Allende*, London: New Left Books
Demas, W G, 1965, *The Economics of Development in Small Countries with Special Reference to the Caribbean*, Montreal: McGill University Press
de Vylder, S, 1974, *The Political Economy of the Rise and Fall of the Unidad Popular*, Cambridge: Cambridge University Press
Di Marco (ed), 1972, *International Economics and Development. Essays in Honour of Raúl Prebisch*, New York: Academic Press
Domar, E D, 1957, *Essays in the Theory of Economic Growth*, Oxford University Press
Don Long, 1983, 'Development and Repression in South Korea', in Jomo, 1983
Dos Santos, T, 1968a, *Socialismo o fascismo: dilema de América Latina*, Chile: PLA
——— 1968b, 'La crisis de la teoría del desarrollo y las relaciones de dependencia en América Latina', *Boletin de CESO*, 3, Santiago (English translation in Bernstein, 1973)
——— 1970, 'The Structure of Dependency', *American Economic Review*, Vol 60, No 21, May
——— 1971, *Socialismo o fascismo: el nuevo carácter de la dependencia y el dilema latinoamericano*, Chile
——— 1977a, Interview in *Economia Informa*, UNAM, Mexico, No 41/42
——— 1977b, 'Dependence Relations and Political Development in Latin America: Some Considerations', *Ibero-Americana*, Vol VII:I
——— 1978, *Imperialismo y Dependencia*, Mexico City: ERA
Drake, P W, 1978, *Socialism and Populism in Chile 1932-52*, Urbana: University of Illinois Press
Emmanuel, A, 1969, *L'échange inégal*, Paris: François Maspero éditeur (English translation, 1972: New York and London: Monthly Review Press)
Evans, D, 1980, *Emmanuel's Theory of Unequal Exchange: Critique, Counter Critique and Theoretical Contribution*, IDS - Sussex (DP 149), March
Fairchild, L G, 1977, 'Performance and Technology of United States and National Firms in Mexico', *Journal of Development Studies*, Oct
Fisk, E K and Osman-Rani, H (eds), 1982, *The Political Economy of Malaysia*, Kuala Lumpur: Oxford University Press
Fleming, M, 1955, 'External Economies and the Doctrine of Balanced Growth', *Economic Journal*, Vol 65 (June)
Foster-Carter, A, 1973, 'Neomarxist Approaches to Development and Underdevelopment', *Journal of Contemporary Asia*, Vol 3, No 1
——— 1976, 'From Rostow to Gunder Frank: Conflicting Paradigms in the Analysis of Underdevelopment', *World Development*, Vol 4, No 3
——— 1978, 'The Modes of Production Controversy', *New Left Review*, No 107, Jan-Feb
Frank, A G, 1967, *Capitalism and Underdevelopment in Latin America*, New York: Monthly Review Press
——— 1969, *Latin America: Underdevelopment or Revolution*, New York: Monthly Review Press
——— 1972, *Lumpenbourgeoisie – Lumpendevelopment*, New York: Monthly Review Press

——— 1973, 'On Feudal Modes, Models and Methods of Escaping Capitalist Reality', *Economic and Political Weekly*, 6 Jan 1973

——— 1977, 'Dependence is Dead, Long Live Dependence and the Class Struggle: An Answer to Critics', *World Development*, Vol 5, No 4

——— 1978, *World Accumulation 1492–1789*, New York: Monthly Review Press

Friedland, W and Rosberg Jr, C (eds), 1964, *African Socialism*, Stanford: Stanford University Press

Fröbel, F, Heinrich, J and Kreye, O, 1980, *The New International Division of Labour. Structural Unemployment in Industrialised Countries and Industrialisation in Developing Countries*, Cambridge: Cambridge University Press

Furtado, C, 1963, *Economic Growth of Brazil*, Berkeley: Berkeley University Press

——— 1964, *Dialéctica do desinvolvimento*, Rio de Janeiro (English translation, 1965: Berkeley: Berkeley University Press)

——— 1969, *Formação econômica da América Latina* (English translation, 1970: Cambridge: Cambridge University Press)

Fyfe, C (ed), 1976, *African Studies since 1945: A Tribute to Basil Davidson*, London: Longman

Galtung, J, 1971, 'A Structural Theory of Imperialism', *Journal of Peace Research*, Vol VIII, No 2

——— 1976, 'Conflict on a Global Scale: Social Imperialism and the Sub-imperialism – Continuities in the Structural Theory of Imperialism', *World Development*, Vol 4, No 3

Gandhi, M, n d, *Speeches and Writings*, Madras

Geertz, C, 1963, *Agricultural Involution. The Process of Ecological Change in Indonesia*, Berkeley: University of California Press

Gerschenkron, A, 1962, *Economic Backwardness in Historical Perspective*, Cambridge: Harvard University Press

Ghai, D, 1974a, *The Social Science and Development*, mimeo, Nairobi

——— 1974b, *Social Science Research on Development and Research Institutes in Africa*, Discussion Paper No 197, Institute for Development Studies, Nairobi

Girvan, N, 1970, 'Multinational Corporations and Dependent Underdevelopment in Mineral-Export Economies', *Social Economic Studies*, Vol 19, No 4

——— 1971, *Foreign Capital and Economic Underdevelopment in Jamaica*, ISER, Kingston

——— 1973, 'The Development of Dependency Economics in the Caribbean and Latin America: Review and Comparison', *Social and Economic Studies*, Vol 22, No 1

Girvan, N and Jefferson, O (eds), 1971, *Readings in the Political Economy of the Caribbean*, Kingston, New World

Godfrey, M, 1982, 'Kenya: African Capitalism or Simple Dependency', in Bienefeld, M and Godfrey, M, *The Sturggle for Development. National Strategies in an International Context*, London: John Wiley

Gutkind, P C W and Wallerstein, I (eds), 1976, *The Political Economy of Contemporary Africa*, Beverly Hills/London: Sage Publications

Gyarmati, G, 1974, 'Development of the Social Sciences in Chile', *Social*

Science Organization and Policy, Paris: UNESCO

Hagen, E, 1962, *On the Theory of Social Change*, Homewood: R D Irwin

Halliday, J, 1975, *A Political History of Japanese Capitalism*, New York: Monthly Review Press

Harberler, G, 1959, 'International Trade and Economic Development', *National Bank of Egypt*, Cairo

Harrod, R F, 1948, *Towards a Dynamic Economics*, London: Macmillan

Heckscher, E, 1919, 'The Effect of Foreign Trade on the Distribution of Income', *Ekonomisk Tidskrift*, XXI

Hettne, B, 1978, *The Political Economy of Indirect Rule. Mysore 1881–1947*, London: Curzon Press

——— 1982, *Development Theory and the Third World*, SAREC Report R:2

Hettne, B and Wallensteen, P (eds), 1978, *Emerging Trends in Development Theory*, SAREC Report R3

Higgins, B, 1968, *Economic Development, Principles, Problems and Policies*, London: Constable

Hilton, R, 1976, *The Transition from Feudalism to Capitalism*, London: New Left Books

Hirschman, A O, 1958, *The Strategy of Economic Development*, New Haven, Conn: Yale University Press

——— (ed), 1961, *Latin American Issues – Essays and Comments*, New York: Twentieth Century Fund

——— 1968, 'The Political Economy of Import-Substituting Industrialization in Latin America', *The Quarterly Journal of Economics*, Vol 82

——— 1971, *A Bias for Hope*, New Haven: Yale University Press

——— 1977, 'A Generalized Linkage Approach to Development, with Special References to Staples', in Manning Nash (ed), *Essays on Economic Development and Cultural Change in Honor of Bert F. Hoselitz*, Chicago: University of Chicago Press

Hodges, D C, 1977, *The Legacy of Che Guevara. A Documentary Study*, London: Thames and Hudson

Hopkins, A G, 1976, 'Clio-Antics: A Horoscope for African Economic History', in Fyfe (ed), 1976

Hoselitz, B F *et al.*, 1960, *Theories of Economic Growth*, Glencoe, Ill.: The Free Press

Huntington, S P, 1971, 'The Change to Change. Modernization, Development and Politics', *Comparative Politics*, April

Hyden, G, 1977, 'Issues beyond the Theory of the Class Struggles', *UTAFITI*, Vol II, No 1

——— 1980, *Beyond Ujamaa in Tanzania. Underdevelopment and Uncaptured Peasantry*, London: Heinemann

James, B J, 1979, 'The University of East Africa in Retrospect', *Mawazo*, Vol II, No III

Jameson, K P and Wilber, C K (eds), 1979, *Directions in Economic Development*, Notre Dame: University of Notre Dame Press

Jefferson, O, 1972a, *The Post-War Economic Development of Jamaica*, ISER, Kingston, Jamaica: University of the West Indies

——— 1972b, 'Professor Lewis and the Caribbean Economy', *Daily Gleaner*, 17 May

Jomo, K S (ed), 1983, *The Sun Also Sets. Lessons in Looking East*, Kuala Lumpur: Insan

Kahl, J A, 1976, *Modernization, Exploitation and Dependency in Latin America, Germani, González Casanova and Cardoso*, New Brunswick, New Jersey

Kaplinsky, R, 1980, 'Capitalist Accumulation in the Periphery – the Kenyan Case Reexamined', *Review of African Political Economy*, No 16

Katz, J, 1978, *Cambio Tecnológico, desarrollo económico y las relaciones intra y extra regionales de la América Latina*, Buenos Aires, Programa BID/CEPAL de Investigaciones en Temas de Ciencia y Techología. Monografía de Trabajo No 30, August

Katz, J and Ablin, E, 1978, *De la industria incipiente a la exportación de tecnología. La experiencia Argentina en la venta internacional de plantas industriales y obras de ingeniería*, Buenos Aires, Programa BID/CEPAL de Investigaciones en Temas de Ciencia y Tecnología. Monografía de Trabajo No 14, April

Kay, G, 1975, *Development and Underdevelopment: A Marxist Analysis*, London: Macmillan

Keesing, D B, 1979, *Trade Policy for Developing Countries*, World Bank Staff Working Paper, No 353, Washington

Kenedy, P, 1977, 'Indigenous Capitalism in Kenya', *Review of African Political Economy*, No 8

Khor Kok Peng, 1983, *Recession and the Malaysian Economy*, Penang: Institut Masyarakat

Kiernan, V G, 1967, 'Marx on India', *Socialist Register*

——— 1974, *Marxism and Imperialism*, London: Edward Arnold

Killick, T, 1975a, *The Economies of East Africa: An Annotated Bibliography*, Boston: GK Hall

——— 1975b, *Past and Future Research on the East African Economies*, Working Paper No 229, Institute for Development Studies, Nairobi

Kindleberger, C P, 1958, *Economic Development*, New York: McGraw-Hill

Kinyanjui, K, 1979, 'The Political Economy of Educational Inequality: A Study of the Roots of Educational Inequality in Colonial and Post-Colonial Kenya', PhD thesis, Harvard University

Klinghaffer, A J, 1969, *Soviet Perspectives on African Socialism*, Cranbury, N J: Fairleigh Dickinson University Press

Kregel, J A, 1972, *The Theory of Economic Growth*, London: Macmillan

Kuhn, T S, 1962 (1970), *The Structure of Scientific Revolutions*, Chicago: University of Chicago Press

Laclau, E, 1971, 'Feudalism and Capitalism in Latin America', *New Left Review*, No 67

Lall, S, 1975, 'Is Dependence a Useful Concept in Analysing Underdevelopment?', *World Development*, Vol 3, No 11

——— 1978, *Developing Countries as Exporters of Technology: A Preliminary Analysis*, Draft, Oxford University, Institute of Economics and Statistics

Lamb, G, 1981, 'Rapid Capitalist Development Models: A New Politics of Dependence', in Seers, D, 1981, *Dependency Theory: A Critical Assessment*, London: Frances Pinter

Langdon, S, 1974, 'The Political Economy of Dependence: Note Towards

Analysis of Multinational Corporations in Kenya', *Journal of Eastern African Research and Development*, Vol 4, No 2

——— 1975a, 'Multinational Corporations in the Political Economy of Kenya', DPhil, thesis, University of Sussex

——— 1975b, 'Multinational Corporations, Taste Transfer and Underdevelopment: a Case Study from Kenya', *Review of African Political Economy*, No 2

——— 1977, 'The State and Capitalism in Kenya', *Review of African Political Economy*, No 8

——— 1980, 'Industry and Capitalism in Kenya: Contributions to a Debate', mimeo, Department of Economics, Carleton University

Leaver, R, 1977, 'The Debate on Underdevelopment: On Situating Gunder Frank', *Journal of Contemporary Asia*, Vol 7, No 1

Lehman, D (ed), 1979, *Development Theory, Four Critical Studies*, London: Frank Cass

Lenin, V I, 1956, *The Development of Capitalism in Russia*, Moscow: Progress Publishers

Lerner, D, 1962, *The Passing of the Traditional Society*, New York: The Free Press

Lewis, W A, 1938 (1977), *Labour in the West Indies. The Birth of a Workers' Movement*, London: Beacon Books

——— 1949, 'Industrial Development in Puerto Rico', *Caribbean Economic Review*, Vol 1, Nos 1-2

——— 1950, 'Industrialization of the British West Indies', *Caribbean Economic Review*, Vol 2, No 1

——— 1954, 'Economic Development with Unlimited Supply of Labour', *The Manchester School of Economic and Social Studies*, Vol XXII, No 2

——— 1955, *The Theory of Economic Growth*, London: Allen and Unwin

Leys, C, 1970, *Politics in Kenya: The Development of Peasant Society*, Discussion Paper No 102, Institute for Development Studies, Nairobi

——— 1971, 'The Role of the University in an Underdeveloped Country', *Journal of African Research and Development*, Vol 1, No 1

——— 1975, *Underdevelopment in Kenya. The Political Economy of Neo-Colonialism*, London: Heinemann

——— 1977, 'Underdevelopment and Dependency: Critical Notes', *Journal of Contemporary Asia*, Vol 7, No 1

——— 1978, 'Capital Accumulation, Class Formation and Dependency – The Significance of the Kenyan Case', *Socialist Register*

——— 1979, 'Development Strategy in Kenya since 1971', *Canadian Journal of African Studies*, Vol 13, Nos 1-2

——— 1980, 'Kenya: What Does Dependency Explain?', *Review of African Political Economy*, No 16

Li Dun Jen, 1982, *British Malaya. An Economic Analysis*, Kuala Lumpur: Insan

Lipset, S M and Solari, A, 1967, *Elites in Latin America*, Oxford University Press

Livingstone, J (ed), 1971, *Economic Policy for Development*, Harmondsworth: Penguin Books

Love, J L, 1980, 'Raúl Prebisch and the Origins of the Doctrine of Unequal Exchange', *Latin American Research Review*, Vol 15, No 1

Lowy, M, 1973, *The Marxism of Che Guevara*, New York and London: Monthly Review Press
Lukács, G, 1923, *Geschichte und Klassenbewusstsein*, Berlin
Luxemburg, R, 1913 (1971), *The Accumulation of Capital*, London: Routledge and Kegan Paul
McClelland, D, 1962, *The Achieving Society*, Princeton University Press
McEachern, D, 1976, 'The Mode of Production in India', *Journal of Contemporary Asia*, Vol 6, No 4
Mahathir, D S, 1983, 'New Government Policies', in Jomo, 1983
Manley, M, 1974, *The Politics of Change. A Jamaican Testament*, London: André Deutsch
——— 1975, *A Voice at the Workplace. Reflections on Colonialism and the Jamaican Worker*, London: André Deutsch
Marcussen, H S and Torp, J E, 1982, *The Internationalization of Capital. The Prospects for the Third World*, London: Zed Press
Marinéz-Alliér, 1967, 'El latifundio en Andalucía y en América Latina', *Cuadernos de Ruedo Ibérico*, Oct/Nov
Marini, R M, 1969a, 'Brazilian Interdependence and Imperialist Integration', *Monthly Review*, Dec
——— 1969, *Subdesarrollo y revolución*, México: Siglo XXI
——— 1972a, 'Brazilian Sub-Imperialism', *Monthly Review*, Feb
——— 1972b, 'Dialéctica de la dependencia: la economía exportadora', *Sociedad y Desarrollo*, No 1
——— 1978, 'Las razones del modesarrollismo (o por qué me ufano de mi burguesia)', *Revista Mexicana de Sociología*, Año XL/Vol XL, Número extra ordinario
Marx, K, 1964, *Pre-capitalist Economic Formations*, London: Lawrence and Wishart
Marx, K and Engels, F, 1960, *On Colonialism*, Moscow: Progress Publishers
——— 1976, *Kommunistiska Manifestet*, Arbetarkultur
Merhav, M, 1969, *Technological Dependence, Monopoly and Growth*, London: Pergamon Press
Metcalfe, J S and Steedman, I, 1972, 'Reswitching and Primary Input Use', *The Economic Journal*, Vol 82, No 325
Minocha, A C, 1970, 'Drain Theory and its Relevance to Present-Day Trade Relations Between Developed and Under-Developed Countries and Rural-Urban Sectors', in *The Drain Theory, Papers read at the Indian Economic Conference*, Bombay: Popular Prakash
Moore, B, 1966, *The Social Origins of Democracy and Dictatorship*, Boston: Beacon Press
Munck, R, 1981, 'Imperialism and Dependency: Recent Debates and Old Dead-Ends', *Latin American Perspectives*, Vol 8, Nos 3-4
Myer, J, 1975, 'A Crown of Thorns: Cardoso and Counter-Revolution', *Latin American Perspectives*, Issue IV, Vol II, No 1
Myrdal, G, 1957, *Economic Theory and Underdeveloped Regions*, London: Gerald Duckworth
——— 1968, *Asian Drama*, New York: Pantheon Books
Nabudere, D W, 1975, 'The Political Economy of Imperialism', mimeo, Dar es Salaam
——— 1977a, 'Imperialism Struggles in Tanzania', *UTAFITI*, Vol 2, No 1

——— 1977b, *The Political Economy of Imperialism*, London: Zed Press
——— 1977c, 'Imperialism, State, Class and Race: A Critique of Shivji's Class Struggles in Tanzania', *UTAFITI*, Vol 2, No 1
Naoroji, D, 1962 (1901), *Poverty and Un-British Rule in India*, Delhi: Publications Division, Ministry of Information and Broadcasting, Government of India
Nash, M, 1977, *Essays on Economic Development and Cultural Change in Honor of Bert F Hoselitz*, Chicago: University of Chicago Press
N'Diaye, J-P, 1973, 'El Problema es la Falta de Visión', *Ceres*, No 34
Nove, A, 1974, 'On Reading André Gunder Frank', *The Journal of Development Studies*, Vol 10, Nos 3 and 4
Nurkse, R, 1953, *Problems of Capital Formation in Underdeveloped Countries*, Oxford: Basil Blackwell
Nyerere, J N, 1968, *Ujamaa. Essays on Socialism*, Oxford: Oxford University Press
O'Brien, P, 1973, 'Dependency: The New Nationalism', *Latin American Review of Books*, Spring
Ohlin, B, 1933, *Interregional and International Trade*, Harvard: Harvard University Press
Omwony-Ojwok, 1977, 'Review of the Debate on Imperialism, State, Class and the National Question', *UTAFITI*, Vol 2, No 2
Oxaal, I *et al.*, 1975, *Beyond the Sociology of Development*, London: Routledge and Kegan Paul
Owen, R and Sutcliffe, B (eds), 1972, *Studies in the Theory of Imperialism*, London: Longman
Palma, G, 1978, 'Dependency: A Formal Theory of Underdevelopment or a Methodology for the Analysis of Concrete Situations of Underdevelopment?', *World Development*, Vol 6, No 7/8
Paris, R, *et al.*, 1973, *El Marxismo Latinoamericano de Mariátegui*, Buenos Aires: Ed de Crisis
Patnaik, U, 1972, 'Development of Capitalism in Agriculture', *Social Scientist*, Sept
Patterson, O, 1967, *The Sociology of Slavery. An Analysis of the Origins, Development and Structure of Negro Slave Society in Jamaica*, London: MacGibbon and Kee
Perceira, H C, 1971, 'The Integration of Research Agencies for African Agricultural Development', *Minerva*, No 1
Phillips, A, 1977, 'The Concept of "Development"', *Review of African Political Economy*, No 9
Pinto, A and Kñákal, J, 1972, 'The Center-Periphery System 20 Years later', in Di Marco, 1972
Prebisch, R, 1950, *The Economic Development of Latin America and its Principal Problems*, New York: United Nations
——— 1976, 'Critíca al Capitalismo Preiférico', *Revista de la CEPAL*, No 1
——— 1978, 'Estructura Socioeconómica y Crisis del Sistema', *Revista de la CEPAL*, No 6
——— 1979, 'Las Teorías Neoclásicas del Liberalismo Económico', *Revista de la CEPAL*, No 7
——— 1980a, Interview in *Third World Quarterly*, Jan
——— 1980b, 'Toward a Theory of Change', *CEPAL Review*, No 9

——— 1980c, Preface to Rodríguez, 1980

Ratliff, W E, 1976, *Castroism and Communism in Latin America 1959–1976*, Stanford (AEI-Hoover Policy Studies)

Robbins, L, 1968, *The Theory of Economic Development in the History of Economic Thought*, London, Macmillan

Robinson, J, 1962, *Economic Philosophy*, London: C A Watts and Co Ltd

Rodney, W, 1972, *How Europe Underdeveloped Africa*, Dar es Salaam: Tanzania Publishing House

——— 1975, *The Groundings with My Brothers*, London: Bogle-L'Ouverture Publications Ltd

Rodríguez, O, 1974, *Sobre el pensamiento de la CEPAL*, Secretaría de la Presidencia, México

——— 1977, 'On the Conception of Center-Periphery System', *CEPAL Review*

——— 1980, *La Teoría del Subdesarrollo de la CEPAL*, México: Siglo XXI

Rosenstein-Rodan, P N, 1943, 'Problems of Industrialization of Eastern and South-Eastern Europe', *Economic Journal*, 53 (June-Sept)

Rostow, W W, 1960, *The Stages of Economic Growth*, Cambridge: Cambridge University Press

Roxborough, I, 1976, 'Dependency Theory in the Sociology of Development: Some Theoretical Problems', *The West African Journal of Sociology and Political Economy*, Vol 1, No 2

——— 1979, *Theories of Underdevelopment*, London: Macmillan

Roy, M N, 1921 (1971), *India in Transition*, Bombay

Rweyemamu, J E, 1969, 'International Trade and the Developing Countries', *Journal of Modern African Studies*, Vol VII, No 2

——— 1971, 'The Political Economy of Foreign Private Investment in the Underdeveloped Countries', *The African Review*, Vol 1

——— 1973, *Underdevelopment and Industrialization in Tanzania*, Oxford: Oxford University Press

Saravanamuttu, J, 1983, 'The Look East Policy and Japanese Economic Penetration in Malaysia', in Jomo, 1983

Schiavo-Campo, S and Singer, H W, 1970, *Perspectives of Economic Development*, Boston: Houghton Mifflin Co

Schumpeter, J, 1934, *The Theory of Economic Development*, Cambridge Mass: Harvard University Press

Schwarz, S M, 1955, 'Populism and Early Russian Marxism on Ways of Economic Development of Russia', in Simmons (ed), 1955

Seddon, D (ed), 1978, *Relations of Production. Marxist Approaches to Economic Anthropology*, London: Frank Cass

Seers, D, 1963, 'The Limitations of the Special Case', *Bulletin of the Oxford Institute of Economics and Statistics*, Vol 25, No 2

——— 1978, *The Congruence of Marxism and other Neo-classical Doctrines*, Discussion Paper, No 136, IDS, Sussex, August

——— 1979a, 'Patterns of Dependence', in Villamil (ed), 1979

——— 1979b, *Underdeveloped Europe. Studies in Core-Periphery Relations*, Hassocks, Sussex: Harvester Press

Seidman, A, 1972, *Comparative Development Strategies in East Africa*, Nairobi: East African Publishing House

——— 1976, 'Changing Theories of Political Economy in Africa', in Fyfe (ed)

Semo, E, 1975, *La Crisis Actual del Capitalismo*, México: Ed de Cultura Popular

Serra, J (ed), 1974, *Desarollo Latinoamericano. Ensayos Críticos*, México: FCE

Serra, J and Cardoso, F, 1978, 'Las desventuras de la dialéctica de la dependencia', *Revista Mexicana de Sociologia*, Año XL/Vol XL, Número Extraordinario

Shivji, I, 1970, 'Tanzania – The Silent Class Struggle', *Cheche*, Dar es Salaam

——— 1973a, *The Silent Class Struggle*, Tanzania Publishing House

——— 1973b, 'Capitalism Unlimited. Public Corporations in Partnership with Multinational Corporations', *The African Review*, Vol 3

——— 1975, *Class Struggles in Tanzania*, Dar es Salaam and London: Heinemann

Simmons, E J (ed), 1955, *Continuity and Change in Russian and Soviet Thought*, Cambridge, Mass: Harvard University Press

Singer, H W, 1950, 'The Distribution of Gains between Investing and Borrowing Countries', *American Economic Review*, Vol II, No 2

——— 1964, *International Development: Growth and Change*, New York: McGraw-Hill

——— 1975, *The Strategy of International Development, Essays in the Economics of Backwardness* (ed by Cairncross and Puri), London: Macmillan

Singer, P, 1976, 'A divisao internacional do trabalho e empresas multinacionais', mimeo, Sao Paulo, CEBRAP

Skocpol, T, 1979, *States and Social Revolutions*, Cambridge: Cambridge University Press

Smith, A D, 1973, *The Concept of Social Change. A Critique of the Functionalist Theory of Social Change*, London: Routledge and Kegan Paul

Smith, M G, 1965, *The Plural Society in the British West Indies*, Kingston: Sangster's Book Stores Ltd

Sofri, G, 1969, *Il Modo di Produzione Asiatico*, Turino: Giulino Einaudi Editore

Stavenhagen, R, 1966, 'Siete tesis equivocados sobre América Latina', *Desarollo indoamericano*, English translation in Petras, J and Zeitlin, M (eds), 1968, *Latin America: Reform or Revolution?* Greenwich Connecticut: Fawcett Pub

Streeten, P, 1959, 'Unbalanced Growth', *Oxford Economic Papers*, Vol 11, No 2

——— (ed), 1970, *Unfashionable Economics. Essays in Honour of Lord Balogh*, London

——— 1974, 'Some Problems in the Use and Transfer of Intellectual Technology', in Ghai, 1974a

——— 1979, 'A Basic-Needs Approach to Economic Development' in Jameson and Wilber (1979)

Ståhl, M, 1980, *Tanzania – Landanalys*, Stockholm: SIDA

Sunkel, O, 1969, 'National Development Policy and External Dependency in Latin America', *Journal of Development Studies*, Vol 1, No 1,

——— 1971, 'Capitalismo transnacional y desintegración nacional en América Latina', *Estudios Internacionales*, No 16

Sunkel, O and Fuenzalida, E F, 1976, *An Interdisciplinary Research Programme on the Transnationalization of Capitalism and National Develop-*

ment, IDS, Sussex, Nov
——— 1979, 'Transnationalization and its National Consequences', in Villamil (ed), 1979
Sunkel, O and Paz, P, 1970, *El subdesarrollo latinoamericano y la teoria del desarrollo*, Santiago de Chile: Siglo XXI
Sutcliffe, B, 1972, 'Imperialism and Industrialization in the Third World', in Owen and Sutcliffe, 1972
Swainson, N, 1977, 'The Rise of a National Bourgeoisie in Kenya', *Review of African Political Economy*, No 8
——— 1980, *The Development of Corporate Capitalism in Kenya, 1918–1977*, London: Heinemann
Sweezy, P M, 1972, 'On the Theory of Monopoly Capitalism', in *Modern Capitalism and Other Essays*, New York: Monthly Review Press
Taylor, J, 1974, 'Neo-marxism and Underdevelopment', *Journal of Contemporary Asia*, Vol 2, No 1
——— 1979, *From Modernization to Modes of Production: a Critique of the Sociologies of Development and Underdevelopment*, London: Macmillan
Thomas, C, 1974, *Dependence and Transformation. The Economics of the Transition to Socialism*, New York: Monthly Review Press
Thorner, A, 1982, 'The Mode of Production Debate in India', *Economic and Political Weekly*, Bombay
Todaro, M P, 1977, *Economic Development in the Third World*, London: Longman
Torr, D, 1951, *Marx on China*, London: Lawrence and Wishart
Tschannerl, G, 1976, 'Periphery Capitalist Development – A Case Study of the Tanzanian Economy', *UTAFITI*, Vol 1, No 1
Viner, J, 1953, *International Trade and Economic Development*, Oxford: Oxford University Press
Villamil, J J (ed), *Transnational Capitalism and National Development. New Perspectives on Dependence*, IDS, Hassocks, Sussex: Harvester Press
Walicki, A, 1969, *The Controversy over Capitalism*, Oxford: Oxford University Press
Wallerstein, I, 1974, *The Modern World-System. Capitalist Agriculture and the Origins of the European World-Economy in the Sixteenth Century*, New York and London: Academic Press
——— 1976, 'Three Stages of African Involvement in the World-Economy', In Gutkind and Wallerstein (eds), 1976
——— 1979, *The Capitalist World Economy*, Cambridge: Cambridge University Press
——— 1980, *The Modern World System II. Mercantilism and the Consolidation of the European World-Economy, 1600–1750*, New York and London: Academic Press
Warren, B, 1973, 'Imperialism and Capitalist Industrialization', *New Left Review*, No 81
——— 1980, *Imperialism: Pioneer of Capitalism*, London: New Left Books
Weeks, J and Dore, E, 1979, 'International Exchange and the Causes of Backwardness', *Latin American Perspectives*, Issue 21, Vol VI, No 2, Spring
Weffort, F C, 1970, *Notas sobre la 'teoría de la Dependencia': Teoría de clase o ideologia nacional?*, FLACSO, December
Weisskopf, T E, 1976, 'Dependence as an Explanation of Underdevelopment:

a Critique', M.S. University of Michigan

Wielenga, B, 1976, *Marxist Views in Historical Perspective*, Madras: The Christian Literature Society

Wuyts, M, 1976, *On the Nature of Underdevelopment: An Analysis of Two Views on Underdevelopment*, ERB, University of Dar es Salaam, March

Wynn, S, 1982, 'The Taiwanese "Economic Miracle"', *Monthly Review,* Vol 30, No 11

Yotopoulos, P A and Nugent, J B, 1976, *Economics of Development. Empirical Investigations*, New York: Harper International Edition